The Gay Man's Guide to Open
and Monogamous Marriage

The Gay Man's Guide to Open and Monogamous Marriage

Michael Dale Kimmel

ROWMAN & LITTLEFIELD
Lanham • Boulder • New York • London

Published by Rowman & Littlefield
A wholly owned subsidiary of The Rowman & Littlefield Publishing Group, Inc.
4501 Forbes Boulevard, Suite 200, Lanham, Maryland 20706
www.rowman.com

Unit A, Whitacre Mews, 26–34 Stannary Street, London SE11 4AB

British Library Cataloguing in Publication Information Available

Library of Congress Cataloging-in-Publication Data

978-1-4422-6801-2 (cloth)
978-1-4422-6802-9 (electronic)

♾ ™ The paper used in this publication meets the minimum requirements of American
National Standard for Information Sciences—Permanence of Paper for Printed Library
Materials, ANSI/NISO Z39.48-1992.

Printed in the United States of America

This book is dedicated to
Mark Thompson (1952–2016)

Contents

Introduction

For centuries, heterosexual people have defined what marriage is. It started out as a type of possession: "I own you." Hardly anchored in love, was it? And yet, this is the model that most of the human race has embraced for hundreds of years. Only in the last century or so has marriage begun to be based on love, mutual respect, and understanding.

As two men considering getting married, we no longer have to do it "that" way. This is a cause for rejoicing! This is real freedom! So why aren't we more excited about this? Because this kind of freedom isn't easy. It's quite daunting to invent or reinvent a cultural institution that's been around longer than anyone alive can remember. It's so much easier to just follow what straight people have been doing and—maybe—modify it a little bit, tweak it just a tad.

This is certainly an option. But given the power of our community to create and invent our own norms and institutions, why would we settle for that?

This book is an invitation—a radical invitation—to you to not settle. Instead, I urge you to examine and investigate the idea and institution of marriage and come up with your own version of what works for you and your husband.

Marriage between two men is—in my experience as a psychotherapist—dramatically different from heterosexual marriage. It's a double testosterone marriage. With all that testosterone, sex is probably going to be handled quite differently for us than for some straight couples or even for some lesbian couples.

Let's be clear, I'm not saying that we are helpless victims of our libidos. Instead, we can be intelligent, aware creators of a new kind of marriage that acknowledges that two men together have unique gifts (and challenges) that other kinds of couples don't. I'll get into this in more detail in the pages to follow, but be prepared to rethink everything you've been told about marriage. The bottom line here is:

Finally, we get to do it our way.

Let's move beyond gratitude into real creativity and come up with two-husband marriages that are unlike anything that's ever come before. Yeah, I know that's a tall order, but don't be intimated. The creativity I'm talking about can be extremely subtle. No one may know how secretly subversive you and your husband are but the two of you.

Or, you can make major changes in the marriage blueprint that rock your world. Either way, it's your choice and it's my privilege and honor to write a book about this new world of double testosterone marriages.

As gay men, our experiences of sex typically differ from those of straight men. For one thing, we can have it more easily and more often (witness the rapid rise in popularity of Grindr, Scruff, Adam4Adam, and all their imitators). Very few straight men expect to be in a relationship with a great woman *and* be able to have sex with other women. Yet, many married gay men expect *just* that kind of freedom in their marriages.

Many of our relationships start off monogamous. However, because sex is so important to a lot of us, it is my experience that about half of our relationships—over time—are not 100 percent monogamous. Whether married or not, many gay relationships begin to "open up" after the first few years. In the book, we'll follow two couples as they explore how to handle the desire for sex outside of their marriages.

Couple #1 is Tomas and Larry. They've been married for eight years. Initially monogamous, they began to find their sex life too predictable after about three years. We'll watch them go through the challenging and sometimes humorous process of navigating an open marriage. For example, we'll look at questions such as

- What can we do about sexual boredom?
- How can we open up our marriage without damaging it?
- Won't one of us get jealous and insecure?

We'll follow Tomas and Larry as they transition from monogamy to an open relationship. This gay couple loves each other deeply: they want to be together and they've learned to trust each other. Yet, to their surprise, their sexual life became the weakest part of their relationship.

So Tomas and Larry decided to try an open/nonmonogamous marriage to see if this would bring them more satisfaction, both as individuals and as a couple. There will be more on them later, in part 2, Exploring Open Marriage, so stay tuned.

Couple #2 is Ethan and Jake. They've been together for about four years and legally married for eighteen months. After three years of living together, they began to grow sexually bored with each other. They considered opening up their relationship, but instead decided to remain monogamous and explore *why* they became sexually bored and *what* they could do about it. In part 3, Exploring Monogamy, we'll watch this couple go through the process of keeping a monogamous relationship sexually alive and fulfilling. With Ethan and Jake, we'll look at questions such as

- Can we, as a married couple, remain faithful to each other while living in a community where sex is so easily available?
- How do we address problems like illness and aging as it affects our sex lives?
- If we have radically different desires for sex, how can we negotiate that and still be monogamous?

Many gay couples *do* want monogamy. But these couples often find themselves smack in the center of a community that only pays lip service to it. These couples want to be faithful to each other, but their community encourages them (both overtly and covertly) not to. Readily available sex doesn't make monogamy very easy.

I've had clients tell me that, shortly after they got married, their friends began to ask them questions such as, "So, are you *really* going to be faithful to (husband's name)?" and "Everyone starts out monogamous at the beginning, but how do you pull that off when everyone around you wants to have sex with you?"

One client even told me, "Now that I'm married, so many more guys are hitting on me at the gym. I guess now that I'm not available, I'm a lot more desirable."

Sound like anyone you know?

For many of us considering marriage—or already married—the question of monogamy or open relationship looms large: it's both terribly important and terribly confusing. Deciding between the joys of infinite sexual possibilities or the security of one person for the rest of your life is a huge catch-22. How do we "win" here?

In this book, we'll explore sexual monogamy, emotional monogamy, and "open relationships" where a gay couple has more than one sexual partner. We'll look at questions and ideas such as

- Is it realistic to have sex with only one man for the rest of your life?
- What if you have different sexual preferences, for example, you're both tops; one of you likes anal sex and the other doesn't; one prefers wild sex, the other opts for tender and gentle encounters?
- How do you resolve incompatible libidos: One of you wants to have sex once a day—minimum—while the other is happy with once a month?
- What role does sex play in your marriage? How does that affect your feelings about being monogamous?
- What is your intention for your marriage? Is it to have fun, share great sex, deepen an emotional connection, stay together for life?
- What would be the purpose of an open marriage? Of a monogamous marriage? What are the pros and cons of each?
- What does "emotional monogamy" mean to you and your husband?
- How can you remain emotionally committed to each other while having sex with other people?

Many of my coupled gay clients, having examined traditional heterosexual marriage-based relationships, find them lacking. Other men, however, think that the idea of "emotional monogamy and sexual nonmonogamy" is a cop-out, a way to rationalize being unfaithful to your husband.

While this is a controversial issue, it's also an opportunity for us as married or potentially married gay men to be social pioneers and make our own way. And I'm not just talking about sex here.

In heterosexual couples, the male and female stereotypes often play out as "Men are from Mars, Women are from Venus." As married gay men, we are inventing our own genres of love, literally making up the rules as we go along.

If you have two men from Mars married to each other, who cleans up? Who is the more nurturing one? Who is the more career oriented?

Then there's what I call the "double testosterone challenge." From my years of working with couples, I've noticed that gay couples typically experience two challenges more intensely than do opposite-sex or lesbian couples: *competition* and *conflict*. And that brings us to the key reason: testosterone.

Biologically, testosterone is crucial in maintaining muscle mass, bone density, and sex drive. It helps keep us youthful and energetic. However, it has its downsides: too much testosterone has been associated with risky behavior—excessive consumption of alcohol and recreational drugs, high-risk sex, driving at unsafe speeds—in many research studies. Anecdotally, I've observed that men with higher testosterone levels typically have a hard time curbing their aggression; this is bound to play out in their marriages.

Science has discovered that men's testosterone levels typically peak in our twenties and thirties, slowly decrease in our forties and fifties, and are noticeably lower from our sixties onward. There are exceptions to this, of course, but this is the general trend. Therefore, it's not surprising to me that these "double testosterone" marriages of men in their twenties and thirties are much more likely to have formidable challenges in the competition and conflict departments.

When we get married young, our testosterone levels are higher, and we're likely to have lots of energy that we may not know how to channel constructively. We bring it into our marriage—and we compete.

We compete with our husbands. A lot. And we compete over silly little things—such as, how to stack dishes in the dishwasher—and some pretty important things—such as, who's the smarter, who makes more money or is more successful.

Competition, in moderation, is healthy. It's the "juice" of being alive, wanting to do well, enjoying success. But too much competition leads to conflict, and conflict in a double testosterone marriage can easily lead to arguments that escalate out of control both verbally and physically.

As a psychotherapist, I've observed that, in heterosexual marriages, our male (testosterone-fueled) aggression is balanced by female (estrogen-fueled) grounding and emotional intelligence. Many of the straight couples I've worked with have demonstrated this: during their counseling sessions, the husband was angry much of the time and the wife kept trying to talk about working together to address their problems. All too often, the husband wasn't having it: he wanted to "win" the argument, "win" the counseling session—his testosterone was running (and ruining) their relationship.

In gay marriages, where is that "female" grounding and emotional intelligence? If we're lucky, each man will be able to access it in himself. But when you're young and have a lot of competitive energy, it isn't easy. We both want to "win," to be "right." The result is a steady effort to prove superiority—and conflict follows soon after.

You could also make the case—convincingly, I might add—that younger married gay couples typically have a lot more conflict and competition due to less life experience. However, I believe that it's also related to those lifetime-high testosterone levels.

On the other end of the testosterone spectrum, I've noticed that decreasing testosterone levels are often related to lower levels of sexual satisfaction (and more open relationships) in gay couples in their forties and fifties. Why? If sex has been a major cornerstone of our marriages/relationships and we hit an age where our sexual desires and libido take a dive, we may hope that opening up our relationship will be just the panacea we're looking for.

To be blunt, testosterone can make us too horny when we're younger (creating trouble in marriages), and too disinterested in sex when we're older.

But never fear! As you'll see in the chapters ahead, the challenges of a double testosterone marriage may be daunting. However, together with this book, you can identify, analyze, and work through them for a stronger relationship.

Legal gay marriage is still a relatively new phenomenon. This book offers married gay couples (and gay individuals and couples considering marriage) an easy-to-follow, practical framework that you can use to create, adjust, and structure your marriage. Part 1 looks at unique challenges for *all* gay marriages (you won't find this stuff in your typical heterosexual marriage manual). Part 2 focuses on how to create and maintain a fulfilling open (nonmonogamous) gay marriage. Part 3 addresses how to keep a monogamous gay marriage lively and fulfilling.

There are currently no "rule books" for how a "double testosterone" marriage could or should work. While there are lots of books about how to plan your gay wedding, there are virtually none that address what to do after the honeymoon is over (literally and figuratively).

This book fills that void.

It is my intention that this book be frank, engaging, and full of practical advice. Toward that purpose, you will find "Questions to Consider" throughout the book that will give you (and your husband) easy ways to talk about the ideas presented in each chapter.

It is to be expected that some readers (and reviewers) may find my posing the question of "monogamy or open relationship?"—in regard to gay marriage—to be controversial. This book may even be disliked. *The Gay Man's Guide to Open and Monogamous Marriage* dares to ask the question, is monogamy or an open relationship (or a combination of both) the best way to structure *your* marriage?

Same-sex marriage has been a long time coming—a few thousand years or so—and now that it's finally here, many gay, bisexual, and transgender men may think that it's a bad idea to "rock the boat" by discussing the kinds of ideas that this book presents.

I believe that *now* is the perfect time to question what gay marriage can, should, and will be, while it is still relatively new, fresh, and malleable.

For the double testosterone marriage, "monogamy or open relationship?" is a question whose time has come.

PART I

UNIQUE CHALLENGES FOR GAY MARRIAGES

CHAPTER ONE

Designing Your Marriage

As married gay men, we have few role models. This is a double-edged sword: we now get to design our marriages on our own terms; on the other hand, it can be very disorienting when there are *so* many choices before us.

And who says we can't take what we like from heterosexual marriage and from same-sex nonmarried relationships and incorporate it into our own special blend of "marriage"? Indeed, for us, the problem isn't a lack of options, it's how to choose among so many options. This is what I call "Designing your marriage." While this phrase may sound funny to you, I like to compare designing your marriage to designing a house you would like to build. Wouldn't you and your husband decide what are the elements/features that you want in your house? What is most important to you both? For some guys, the kitchen may be really important, for others, it may be low on the priority list.

I encourage you to look at your marriage in the same way: What elements of your marriage are most important to you? Which ones don't matter so much?

Questions to Consider

- What is important to you in your marriage? (Make a list and have your husband do the same.)
- What are your priorities? Number the items from "1" (most important) and work your way down the list.
- Compare the two lists: Where do they overlap? Where do they differ?

Your responses will begin a conversation that will help to determine how you two will design your marriage. Ironically, very few couples—gay or straight—are ever encouraged to do this. It's a very helpful process—I use it in my work with couples—but it's not always a smooth process. If the lists jibe quite nicely, then it's great. But what do you do when they don't?

You talk about it.

Let's look at our first case study couple, Tomas and Larry.

When they first were married, they came to me for premarital counseling. They'd made their lists, and the lists did not overlap as much as they'd expected. They were surprised by this; they had assumed (after dating for over a year) that they knew what each other wanted.

Surprise!

They did know a lot about each other, but few of us ever sit down—on our own or with our husband—and make a list of what we want in our marriage.

For example, here was Tomas's list.

1. Security
2. Ease of adopting or having children
3. Legal/financial rights
4. Someone to grow old with
5. Get to know my partner sexually and vice versa and be very comfortable with each other
6. Monogamy and no risk of STDs or HIV ever again
7. My parents will finally get off my back now that I'm married

Here is Larry's list.

1. Want to be with you forever
2. Want our relationship to be the "rock" in my life
3. Possibility of children
4. Someone who will be my #1 and always have my back
5. Someone to buy a house with
6. Someone to explore an open relationship with (when the time is right)
7. Financial benefits (social security, taxes, etc.) and someone to plan/save for an early retirement with

Some differences: Tomas definitely wants children; Larry is open to it. Tomas is very keen on monogamy; Larry isn't so sure. Both men have a lot of overlap: each wants to be with the other "forever" and wants their relationship to last so they can grow old together, but can you detect other, more subtle differences? Like their attitudes toward money, family, and their sexual "ideals"? They did too. The list provided a foundation for them to begin to talk about what they wanted from their marriage. Every couple is going to have their own unique combination of goals. We'll return to Tomas and Larry in part 2, Exploring Open Marriage.

Questions to Consider

- What goals are nonnegotiable (i.e., they are crucial to you and you must have these in your marriage)?
- What goals aren't so important (i.e., it would be nice if you both were into them, but it's okay with you if they're not realized)?
- Write these down or talk about them with your husband/fiancé.

I urge the couples I work with to be aware that these goals are likely to change over time. What we see as "crucial" today may be optional next month/year. Knowing this—and reminding yourself about it—can help you from becoming too rigid and attached to having it your way. I've seen these goal "discussions" become power struggles; they certainly don't have to be.

If you feel that you must "win," that means your husband is going to lose (and vice versa). The only way for your marriage to "win" is for both of you to give up needing to be right. This sounds simple, but it's not so easy. As men, many of us have been trained to "win" and be "#1." This may be helpful in an aggressive work environment, but it will not be helpful in creating a happy, loving marriage.

A couple I worked with, Adam and Seth, found that in setting their goals, that Adam—a corporate lawyer—tended to dominate the conversation while Seth—a musician—allowed him to do so. This would have been fine had it been pleasing for both men. However, as is usually the case, the "quieter" husband eventually grew resentful and angry at being dominated, but didn't speak up about it until he had had enough and he "blew" (like a volcano) in my office. Not so unusual.

With these clients, I helped them talk about Seth's need to be heard and his opinions valued and Adam's belief that "aggression equals success." Adam had a hard time turning off his aggression when he left the office, while Seth had been trained to be a "good" boy his whole life, which sometimes meant letting others dominate him or putting his own needs aside.

One of the best things about premarital counseling is that you get to see your shit before it hits the fan. Adam and Seth saw that, if they designed their marriage along the lines of what they were used to, the power struggle would neither be acknowledged nor addressed, and would cause them both a lot of suffering. We'll look at power struggles, competition, and conflict in detail in chapter 2.

Just to let you know how things turned out for Adam and Seth: while each man struggled with his old, habitual patterns, they were willing to change and work together. Initially, they didn't know how to change, but their willingness was enough to begin the process. Today, while Adam is still an aggressive attorney and Seth is still a soft-spoken musician, when they are together, Adam is more receptive and cooperative and Seth is more quietly assertive and active in the relationship.

Let's not be naive here. It's my experience as a psychotherapist that our basic personalities don't easily change. However, over time, if we are *willing* to change, change happens. Not quickly, not easily—but it *does* happen.

Meet Ethan and Jake

Just as Tomas and Larry were our case study couple for an open marriage, Ethan and Jake are our case study couple for a monogamous marriage. Ethan and Jake had been together as a couple for about three years when they came to me for help with their marriage.

> Ethan: "Our first two years were exciting: we moved in together, bought a house together, and shortly after, got married. Buying the house was really great, because we'd both only lived in apartments up until then. Everything seemed to be a new adventure, but not anymore."
>
> Jake: "Now that we've been together for about three years, the glitter has definitely worn off. Neither of us has ever lived with anyone before. I thought we'd always be really in love and happy together, but I think we're both beginning to be bored with each other."

As I began to get to know Ethan and Jake, I learned that each of them had—rather unconsciously—designed their marriage in ways that didn't really work for them. They expected that the newness and excitement of moving in together, buying a house, and getting married would be enough to keep them from being "bored with each other" (Ethan's words). When things stopped feeling like "a new adventure" (Jake's words), neither of them was sure what to do next.

When we jump into marriage without much conscious intention, this is often what happens: the momentum of newness keeps us revved up and excited for a while, but it cannot last.

We'll pick up again on Ethan and Jake's marriage in part 3: Exploring Monogamy.

As you and your husband are together—over time—you can help each other change. In fact, often, in the happiest couples, each man takes on some desired characteristics of his partner. I like to use the analogy of marriage as similar to the process of polishing gemstones. I am told that to polish gemstones, the rough stones are put in a contraption that makes them tumble against each other. In the process of tumbling, the gems rub up against each other and rub each other's rough edges off. The longer they tumble together, the fewer rough edges and the shinier the gems become.

A good marriage is like that: the longer we "tumble" together, the more we can help each other lose our rough (primitive) habits and behaviors. As we rub up against each other, each of us becomes shinier, more brilliant, and happier.

Now that you've taken some preliminary steps to "design" your marriage, I'd like to offer some ideas for your consideration. These are the most popular reasons for getting married that I hear from my gay clients.

- Emotional bonds
- Legal rights
- Raising children
- Feeling legitimized in the eyes of society

Let's take a good look at each of these and see if they are important to you and your husband (you can always add them to your lists, if you like).

Emotional Bonds

Over the years, I hear many couples—gay and straight alike—talk about commitment and the power of a commitment. But what does that word mean? A commitment can mean dedication and devotion to your husband/marriage. It can mean loyalty and faithfulness. It can mean an obligation that expands your freedom (e.g., "I will be your #1 man, whomever else you sleep with") or restricts it (e.g., "You will not have sex with anyone else but me").

A commitment is an emotional bond. We want to be with our husband and we want him to know that, so we "commit." Any commitment is a kind of structure, as opposed to keeping everything loose and "free." In my experience, a certain degree of structure is helpful in a marriage. Just how much structure is best depends on the two men involved. It takes a certain type of guy to be comfortable with a lot of uncertainty; if this is true for you and/or your husband, you may bridle with too much structure. One couple I worked with—Devon and Carlos—had strong emotional bonds, but wanted very different amounts of structure in their marriage. Carlos said, "I feel smothered with too many shoulds and have-tos." Devon said, "But I want to feel secure and safe, so I need that structure."

What to do? In this case, I helped Devon and Carlos find a balance of structure/freedom that assuaged most of their needs. In some areas, Carlos had freedom (e.g., "When you're on a business trip, it's okay to hook up with guys, as long as you play safe"), while, in other areas, Devon got the emotional structure that he needed (e.g., "When you're away on a business trip, you'll call me every night so we can touch base").

See the different ways that emotional bonds can be structured so that they work for both men? Now, let's take a leap into another type of emotional bond. Let's talk about love.

I learned long ago that, if you really want to mess with someone's head, ask them to define love: it's pretty much impossible. Yet, when I talk with a gay couple in a counseling session, and ask them why they're still together—after going through their own private hell—one of them inevitably says, "Because I love him."

Sounds good, but what does that mean? Should we stay in a difficult relationship because we love our husband? Is love the glue that holds things together when times are rough? It is beyond me to come up with a great definition of love. Perhaps it's more helpful to call love the mystery ingredient in a good marriage: you can describe it (sorta, kinda) but you can't really define it. That said, in the context of this book, I'll be brave (and stupid) and offer a tentative definition of love: a cluster of feelings having to do with a strong, tender, passionate affection for another person.

It is beyond anyone's abilities to really—ultimately—define love. And yet, it's love, this hard-to-define experience that motivates so many of us to consider marriage. We love him; we want to be with him. We have this combination of emotions—attraction, respect, admiration, comfort, desire, and friendship—that we decide is our experience of love. And no one else can really tell us we're right or wrong.

I invite you and your husband to talk about what love is for each of you.

Questions to Consider
- Define "love" for yourself. Have your husband do the same.
- Compare notes. Where do you overlap? Where do you differ?

Have you ever been to a wedding and heard the couple make the vows: "Till death us do part"? I don't know about you, but for me, that's a huge emotional commitment. For some of my clients, a lifelong commitment is what they want. They aspire to achieve that. For other clients, it's not a good fit. One couple I worked with, Alex and Kevin, had a definite opinion about this. Alex told me: "There is no way I want to make that 'till death us do part' commitment. It's completely unrealistic." Kevin said, "It's a nice idea, but isn't it really setting yourself up to fail? I mean, how many people can pull this off?"

I once heard a wise woman—happily married to husband #2—say that the ideal marriage vow would be: "I like you a lot; let's see how it goes." Awfully loose, right? But perhaps this taps into the bottom line: marriage is uncertain. We can promise to be together until death separates us, but can we actually pull this off?

Questions to Consider
- Ask your husband (or potential husband): "What do you think of 'till death us do part'?"
- Discuss: What do you think are/will be the biggest obstacles for us to happily stay together?

Legal Rights

As gay men, what does marriage mean to us legally? For some of us, this is the most important reason to get married. Another couple I worked with—Sam and Will—were very keen on the legal and financial benefits of gay marriage. Sam, an elementary school teacher, told me: "I couldn't care less about marriage from a commitment point of view; my husband and I would be together anyway. What *does* matter to me are all the legal rights that we wouldn't have otherwise."

Will, an investment banker, said, "My husband and I have been together for nineteen years; legal marriage isn't going to change that. But what it *does* change are all the financial benefits that we are now eligible for. That alone makes it worth doing."

According to the Human Rights Campaign website (hrc.org, accessed March 23, 2016) there are 1,138 benefits, rights, and protections provided on the basis of marital status in federal law. Let's look at just a *few* examples of these 1,138 legal rights, benefits, and protections that you and your husband will—or do—enjoy.

- Veteran's disability
- Supplemental Security Income
- Disability payments for federal employees
- Medicaid
- Property tax exemption for homes of totally disabled veterans
- Income tax deductions, credits, rates exemption, and estimates
- Employment assistance and transitional services for spouses of members being separated by military service; continued commissary privileges
- Per diem payment to spouse for federal civil service employees when relocating
- Indian Health Service care for spouses of Native Americans (in some circumstances)
- Sponsor spouse for immigration benefits
- Exemption from federal unemployment tax for an employee working for his spouse

Joint and family-related rights:

- Joint filing of bankruptcy
- Joint parenting rights, such as access to children's school records

- Family visitation rights for the spouse and nonbiological children, such as to visit a spouse in a hospital or prison
- Next-of-kin status for emergency medical decisions or filing wrongful death claims
- Custodial rights to children, shared property, child support, and alimony after divorce
- Domestic violence intervention
- Access to "family only" services, such as reduced rate memberships to clubs and organizations or residency in certain neighborhoods
- Preferential hiring for spouses of veterans in government jobs
- Tax-free transfer of property between spouses (including on death) and exemption from "due-on-sale" clauses
- Special consideration to spouses of citizens and resident aliens
- Threats against spouses of various federal employees constituting a federal crime
- Right to continue living on land purchased from spouse by National Park Service when easement granted to spouse
- Court notice of probate proceedings
- Domestic violence protection orders
- Existing homestead lease continuation of rights
- Regulation of condominium sales to owner-occupant's exemption
- Funeral and bereavement leave
- Joint adoption and foster care
- Joint tax filing
- Insurance licenses, coverage, eligibility, and benefits organization of mutual benefits society
- Legal status with stepchildren
- Making spousal medical decisions
- Spousal nonresident tuition deferential waiver
- Permission to make funeral arrangements for a deceased spouse, including burial or cremation
- Right of survivorship of custodial trust
- Right to change surname upon marriage
- Right to enter into prenuptial agreement
- Right to inheritance of property
- Spousal privilege in court cases (the marital confidences privilege and the spousal testimonial privilege)

For those divorced or widowed, the right to many of ex- or late spouse's benefits, including:

- Social Security pension
- Veteran's pensions, indemnity compensation for service-connected deaths, medical care and nursing home care, right to burial in veterans' cemeteries, educational assistance, and housing
- Survivor benefits for federal employees
- Survivor benefits for spouses of longshoremen, harbor workers, railroad workers
- Additional benefits to spouses of coal miners who die of black lung disease
- $100,000 to spouse of any public safety officer killed in the line of duty
- Continuation of employer-sponsored health benefits
- Renewal and termination rights to spouse's copyrights on death of spouse
- Continued water rights of spouse in some circumstances
- Payment of wages and workers' compensation benefits after worker death
- Making, revoking, and objecting to postmortem anatomical gifts

And, dear reader, this is just a small sample of the legal rights and financial benefits that legal marriage offers us. Did you realize just how many benefits there were? I didn't until I began researching this book. So, in light of that, it's undoubtedly worth your time to talk with your husband about what many consider "too unromantic" a topic.

Questions to Consider

- What legal rights matter most to you and your husband?
- Why?

Raising Children

For several years I was a clinical consultant to an organization called COL-LAGE: Children of Lesbians and Gays Everywhere. I also did research for my master's thesis on the psychological effects of having same-sex parents and how these children might be different (or not) compared to the children of opposite-sex parents.

For many years, gay men were not seen as good parent material. It was long thought by child psychologists that a child needs a male and female parent to be happy and well adjusted. This, of course, portrayed any relationships outside of that norm—including single parents or same-sex parents—as bad for the child.

Until relatively recently, most gay dads had become dads in heterosexual marriages. I wanted to be a gay dad when I lived in San Francisco in the 1980s, so I went to a group called "Gay dads and those who want to be." I was surprised to find out that every man in the room had become a dad in a relationship with a woman (mostly through heterosexual marriages) and, after coming out, found themselves to now be "gay dads."

Much has changed in the past thirty years, and yet I still meet many gay dads in their thirties and forties who became fathers in a heterosexual marriage and, upon coming out and entering happy gay relationships, were the 2017 version of gay dads.

In some ways, things have changed; in others, not so much.

From my experience, younger gay men are much more interested in becoming gay dads in the context of their relationship with another man. We can, in essence, "skip" the heterosexual marriage phase and become parents with our husbands. But of course, there are challenges here. A huge one is the challenge of *how* to become gay dads.

In a heterosexual marriage, fatherhood is usually pretty straightforward: you and your wife have intercourse, she becomes pregnant and, if all goes well, nine months later, you're a dad. In a gay marriage, it's usually a lot more work and much more complicated: obviously, there is no "wife" to have the baby, so, if you want a biological baby, you'll need to find a woman to have your child. This alone is quite a daunting task, requiring much time, money, and effort. There are many good books on this subject, so I won't go into further details here.

However, two gay fathers-to-be have some pivotal questions that I will address. For example: Whose sperm will be chosen for biological fatherhood? I've facilitated some intense (and tense) discussions on that question in my office. If having a biological child is important to one or both of you, how is this to be brought about? One couple I worked with—Patrick and Jonathan—could not come to an agreement. *Both* of them wanted to be the biological dad. When one of their friends jokingly said that they should flip a coin, they both just about bit his head off. This was a big issue for them.

Over time, neither of them was willing to let the other be the biological dad. So, I, playing King Solomon (not really), suggested that they have two children, so that each man would get to be a biological dad. Miraculously, this worked for them and today, they have two children, and it is amazing how each child looks like their respective biological dad.

Both men are very happy.

Adoption is another avenue for gay dads, and yet, as anyone who's adopted (or tried to adopt) a child knows, it is usually a long, challenging, and expensive path. It's hard enough if you're a straight couple, but for gay couples it's even more difficult. While it's true that, in many parts of the United States, gay couples are legally required to receive the same treatment as straight couples, in reality, we often have to jump through more hoops to prove our "worthiness." Legally, this shouldn't be happening, but anecdotally, in speaking with clients who have adopted and friends who work in adoption placement, the reality is catching up (slowly) with the theory. Let's hear from two couples on this topic: Thomas and Michael and Billy and Khaleed.

> Thomas: "In our state, gay couples supposedly have all the same rights as straight couples. In reality, it ain't so."
>
> Michael: "From the first day the county social worker came to our home for the initial assessment, I could feel that she didn't like us. It wasn't anything like the experience that my sister and her husband had—and they had the same social worker!"
>
> Billy: "We live in a good-sized urban area, so we didn't think that adoption would be that different for us than it is for our straight friends, but boy, were we naïve. Not only are we gay but we are an interracial couple and Khaleed is about fifteen years younger than I am. I don't think any of these helped our cause."
>
> Khaleed: "The social worker seemed to be really accepting and we thought that everything was going well. However, as the other couples in our adoption support group began receiving placement possibilities, we were not. The social worker kept saying stuff like, 'It just takes longer in some cases; don't be discouraged.' But finally, when we were almost the last couple to be considered for a placement, one lady in our group, who had adopted two kids already, took us aside and told us, 'Between you and me, there are all kinds of unspoken prejudices on the part of the social workers, and you guys have several things going against you:

you're gay, you're mixed-race, and there's quite an age difference between the two of you. Get real, guys. You're gonna be pretty far down the priority list.' "

I don't mention these examples to dissuade you from wanting to become dads; I include them to present the possibility that the reality of adoption doesn't always match the (theoretical) way it's supposed to go. The path to fatherhood can be much more difficult than you expect. Be prepared.

Becoming parents is a big deal for a gay couple; indeed, for any couple! For gay couples, there is a myriad of decisions that the couple must make and, in many cases, there are decisions to make that most straight or lesbian couples may not need to address (e.g., surrogacy, adoption, financial and emotional costs). The joys of parenthood can be amazing, but the process of parenthood usually puts a lot of stress on the relationship. How can you minimize the painful parts and maximize the enjoyment?

I recommend that you and your boyfriend/potential husband talk about children when your relationship begins to get serious. I also recommend that you establish your emotional balance as a couple *before* you begin the path to fatherhood. Tackling fatherhood too soon can put unnecessary stress on a new marriage. Don't go there prematurely! In my experience, it seems best for a gay couple to wait two to three years before they begin the process toward parenthood. By this time, your relationship has usually stabilized to a large degree—you and he know each other pretty well and have already worked through some (if not many) difficult, stressful situations.

And what about once you and your husband become parents? How supportive is your community? We'll look more at this phenomenon in chapter 4, "Soul Mates, Family, and Community Support," but many of my gay dad clients report a huge shift in their relationship with the single gay community.

Todd: "My (gay) friends were really excited when Eddie and I adopted (five-year-old) Gayle, but now—two years later—they complain that we never go out with them. Honestly, most of the time, we're just too tired."

Juergen: "Van [his husband] and I are closer to the straight couples whose kids play with ours then with our single gay friends. We sure didn't expect that, but we have so much in common with them and not so much anymore with our single friends."

Bob: "Our social life has completely changed since becoming gay dads: our (single) gay friends dropped us and the only people who seem to want to hang out with us also have kids. I'm glad we didn't know this before we adopted, because it may have made us think twice to know that we'd lose most of our single gay friends."

Becoming parents usually brings about huge changes in how you live your lives as a couple. Your time is no longer your own and you probably don't have much of it to spare. You may be exhausted from parenting duties and not have the energy to go out on a weeknight (or even a weekend night). In some ways, this isn't so different from what happens to straight couples who have kids; their single friends often don't know how to "fit in" to their old friend's new child-oriented lives. Some friendships make it; others don't.

If you and your husband are considering parenting, please talk with other gay parents (and straight parents too) and ask them about how their social life has changed and how they managed it. I also urge you to see if there are any gay parenting groups near you. If there aren't, consider connecting with a (predominantly) straight parenting group: you may be surprised how much you have in common and the kind of support you can get.

Once you have kids, how do you and your husband choose the kinds of parents you want to be? Traditional psychology usually claims that every child needs a loving, nurturing mom and a loving, supportive dad. As a former preschool teacher, middle school counselor, and *Sesame Street* intern, it is my experience that every child needs someone who provides comfort and reassurance as well as someone who "gently kicks his butt" as one of my clients so aptly puts it.

Linc: "With Kelly (our son), I am the dad who will comfort him, tell him it's gonna be okay, wipe away his tears, clean up his knee when he scrapes it and put the bandage on. Gary, my husband, is the dad who tells him, 'Okay Kell, you're fine now, get back out there and keep going.' We split these roles pretty well down the middle. I guess you could say I'm more like my mom and Gary is more like my dad. That's just our personalities."

In a household with two dads, who is the more nurturing dad? Who is the more independence-encouraging dad? Do you both try to take on both aspects of parenthood, or do you each find yourself gravitating more toward one or the other? We'll go into this in more depth in chapter 3, "Redefining Gender-Based Roles."

Regardless of how you and your husband determine your parenting roles, I urge you to question traditional child psychology on this topic: while gay *marriage* hasn't been around long enough for there to be much research on how it affects children, gay *parenting* is a phenomenon that's been around for quite a while. I would like to say a bit about my own experience doing research on how children of same-sex parents fare psychologically (this was the thesis subject for one of my master's degrees).

For many children with two dads, what was noticeable to me in my research was that these children *knew* they were *wanted*. Two men together usually have a very challenging time becoming parents. In heterosexual and lesbian relationships, where one or more of the partners is a woman, a woman has the option of being the child's biological mother. As married gay men, we need to either find a surrogate mother or pursue adoption. It takes a lot of time, energy, money, and desire for a gay couple to become parents. I found that children with two gay dads knew they were wanted, and this usually had a positive effect on their self-esteem.

Gay parents are usually *very* motivated parents. If it takes years to adopt or find a surrogate mother before a child is brought into the marriage, these men must *really* want to be dads, and very motivated dads tend to be devoted dads.

Questions to Consider

- Do you and your husband want children? If so, how many?
- How would you like to become parents (adoption, surrogacy)?
- When would you like the parenting process to begin?
- What do you think you'll enjoy the most about being a father? The least?

Feeling Legitimized in the Eyes of Society

This is a rather controversial subject for many of my clients. Many of them, particularly the younger ones, say things like, "It doesn't mean shit to me what society thinks of my relationship or marriage. It's none of their damn business and I couldn't care less."

Other clients, usually in their late thirties or forties, frequently sing a different tune. One newly married gay man told me, "It makes a huge difference to me and my husband that we are legally married. It just makes everything so much easier. I can introduce him as my husband and not come up with some stupid-sounding substitute like 'partner' or 'other half.' And I feel proud that I can say the words 'married' and 'husband' just like the rest of my straight friends and siblings."

It's not surprising that age makes a big difference here. For those of us who grew up in a time when homosexuality was something to be ashamed of, legal gay marriage is amazing. I can honestly say that, at my age (sixty-three), I never expected that same-sex marriage would be legal in my lifetime. It was a pipe dream, but not anything I thought I'd live to see.

Not surprisingly, then, for many of us older gay guys, to be able to get married and call our husband "husband" is pretty earth-shattering. I still get a little thrill when going to social events and someone introduces me to his husband. It still sounds new and fresh and, yes, exciting. And I know I'm not alone.

I would say that the "dark" side of this excitement (and, yes, every "wonderful" thing has a dark side), is our tendency to overvalue it, to come from an "I'm so grateful; I'm so grateful" position, rather than a "We deserve this; we deserve to be equals" point of view. When gay marriage wasn't legal, our relationships were seen as not as valid as those of straight folks. Domestic partnerships and other kinds of legal (albeit second-class) designations were a step in the right direction, but they were still a substitute for the real thing. Now that we have the real thing, what are we going to do with it? That is basically the subject of this book!

Questions to Consider

- Does your relationship feel more "validated" now that you can get married legally?
- How so?

We have a whole range of choices about how we can create/design our marriages. In this chapter, we looked at many options and—hopefully—used the exercises and questions as tools to talk with our actual or potential husbands about how to best design our marriage so that each of us is pleased with what we're creating (at least, most of the time).

While we've identified some of the design elements you can choose from, in reality, we are consistently designing and redesigning our marriages over time. As situations change, and we change, we want different things. In many cases, we achieve our goals and then are in a good place to set new ones.

Now, let's look at a problem that is all too common, but seldom addressed, in many gay marriages—how to deal with conflict and competition.

CHAPTER TWO

Competition and Conflict

Have you ever noticed how much competition there is in gay male couples? It's just beneath the surface, and something I see a lot as a psychotherapist to the gay community.

It seems easier for opposite sex couples not to compete. Perhaps it's because they look at their partner across the breakfast table and that person looks so different that they don't feel what I call that "testosterone grunt" of competition that we gay couples do.

What's a healthy gay couple to do when you or your man find yourselves thinking some version of: "You think you can make more money than me?" or "Oh really, you think you do (fill in the blank) better than I do? Watch this."

Why do we compete anyway? What drives us? What is the essence of competition?

I love this definition of competition: a rivalry between two or more persons for an object desired in common, usually resulting in a victor and a loser but not necessarily involving the destruction of the latter.

Isn't that great? Not necessarily involving the destruction of the "loser." And yet, in our marriages, where does competition take us?

Must there be a winner and a loser? Is that endemic to competition? In a relationship, what does the loser usually do? In my experience counseling couples, the loser usually exacts some sort of revenge on his partner, often through passive-aggressive means. "Oh, you got away with _____, well, I'm gonna get you back, just you wait." I see this over and over in my work with gay couples and no one wants to talk about it.

And what about the "winner" of the competition? Today's winner is tomorrow's loser. It may feel good to win, but if you love your husband, don't you feel bad when he loses? And in reality, don't you lose too?

If both of you don't "win," the outcome is destructive.

"Winners" only get the booby prize: the real prize is when two men work together to find a solution to a problem that they can both live with. It may not be perfect; it may be a major compromise for both of you, but no one "loses" and no one "wins"—you're both in the same boat: "I gave a little; you gave a little and we both got some/most of what we wanted."

Competition—whether in a marriage or a friendship—doesn't lead to happy endings. What else is there? How about cooperation and compromise? Cooperation is about working together to the same end. Compromise is a settlement of differences by mutual concessions.

I've been told by some male clients that compromise is for cowards and cooperation is for new-age types who are afraid to take a stand. That point of view is so twentieth century. Modern organizations and modern life aren't set up for competition without cooperation and compromise. Even the most cutthroat businesses cannot survive purely on competition: everyone would burn out and only one person would ultimately "win." There's nothing wrong with a little friendly competition, but when it becomes your main way of getting through life, you're going to leave an awful lot of unhappy people in your wake.

In gay marriage, cooperation and compromise are the building blocks to long-term mutual happiness. Think of the relationships in your life that have stood the test of time and made it through arguments, hurt feelings, and anger. There's no way you can make it through the inevitable difficulties and disagreements of marriage if competition is your main coping strategy. In any good, ongoing relationship, both people are bound to piss each other off. It's part of life; there's no avoiding it.

Competition, like high-calorie desserts, isn't a bad thing. In moderation, it gives life a little "pow!" And it's a funny thing about the word "competition." The root of the word is from the Latin *competitionem*, the past participle of *competere*, which means to meet, to come together. And that's exactly what good relationships are all about.

Even in the best marriages, conflict is inevitable and the often resulting competition between two men is typically seen as masculine and manly. When we "win," we feel pride in our victory. Cooperation is often seen as girly and new age-y. Men who cooperate are sometimes described as too "soft" or even, as "losers."

As a sixty-three-year-old gay man raised on a farm in Ohio, I considered competition and conflict a part of life; I was encouraged to "buck up" and "if he hits you, hit him back harder." There are obviously pros and cons to this approach to life. When viewed in the context of gay marriage, cooperation is an extremely useful skill to develop. If you and your husband can work *together* to resolve your conflicts and competitions, you're much more likely to find marriage satisfying than two guys who are constantly at each other's throats.

It is my experience that conflict and competition are inevitable in even the happiest marriage. So how do we deal with them? We can start by acknowledging and talking about it.

Questions to Consider

- What triggers you to want to compete and "win" in your marriage?
- When do you feel a strong need to be "right"?
- When is it easy for you and your husband to work together?
- In what situations is it difficult for you and your husband to work together?

Competition is not all bad. At its best, it has a healthy, playful, male energy. It takes the form of gentle teasing for some couples. Here are a few examples of healthy competition.

Dalton: "My husband and I often have some kind of friendly competition. Our most recent one is who can lose the most weight and look better? We encourage each other and complement each other as we're both exercising more, losing weight, and showing more muscle. We also tease each other (good-naturedly, of course): 'Oh really, you're skipping the gym today? Well, I'm not.' This may get him to come with me, or not. Either way, we're encouraging each other."

Silas: "My husband and I have always playfully teased each other since we met. It's just how we are. We both like to bicycle, so our latest 'contest' is who can bicycle the farthest? We ride together—and separately—and keep track of how far we ride. At the end of the month, whoever's ridden the farthest has to buy the other a nice dinner at the restaurant of his choice."

Taylor: "My husband and I are real jocks; we're always competing with each other in baseball, tennis, swimming, skiing. We compete with our friends too. It's just part of who we are and it works for us. Lately, we've decided that we want to buy a house, so we've shifted our competition from sports to 'who can save the most money for the house?' Each of us is putting money aside for the house and we'll both win when we have enough for a down payment."

Let's talk about conflict. Learning to work through conflict is a major goal of any long-term relationship. In a marriage, our old unresolved stuff is bound to come up and, if we can work with it consciously and respectfully, we can use our marriage as a kind of "informal therapy" to help each other unravel the tangled webs of old trauma and hurts.

Conflict can be healthy. It's a constructive way to test your limits. It lets you learn where your boundaries are. Conflict lets you know: this is not okay with me. That doesn't mean that you're "right"; it simply shows you where you've hit a wall and something's got to give.

Through conflict and competition ("C&C") in a marriage, we learn about each other and ourselves. Our husband will learn more about us than anyone else. He may learn all of our weakest spots and greatest vulnerabilities. In a marriage, we often say hurtful, mean things. We know just where to really hurt our husband.

In some ways, it's easier for two men to work through C&C: we both know what it's like to be a man; we know how hard it is to be open and vulnerable. We know how we may be silent in our pain and hurt. This is really good. It builds empathy. We see ourselves across the breakfast table and we know the joys and sorrows of being gay men.

A little C&C is good: it keeps us sharp and awake. It lets us learn where our "edges" are—where our rough spots remain rough and could use some help. Too much C&C inevitably leads to anger, hurt, cruelty, and a breakdown of the marriage. So find your balance: if you and your husband like to tease each other, great. It can be playful and fun. If you or your husband find that teasing hurts and pushes old buttons, enough said.

Hurt can always be followed by repair. Repair is a crucial part of any marriage. We are bound to hurt the man we love (and vice versa), but what do we do about it?

Dex: "I know that I sometimes hurt Jared [his husband], but I don't always know what hurts him and what doesn't. So we've gotten good at reading each other. I know that when he goes silent and withdraws, that he's hurt. I can ask him about it and he'll tell me, but he usually doesn't bring it up himself. That's okay; we've learned to work together this way."

Welison: "My husband is really resilient; almost everything slides off his back. Not me—I am more sensitive than I'd like to be, but I've learned to live with it. For me, it's hard to tell him that I feel hurt by something that he said or did, but if I don't, he probably won't notice. So I *have* to say something, or it won't get addressed. This is good for me because it forces me to speak up, something I'm not too good at (yet)."

Jahleel: "My husband and I are both really sensitive; we notice everything and nothing gets by us. On the plus side, this means we can easily read ourselves and each other; on the downside, it means we both easily feel slighted. We're working with this, learning to bring things up, not let them fester, so that we talk them out and let them go. It makes for a lot of talking through stuff, which can be a drag, but it also makes for a lot of healing, which is great."

As you can see from these examples, every couple will have their own unique "repair dynamics." There is no right or wrong way to do it; what matters is that you and your husband come up with a structure that works for you. Here are some general guidelines to consider.

If you did the hurting

1. Apologize—Only if you mean it. If not, wait until you do.
2. Time-outs—Get away from each other for a bit; let things cool down.
3. Don't rush the process—Some of us can process our emotions on the spot, others need a few days to get clear on what we feel. Let your husband have the time he needs, even if seems to take "forever" for you. Everyone has his own timetable.
4. Take action—Healing isn't always verbal; actions may be the way it plays out (especially with men). Some of us have trouble finding the right words; we're better at demonstrating our regret. One client of mine gave his husband a little plant from Home Depot and, in his case, that spoke more eloquently than words.

5. Ask your husband what you can do—We often don't consider this. After you've apologized, ask your man: "What can I do right now to help you feel better?"

If you were hurt

1. Admit it—"Wow, that really hurts." Surprisingly, a lot of men skip this step. Don't expect your husband to be a mind reader. Speak your truth as calmly and respectfully as possible.
2. Time-outs—If you're really mad at him, don't talk then. If possible, let yourself cool off before you say much. Just let him know that he's hurt you and you need some time to process/think/feel it.
3. Talk with a trusted friend—I recommend you only talk with *one* friend. Don't broadcast your unhappiness; vent it with one loyal person who can keep it to themselves.
4. Exercise/walk—Something physical can help quiet your mind. The endorphins of exercise can lift your mood and stop your mind from obsessing on "He done me wrong."
5. Comfort yourself—Do something that makes you feel better.

How to Fight Fair

Sometimes I wonder: Why do we fight, argue, or disagree?

- We want our way.
- We want to be right.
- We want to get something.

Are we willing to get it at any cost? For most of us, the answer is no. In any relationship of worth, we want the relationship to prosper more than we want to "win." However, in any important relationship, like marriage, we have disagreements that we want to resolve. How can we do this so that both of us feel good (or, at least, pretty good) about the final result?

We fight fair. Let's look at three aspects of a good, fair fight.

Part I: The Setup

Ask yourself, "What exactly is bothering me? What do I want my husband to do or not do?" Write this down.

Know what your goals are before you begin. What are the possible outcomes that would be acceptable to you? Write this down too.

No surprise attacks. Set a time for a discussion with your husband, hopefully as soon as possible. Don't wait until the mood is "perfect" (it never will be).

Set boundaries together, for example, "This (behavior) is acceptable, but this (behavior) is not. If it happens, we will (appropriate action)." Good, clear boundaries make you both feel safer and provide an "emergency safety valve" if things get too intense.

Watch your mouth: the words you speak have great power to harm. Things said in anger can linger for years and are impossible to "erase."

Part II: The Process

Throughout the whole process, monitor your anger level. No one but you can know how close you are to losing it (or not). If you know you are going to lose self-control, take action before you say or do something you will later regret.

State the problem clearly. State the facts; then, state your feelings.

Use "I" messages to describe feelings of anger, hurt, or disappointment. Avoid "you" messages such as, "You make me so angry."

Avoid all-or-nothing terms like "always" or "never."

When you're listening to your husband, really listen. Don't rehearse your response and don't interrupt.

If you and your husband have a history of misunderstandings, it's usually helpful to restate what you heard, so he knows that you got it. Ask him to do the same for you.

Be specific about what is bothering you. Vague complaints are hard to work with.

No playing dirty and attacking your husband where you know he is vulnerable. This can quickly destroy a trust that may have taken *years* to build.

Don't machine gun: storing up lots of grievances and then letting him have it doesn't work. If you've got a list of issues that are unresolved, stick to two or three things *maximum* at any given discussion.

Avoid power-pouting: take turns talking and listening. If one of you gets pissed off and goes silent, nothing will get resolved.

Come up with more than one (possible) solution: allowing your husband only one option will make it difficult to resolve the concern.

Part III: Afterward

When you reach an agreement on a way forward, give yourselves credit (and a hug or something pleasant).

Decide together on a future time to check in and see how things are working. You can always modify any previous decision.

If no solution has been reached regarding the original problem, schedule a time to revisit the issue (usually in a few days, after you've both had time to reflect on what happened) and continue your discussion.

Sometimes, despite our best fair-fighting efforts, a disagreement or conflict seems insurmountable. Working with a good psychotherapist can help both of you communicate more effectively and deal with intense emotional reactions that often sabotage the process.

This sounds like a lot of work, right? Well, ironically, fighting fair is actually good for you and your marriage.

Conflict is an inevitable part of even the happiest marriage; we can't avoid it (no matter how much we try). When we have the courage to resolve problems with people in our lives, we build more trust in the strength of our relationships and feel better about ourselves (and those we love). It makes us more confident, knowing that we can—if we need to—go through the process again.

Like any skill set, fighting fair gets easier with practice. So don't avoid it; instead, accept it as an inevitable part of life and get good at it. Your marriage—and all of your relationships—will benefit.

How to Work with Your Anger

Dear Michael:

I am embarrassed to be writing to you, but so what? I am thirty-seven years old, and angry all the time. The weird thing is, I don't know exactly what I'm angry about, but I have to admit that lately my anger seems out of control. I blow up at everybody, in the car, with my husband, friends, and people at work. Some days, everything just pisses me off!

My husband told me I need "anger management" classes, because I'm always going off on him and he's fed up. I think he's right, but what exactly is "anger management"?

Ready to Explode in Hawaii

Dear Ready:

When someone treats you badly, it's natural and even healthy to feel angry. Instead of stuffing your anger until it builds (like a volcano) eventually to "explode," anger is a sign that you have needs that aren't being met.

When you act out your anger, usually it's you who suffers the most. You may yell at your husband, give the finger to another driver on the road or insult a colleague at work, but in the long run, it will come back to hurt you more than it will them. Out-of-control anger is destructive. Anger expressed responsibly is constructive and healthy.

Anger that gets pushed under always finds its way to the surface and will eventually "explode" with damaging results. Being able to responsibly express anger is part of being assertive. If you can't assert your needs, wants, or desires, you're going to get frustrated, annoyed, and angry. This doesn't mean you always get what you want; you ask for what you want or tell someone what you don't want, and see what happens.

For example, if your husband does something you don't like, you can be passive (stuff it and say nothing), aggressive (overreact and yell at him, "You idiot, I told you not to do that"), or assertive ("Remember that I told you how much that annoys me. I'm starting to get angry because you're doing it again").

Anger management is about responsible and timely expression of anger. This doesn't mean going off on your husband whenever you feel like it. It means finding a way to maturely and respectfully express yourself when someone or something is bothering you.

When I work with clients on anger management, I help them figure out what to do with their anger, how to control it (not vice versa) and where it comes from. Where *does* your anger come from? Anger management asks you to *think*, not *react*. Your thoughts create your emotional reaction, not vice versa.

The next time you're angry, think before you react. Ask yourself

- What am I upset about?
- What need of mine is being ignored/denied?
- What do I want to be different?
- How do I want to be treated?

When you are clear on what you want, you can ask for it. You can let others know when you don't like what they're doing/saying to you.

However, if you're angry almost *all* the time, this is different from situational anger.

Chronic, ongoing anger is almost always a reaction to events from your past; it's important to figure out where it comes from. This doesn't mean that you blame your parents, teachers, or whomever for past poor behavior. It means that you take responsibility for yourself by (1) admitting that you have valid reasons to be angry and (2) finding healthy outlets for that anger.

The worst way to channel your anger is to aim it at your husband (or someone else) by yelling at or blaming him. Usually, our nearest and dearest get the worst of our anger. This can destroy a good relationship, so it's crucial to find other ways to channel your anger. Here are a few.

- Get some intense physical exercise: drop to the floor and do push-ups until you're exhausted. Then see how angry you feel. Run, jog, lift weights—it's really hard to be angry when that endorphin "high" kicks in.
- Write about it: uncensored writing that you don't show to anyone can be a good release. Be as pissed off as you want to! It won't hurt anyone (just don't text or e-mail it).
- Hit an inanimate object with your fists or a tennis racket; it's a good physical release for anger. You can beat pillows, hit the bed, or slug a punching bag.
- Scream in the car (while you're alone, of course). Ignore those strange looks on the faces of your fellow drivers—they're just jealous that you can scream so well.

Here's what *not* to do.

- Drink alcohol or take drugs: this lowers your impulse control and encourages you to "explode." Domestic violence often involves alcohol or drug use.
- Get in your car and drive. Sometimes driving can calm you down, but if you're really angry, your ability to drive is impaired and you're

likely to get angrier when other drivers don't vacate the freeways for you. Go for a walk instead.
- Yell at people or "tell someone off": you'll feel better for, oh, about five seconds. And then the repercussions come: you can't undo cruel things you say or do.
- Break things. You'll just have to clean up and replace them.
- Give someone the finger in traffic: How do you know that the other driver isn't high on crystal meth or has a gun in his glove compartment? Don't risk pissing off some crazy person who might follow you home.

Anger can be an asset: it's one way to let other people know where you stand (e.g., "this is not okay with me"). Anger clarifies what you think and feel; it can help you to identify the source of your conflicts with others. You can say to your husband, "This matters to me; I need to be able to talk with you about it, because if I don't, I'm going to resent you." Unexpressed anger causes resentment, and too much resentment results in the kind of emotional "explosion" that Mr. "Ready to Explode" mentioned in his e-mail.

Let's be real. If your goal is to express your anger responsibly, in all conditions, at all times—good luck! No one I've ever met has pulled this off. But it's a good goal. Anger management is about gaining control over your emotions so your brain can short-circuit your impulsive reactions to say and do hurtful things. In the long run, learning to manage your own anger is one of the best things you can do for *you*—and, of course, your husband will be happy too.

Maintaining Your "Good Boy/Bad Boy" Balance

Recently, I've seen quite a few of my male clients who find that their balance is off. The balance I am talking about is the balance between excitement and safety, spontaneity and predictability—between being a "Good Boy" and a "Bad Boy."

If we try to ignore our Bad Boy side, it's going to find a way "out" and likely result in unpredictable (and unconscious) aggression, anger, acting out behavior, and—you guessed it—increased competition and conflict in our marriage.

As men—no matter how old we are—we need to embrace our inner Bad Boy. You know him, he's the one who has so much fun and sometimes goes too far and drinks a bit too much and may be too blunt or too loud for his own good. Don't think you have one? You're lying to yourself. We *all* have one. Okay, don't call it Good Boy/Bad Boy. Freud called it the id/superego balance. The id is the instinctual, primitive part of us that wants to eat when we want to, sleep when we want to, have sex when we want to, and never have to compromise or wait for anything. We want it *now*, dammit! That's the voice of the "Bad Boy" id.

The superego is the "Good Boy" voice of caution, worry, and concern about future problems or dangers. It's the voice that says, "You'd better not do that; you'll be sorry tomorrow" or "Doing that is going to get you in trouble." It wants to protect us and keep us safe. Meanwhile, the id wants us to have nothing but fun, fun, fun. These two need to balance each other. If you go too far in either direction, you end up unhappy: either you're indulging all your impulses and already regretting the trouble you've made or you're so good and sweet that you're bored out of your mind.

Freud didn't leave the id and the superego to battle it out alone. He created the concept of the ego: the mitigating force between too much "Good Boy" or too much "Bad Boy" behavior. When we go too far in either direction, our ego warns us: "Hey bro, your balance is off. You better do something to get back to a happy medium. Now, what's it gonna be?" The Buddhists call this happy medium "The Middle Path"; it allows you to have healthy helpings from the Good Boy and Bad Boy smorgasbord of life.

When a client tells tell me, "I'm so worn out from just living my life," it may be because he's bouncing back and forth between extremes; he hasn't yet found his Middle Path.

For example: Mr. A tries so hard to do the right thing: eat right, volunteer for a worthy cause, be the perfect husband, work overtime whenever the company needs it—you get the picture. However, Mr. A hardly ever lets himself go. His superego is so strong that he is locked into perpetual Good Boy mode. If he keeps this up, eventually he's likely to have a strong reaction in the opposite direction. He's likely to get fed up with being so good that he may do as one of my clients did recently: drink too much, score some crystal meth and cheat on his husband. And then he'll come into my office and ask me, "How did I let that happen? I know better than to do that." And he'll be full of grief, sorrow, and self-punishment. He ignored his inner Bad Boy for so long that it came out with a vengeance!

Then we have Mr. Z, the perpetual Bad Boy. He hates to wait—for anything. He almost always finds a way (through money, charm, personality) to get whatever he wants. He's the man who's done it all, had it all, and is bored to death. The idea of doing something purely generous and kind for someone else rarely enters his impatient, self-centered head. He's living the id-driven life and it's not making him happy. He's often disgusted with himself and with his husband and friends for letting him get away with so much. But he'll come in for therapy and tell me, "I don't know why I feel so depressed, I have everything I want." His inner Good Boy is pissed as hell: he wants to see some kindness and compassion for others.

The Middle Path is a path of balance. You get to be both the Good and Bad Boys, sometimes even at once. You get to be outrageously sexy, goofy, loud, and blunt and then pull back and be considerate, thoughtful, polite, and kind. You get to have wild, uninhibited sex with your husband and then go to church the next morning. You get to buy super-expensive, sexy underwear and wear it to work beneath your conservative business suit, smiling to yourself because your man will get to (slowly) take it off you that night. You let yourself have that tattoo or motorcycle you've been wanting, but you also pay your bills on time and call your grandmother in Omaha on her birthday.

It's good to shake things up and kick yourself in the ass when you get too "good" and things get way too predictable (too much Good Boy energy). On the other hand, when you get too out of control and selfish (too much Bad Boy energy), you may need to pull back, be quiet, and have a good honest talk with yourself. Whoever you are—and however old you are—why not embrace both your Inner Good Boy and Bad Boy? Your life will open up, you'll have a lot less conflict and competition in your marriage, and you'll find your own Middle Path. When you balance it out, you and your husband can have a hell of a lot of fun—and few regrets.

More Happiness; Less Conflict

It may be overly simplistic to say so, but I like to simplify things: the happier you are as a person, the less conflict you're likely to create in your marriage. When you're happy, you don't *need* conflict. Conflict is a way of playing out and expressing your unhappiness. Many couples focus on reducing the conflict, but they rarely focus on bringing more happiness into their lives. Here are seven "steps" that you and your husband can take—individually and as a couple—to have more happiness and less conflict in your marriage.

Step 1: Let go of your stories—Our words are very powerful. What we tell ourselves is amazingly self-fulfilling. If we keep telling ourselves the same stories over and over, we are pretty much doomed to keep having the same experiences over and over. Our stories create our experiences. If you are willing to release your old stories about yourself and your husband, you are opening the door to a happier marriage. Begin the process by noticing the stories you tell yourself about how your husband has hurt or betrayed you. Start to notice what you are perpetuating in your marriage by the stories you tell yourself.

Step 2: Forgive people—I wish this weren't true, but holding grudges against people ultimately harms only you. I have held a lot of grudges in my time and none of them did me any good. While I was angry at people who I thought treated me badly and should be "punished," these people were off having a great time without me. Who suffered? You don't have to know *how* to forgive, just be *willing*. Even if you are so mad at your husband that you are spitting bullets, if you are willing to forgive him, it will start the ball rolling.

Step 3: Embrace peace/release drama—For some couples, drama gives them the illusion of feeling "alive." These people are confused (or very, very young). Drama is not aliveness; it is a substitute for aliveness. Aliveness is a marriage full of opportunity and possibilities. Drama sucks the energy out of you. Aliveness gives energy to you and your husband. Drama is often a diversion from looking at deep (old) pain in your life. Face your pain, clean it up, and reduce your drama.

Step 4: Learn more sophisticated ways of functioning—Are you and your husband doing the same old stuff over and over? Is it working? I didn't think so. As we age, the Universe/God keeps showing us what we need to let go of in order to embrace something better. It's like the Buddhist idea of the empty rice bowl: if you're holding on to stale old rice in your bowl, there's no room for fresh, new, delicious rice. You've got to dump that stale, moldy, old rice so there's room for something new and wonderful. Scary? Sure. Productive? Absolutely.

Step 5: Polish your rough edges—We all have areas where we're not so smooth or high functioning; start to notice them. If you really want to discover your "rough" spots, ask your husband: he probably sees them much more clearly than you. And don't beat yourself up for them; instead, just notice them and be willing to change. Start with compassion—not punishment—for yourself. Ideally, you and your husband could help each other get rid of your sharp edges; wouldn't that be a terrific benefit of your marriage?

Step 6: Empty yourself—Try saying some version of "I am empty," meaning, "I am open, I am willing to let go of preconceived ideas." It's a really interesting phrase that I've been working with, personally and with clients. It can be helpful in letting go of upset and instead feeling calm and spacious. Often our mind feels so full of thoughts that we can't let go. These thoughts can keep you from falling asleep or enjoying time with your husband and other loved ones. Emptying yourself lets you dump all that mental junk and see how you feel without it. Try quietly and peacefully telling yourself, "I am empty" and see where it takes you.

Step 7: "I don't need to know"—This is another phrase that I frequently tell myself. Many of us think that more information will bring us happiness. Usually it doesn't. In fact, you and your man will *both* be happier if you can let go of having to "know" and "be right." Wanting—no, needing—to be right is the cause of many, many marital conflicts. Information is useful, but only if you use it in a way that works for you and your husband. Too much information can actually be unhelpful. Try saying "I don't need to know," and feel how freeing it is. Encourage your husband to try it too. You may both be surprised to find out that it's true.

Perfectionism, Conflict, and Competition

Do you feel like you're always judging/critiquing/evaluating yourself or your husband? Are you afraid to do something you may not be good at? Are you afraid to take risks? Do you have unrealistic expectations of your husband and yourself? Congratulations! You're probably a perfectionist.

There is a strong link between perfectionism and marital conflict: when we *have* to have things a certain way, it's no surprise that our husband is not always going to be able to do things *exactly* as we want. Plus, when we put this same set of unrealistic demands on ourselves, we perpetually disappoint ourselves. Perfectionist husbands are not happy husbands: they criticize themselves, their mates, and most of the people around them. The result? Increased marital conflict and competition.

Walton: "Did you ever read that book *The Best Little Boy in the World*? That's me. I am *always* overcompensating for not feeling good enough. I've done it since I was eight and my Mom caught me messing around with another boy, rubbing up against him. I tried to make up for being gay and now I've done it for so long it's a pattern. I wish I could relax and loosen up, but I can't."

Miguel: "I never thought I'd get married: Who could stand living with me? I have to have everything just so, and, if it's not, it makes me anxious. Thank God my husband Jim doesn't care about stuff like that. He lets me be in charge of our house and even the clothes he wears; he just doesn't care about how things look. He's perfect for me; who else could stand being married to me?"

Tomson: "My family was dirt poor and I am the only one who 'escaped' and got an education. When I go back home to visit, I see chaos and confusion. *This* is why I became a neat freak and super-organized. My husband Craig is the same way; between us, our home is always perfect and everything is organized. When something goes wrong, we *both* spring into action to fix it. We're a good match."

These married gay men have come to terms with their perfectionist tendencies, each in his own way. Contrary to popular belief, perfectionists are made, not born. It is a *learned* set of behaviors and can be *unlearned*. The bad news: it's not so easy to unlearn it. How do we become perfectionists? For some of us, our parents set us up. They put a lot of pressure on us to achieve and succeed. We came to believe that if we weren't "superstars" in everything we did, that we were "nothing."

Some of us had laid-back parents; it was we who made an unconscious choice to be perfect. Maybe we wanted attention and only got it by being a star. We wanted to make Mommy and Daddy happy. Maybe we had to be better than all the other kids just to get Mommy and Daddy's attention.

Perfectionism is an endless report card. We never really "graduate" and get to a place where we can relax and stop critiquing ourselves. We always have to be the A student—in our marriage, at work, with friends, in sports, with hobbies. Getting a B is never enough. Our lives become a continual pressure cooker to be better and better—at everything.

There's no fun or playfulness there and it's a setup for high blood pressure, strokes, anxiety, panic attacks, and constant worry. But fear not, there is a way out. Here are some steps you can take to ease up on your perfectionism.

- Be willing to redefine "success" and "failure": failure is not the end of the world; it's merely useful information. Instead of saying, "Oh, I'm such a loser," when something you do doesn't go perfectly, you could say, "Hmmm, that strategy didn't work so well, what can I do differently next time?" See how that approach has a completely different emotional tone?
- When you don't get an A, ask yourself: "Does my husband think less of me? Does he think I'm a failure?" Perfectionists are often insufferable because they have to do everything better than everyone else. They're not easy to love (just ask their husbands). It's easier to love people who make mistakes. Try telling yourself: "It's human to not win every time. It actually makes me more lovable. We all get our turn to win; this time wasn't my turn." and don't be surprised when your husband feels great relief as you really start to believe it.
- Stand in front of a mirror and tell yourself: "I am lovable exactly as I am" or "I am always good enough no matter what I do." You could also ask yourself questions like: "How can I be kinder to you today?" and "What would make you feel better right now?" Kindness and compassion are great enemies of perfectionism: over time, they dissolve it bit by bit.
- Participate in an activity—alone or with your man—that doesn't trigger your perfectionism, like watching a movie or walking along the beach. Notice how much pleasure you get from it and that it's not a competition.

Reading this, you may have wonder: "Why should I lower my standards? Perfection leads to high achievements, more money, and prestige. I want that." Fair enough, but consider this: an obsession with perfectionism does not make a happy marriage or a relaxed husband. Husbands of (unreformed) perfectionists tell me:

Bob: "It's like walking on eggshells. I never know when the littlest 'imperfection' is going to set him off. And then he pouts like a little kid, for hours. It's like being married to a man who occasionally becomes five years old whenever things don't go *exactly* the way he thinks they should. It makes me want to tear my hair out, sometimes."

Webber: "I feel like I can never do anything right. I am not an incompetent person. In fact, most people think I am pretty good at a lot of things. But with Manny, my husband, it's never good enough. There's always some 'flaw' that he points out. I think if he ever told me, 'Wow, that's great,' I'd fall over dead from shock."

Kish: "He's always judging me according to some unattainable standard. And the sad part is, he judges himself like this too, which is why he's always so tense and worried about everything."

Perfectionism does *not*, in the long run, lead to success in life. Success in life isn't about doing everything right (which is impossible); it's about what you do when things go wrong (which is inevitable, especially in a marriage).

Real success in love, marriage, and career comes from being resourceful, hard-working, and good at problem solving. The perfect marriage, gorgeous home, lots of money, and the corner office may sound good, but if you can't enjoy them, what's the point? Being able to relax and enjoy your life, trying new things and seeing what happens, being spontaneous and playful—this is where the joy of life comes from.

You and your husband deserve this.

What is the opposite of conflict and competition? For many of us, the answer is peace.

Oh sure, we'd like more money and a better body and a perfect marriage and the most fulfilling job possible, but if you dig deeper, the reason we'd like most of this stuff is that we think that, if we had it, we'd feel a wonderful, deep sense of peace. And we could relax into that peace and maybe, for the first time in our lives, not be so stressed and anxious and worried.

Sound good?

Peace is one of those words that a lot of us throw around without really knowing what it means. My friend Phil told me recently that he was meditating on peace (he's a deep thinker kind of guy) and that he broke "peace" down into five key components. Ironically, these components are crucial to a happy, peaceful marriage.

- P is for patience—being willing to wait for something that I want right now. I don't need to push myself (or my husband) or worry that things are going to be a mess. I can just put one foot in front of the other and walk my path, knowing that even if the current part of the path is rocky and steep, I *will* get through the tough stuff if I am willing to be patient.

- E is for empathy—understanding that it's not all about me, it's about *us*. I can ask for what I want, knowing that I am an integral part of a marriage, a family, a community, and a great big world of many, many people, and that we all want the same things: to feel safe, loved, and secure. I can focus more on how we—as human beings—are all alike, rather than how different (e.g., better or worse) I am, compared to you. I can open my heart to understand what my husband is going through and, even if I don't agree with him, I can respect him and honor his opinions and beliefs.
- A is for acceptance—for me, this is a tough one, because I like to think that if I try hard enough, I can get what I want. It's easy to accept things when life is flowing smoothly. I don't know about you, but that smoothness eventually gives way to challenges. How do I accept things that I don't like or want? Can I accept that painful experiences in my marriage can ultimately be good for me, or will I fight them tooth and nail?
- C is for calm—easy, serene, contented. *Calm* is one of my favorite words. It's the opposite of worry, anxiety, and panic. Not only does a calm state allow our mind to relax, thoughts to slow down, and obsessive thoughts to disappear, but our body calms down too: our heart rate slows and all our organs work better. When we're in a calm state, we make better decisions, take good care of ourselves, and treat others respectfully. Calm is really, really good for our marriages.
- E is for enlightenment—I think this is one of the most misunderstood words around. I think it means to be full of "light" and clarity, without heavy, depressing thoughts and emotions. It means realizing that I am on a very long path that is eternal (yes, I think that this is not the only life we will ever live) and that with each life we have another opportunity to "wake up" and know the truth. And the truth shall set us free . . .

I hope that breaking down that old, familiar word *peace* into P.E.A.C.E. has given you another way to look at it. In my experience, once you've got peace, you've got the perfect antidote to conflict and competition. It makes everything better. Peace is the bottom line.

The Power of Silence

Recently, I was asked to co-facilitate a workshop with the above title. I wasn't sure I really wanted to do it. After all, I thought, what's so great about silence? So I did some research and was surprised at what I found.

I discovered that silence has great power to make our marriages calmer and better. No matter where we live and who we're married to, there's a tremendous amount of "noise" in our lives: both internal (our racing, over-analytical minds) and external (the intense, crazy world that's all around us). How can we find some silence or do we even want to? Are we afraid of silence? After all, what would we do with an empty space, with all that nothingness?

Finding silence in your marriage is surprisingly helpful. It's easy to get lost in other people's expectations. All the "shoulds" can make you crazy: You *should* be a wonderful partner. You *should* be happy in your marriage. You *should* easily forgive your husband when he does things that drive you crazy. You *should* be generous to him. You *should* forgive him for being selfish/mean/foolish. See what I mean?

All this emotional "noise" is confusing and disorienting. It's an example of what my Buddhist meditation teachers call "monkey mind": our mind just bounces all around from one thing to another and—as a result—our thinking often feels out of control. If you ever find it hard to stop worrying/analyzing when you want to fall asleep, it's your monkey mind that's in control.

This is where silence can be useful. Take a moment before you read any further and define "silence" for yourself. Close your eyes and ask yourself, "What is silence for me?" Then just listen and see what you get. Be willing to be surprised. Done that? Okay, here are some definitions I found: peacefulness, quietude, stillness, and tranquility. Sounds pretty good, doesn't it? Well, how do we get there? Consider these questions as a starting point.

Questions to Consider

- When is silence easy for you? When is it difficult?
- What helps you to enjoy silence? What makes it hard for you to enjoy it?
- How can silence make your life better?

When you answer the questions, write the answers down in your phone or on paper, so you can come back to them later. The answers can help open the door to more—and deeper—moments of silence in your life.

Here are two ways to experiment with the power of silence. I use these with my clients because most of us—no matter how hyper we are—will benefit. The first one only takes a few minutes; the second one—a silent wandering—takes a bit longer.

First: a quick-and-easy silent meditation. This is especially good to do with your husband.

1. Take three deep breaths. Enjoy them. Invite your body to relax (it just might do it).
2. Check in with your emotions: notice if you're relaxed/sad/angry/bored. Don't judge it, just notice. This is what is often called "mindfulness."
3. Check in with how your body feels. What do you notice? Is there tension anywhere? Is your body more relaxed than a moment ago? Just notice.
4. Check in with your thoughts: What are you thinking? Again, just be mindful (no need to change anything).
5. Slowly allow your eyes to open and come back to the room. Take your time. If you like, you and your husband can talk about how this was for you. It can be a really positive bonding experience.

Silent wandering: this is another type of meditation you can share with your man.

1. Give yourselves about half an hour to "wander" together in silence: you can walk through a park, your neighborhood, a busy urban area, or an open field. Wherever you choose to wander, notice what it's like to do it in silence. Try to keep your mind silent too (that's not so easy) and be aware of the temptation to have a goal: instead, just wander.
2. During your wandering, you and your husband might each like to bring back an object to represent your silence (e.g., a leaf, flower, or found object). Let an object speak to you. If you are quiet enough, it will.

3. When you get home, the two of you can put your objects somewhere where you'll see them often, so they can remind you of your silent wandering, and—perhaps—encourage you to do it again.

Let the power of silence be your teacher.

Increasing your personal self-esteem reduces the conflict and competition in your marriage. Think about it: anything you can do to feel better about yourself is bound to have a positive effect on your marriage. The same goes for your husband: when he's happier with himself, he brings a lot of good energy and experiences to your marriage too. The personal becomes the communal!

When I worked for Kaiser-Permanente Psychiatry and Addiction Medicine, I originated and facilitated the "Healthy Relationships Support Group." A key concept of the group was: without healthy self-eeem, a healthy relationship is almost impossible.

That said, I invite you to take this Self-Esteem Quiz. Read the following statements and rate them on a scale of 1 (totally true) to 10 (totally false). Answer the questions as you honestly feel today, right now.

1. I feel positive about myself most of the time.
2. I believe in myself.
3. I know that I am a good person.
4. I have an inner sense of pride.
5. I take excellent care of myself.
6. I treat myself as I would a beloved friend.
7. I deserve great things to happen to me.
8. I love myself.
9. I know I am precious, wonderful, and truly unique.

Done? Good. Take a look at your answers.

If most of your answers are between 1 and 3, you have high self-esteem. Put this column down and go share your wonderful self with your lucky husband!

If most of your answers are between 4 and 6, your self-esteem is average. It could use some work, but—overall—it's okay.

If most of your answers are between 7 and 10, dude, we gotta talk. Your self-esteem is low and you deserve to feel better.

So, what is self-esteem? Reread the nine questions; to me, they summarize the major elements of self-esteem. One of the best ways to increase your self-esteem is to be willing to help yourself. This is not good news for chronic complainers. If you continually see yourself as a victim of unfair circumstances and tell your friends how things suck for you, you probably got a lot of 7s and 8s on the quiz.

We need to stop blaming others for our situation if we want to raise our self-esteem. This kind of change is usually uncomfortable at first. For some of us, as our self-esteem rises, we get scared. "It would scare the shit out of me to like myself," one client told me, "Who would I be then? Would anyone like me?" Ironically, other people usually like us better when we like ourselves.

Here are some more specific suggestions for raising your self-esteem.

- Self-assessment. Ask yourself questions such as: What is it I want? What am I afraid of? How would my life change if I liked myself more? Learning more about yourself is a crucial part of improving your self-esteem.
- Get new information. Reading and listening to books/CDs/MP3s are great ways to allow new information to flow through your subconscious, slowly changing how you feel about yourself. It is especially helpful to listen to them just after you wake up and right before you go to sleep; these are times when your subconscious is particularly receptive to new information.
- Write. Introspection put to paper is usually more powerful than just having thoughts about something. Writing things down makes them more concrete. It's a great way to learn more about yourself and monitor how your self-esteem improves over time.
- Changing behavior. Great ideas are nice enough, but you want to (gradually) change your behavior to make them real. Insights come, but what do you do with them? Begin to do things differently. Changing your behavior usually happens slowly; don't give up too soon.
- Get support. A good therapist, friend, or maybe even your husband (if you're both comfortable with it) will be able to encourage you, hold you accountable, and kick you in the butt when you need it. This stuff is too hard to do alone; get help.

"Why bother?" you may ask, "Raising my self-esteem sounds like a lot of work." You're right. It is. But what's more important than how you feel about yourself? Raising your self-esteem isn't selfish either: when we love ourselves more, we have more to give to others. We are more secure, kind, and forgiving men when we are strong, centered, and full of good feelings for ourselves. When we like who we are, we are happier husbands; we have more to give and are generous with our gifts and talents.

You *can* raise your self-esteem. Try these ideas and watch it rise.

Healthy Boundaries = Happy Marriage

If you listen to any kind of psychological advice show—from Dr. Phil to Dr. Drew—you'll hear the therapist talking about "healthy boundaries." A boundary is a marker, a dividing line. It tells me where my property stops and yours starts. Psychologically, it tells me when something is okay with me and when it's not.

A boundary is a kind of defense: it's a way for me to take care of myself. Taken too far, however, it can be a way for me to not let anyone—even my husband—into my inner world. People who have been hurt deeply often carry wounds that keep their boundaries very strong: "I'll never let anyone hurt me like that again."

Rigid boundaries may keep us from getting hurt, but they also keep us from getting love. We want to let more love in, but we're too afraid, so we keep our husband and others who love us at a distance, never letting them get too close. Holding onto rigid boundaries for a long time makes us into bitter, cynical, isolated elders.

Flexible boundaries let some people in, but not everyone. Flexible boundaries let us decide, in the moment, what we are able and willing to accept. Today I may be able to let my best friend vent for an hour about what his boyfriend did last night. Tomorrow, I may only be able to tolerate listening for a few minutes. People with flexible boundaries usually take good care of themselves and have strong, long-lasting friendships.

Wimpy boundaries are too weak. We want to stand up for ourselves, but we don't. My Grandma in Ohio used to call it "not having a backbone." People with wimpy boundaries are often seen as easy to manipulate (lend you money, let you verbally vent to them for hours, drive you to the airport at 3:00 a.m.) because it's hard for them to say "no." They are also known as "people-pleasers" who are terrified of any type of conflict or disagreement.

Marek: "My childhood was a real mess: my parents were too young and didn't know what to do with us kids, so someone had to step up and take control. Guess who? Yep, it was me. I started to take care of my little brother when I was about seven or eight, because Mom worked so much and Dad just wasn't that interested. So I became Mr. Rigid, as my husband calls me. I organize things and goddamn it, they better happen or I get pissed off."

Darryl: "I grew up with parents who were really relaxed, so I and my sibs are pretty relaxed too. We know when to say, 'no' but we rarely get bent out of shape. I don't know why Dathias (my husband) can't just let stuff roll off his back, like I do, but he can't. Sometimes I'm probably too laid-back, but Dathias and I balance each other out, so it works for us."

Jared: "I was always the quiet kid; I never had many friends. I did better with adults and books. I could always converse better with older people than with my peers. I still have trouble with people my age: they seem louder and drunker and more out of control than I am. It's hard for me to stand up for myself. My husband Dennis is always telling me, 'Speak up, let people know where you stand,' but it's so hard for me to do."

If your boundaries are flexible like Darryl's, hooray for you! You're probably enjoying yourself, have plenty of friends, and feel pretty good about your life. But if your boundaries are rigid or wimpy, what can you do?

If your boundaries are rigid like Marek's, notice how fearful you are and how you keep people at a distance. Your rigidity was probably once a good thing: it kept you safe in unsafe times. However, what once was your friend has now become a problem—you've outgrown it.

Ask yourself, When did I start to be so rigid? What was going on in my life back then? You became this rigid person so you could feel safe. The good news: there are other ways to feel safe. Try this exercise.

Find a picture of yourself at the age that you were the most frightened (it's usually childhood). Take that picture out and start to talk to this scared little child. Find out what terrified him. Let this child speak to you. You are carrying this child around with you and it is his fear that has kept your rigid boundaries in place. Begin to tell this child that he is safe, that you—the big, strong adult—will take care of him from now on. As your frightened inner child feels safer, the rigid boundaries begin to come down.

And what if your boundaries are too wimpy, like Jared's? Somewhere in your early life you were taught that you had no right to have needs or want things. You believed this and let this become your credo—until now. Most wimpy people have a lot of unexpressed anger and are afraid that if they let it out, it will overwhelm them and they'll become evil, vengeful people.

They won't. But that's the fear.

Find a picture of yourself at the age when you started to become a wimp and talk to this child. Tell him that he has a right to say "no," to be angry, and that it's safe to begin to let that anger out. Listen to his anger: it's in there and it needs to come out! Once your child starts to express his anger, the wimpiness will begin to melt and boundaries become stronger and more useful and flexible.

Healthy boundaries—flexible yet strong—make for healthy marriages. We need to be able to say "no" (calmly, of course) and mean it. On the other hand, it benefits us to be flexible and let people into our lives to love us and get to know us. If your boundaries can use some work, try the exercises above. Encourage your husband to try them too.

How to Lower Your Relationship Drama

You've probably heard some people describe their relationship as "high drama." Drama loves lots of conflict and strong emotion; it feeds on jealousy, envy, and resentment. It loves an intense competition with a glorious "winner" and a defeated "loser." These are *all* extremely unhelpful if your goal is to have a happy and loving marriage.

Why do some people love drama? They're used to it: it's their "normal." They were probably raised in it and it feels like "home" to them. Often, in my therapy practice, I work with people who find that peace and stability make them nervous; they're used to upset, chaos, and crisis. This is what they know, so they keep recreating it in all their relationships.

Until something snaps. Some line is crossed and they see that how their drama sabotages everything that they say they want: a good job, happy marriage, nice home, financial success. Drama says, "Let's stir things up. Let's make a mess. Let's pick a fight. Stability is boring. Let's have some crazy fun."

Mykola: "I don't know what peace is (laughs). My family is funny and loud and full of big personalities. I'm just that way too. I like to clown and make people laugh. I considered acting when I was younger, so I'd have an outlet for all that intense energy. Now that I have a more conservative job, I like to go out in the evenings with Chet [his husband] and our friends to our favorite bar, have a few drinks and go a little crazy. I need my outlet!"

Denny: "My family is very religious and everything looks calm and serene on the surface. But dig a little and you've got tons of drama. My Mom and her family all yell and scream at each other; then they just laugh it off. None of them takes it very seriously, but it gets really loud and intense. I'm used to it, but when I start to get dramatic with my husband Gary, it really upsets him. He says it's just too much."

Oak: "My dad was very calm, but my mom was super-dramatic. When they divorced, I ended up living with her and, unfortunately, I became a lot like her. When I first started dating guys, I'd pick men like my dad and end up playing my mom's role over and over again. Therapy helped me break this pattern, but it still comes back to haunt me in my marriage, sometimes with a vengeance."

If you have a history of high-drama relationships, how do you change? How do you replace drama with peace? First of all, realize how you create drama. Take responsibility for the drama in your life. See how you are the catalyst. No matter what situation you've created, it all starts with you.

That's actually good news, because it means that since you started it, you can stop it.

For some drama addicts, peace makes them nervous; they're just not used to it, so they call it "boring" or "not good enough." Getting used to calm may take a while and it may increase your anxiety as it becomes your new "normal."

Physically, drama triggers your sympathetic nervous system to go into survival mode. Drama actually shuts down the smartest part of your brain—the higher cortical functions like reasoning, problem solving, intuition, and creativity—so you can't think clearly.

Here are some ideas to reduce the drama in your relationships.

- Don't judge yourself or your husband for creating drama. It won't help. We're all doing the best we can until we become more stable and secure. Try compassion instead of judgment and you'll change faster and more easily.

- Get good at recognizing your own version of what I call "The Drama Sequence": Something happens, your mind starts to feed on it, you build a story in your head and get worked up about it. Result: high drama.
- Notice your motivation for creating drama: You won't do anything repeatedly unless there's something in it for you, so, what's the payoff? Are you looking for attention or excitement? If so, can you get it more directly? If you're bored, what new adventure(s) can you create in your life?
- Don't take things so personally. When we're mentally overstimulated from drama, it's easy to overreact instead of respond calmly.
- Get out of your head and into your heart. In an emotional situation with your husband, don't just vent. It often makes things worse. Instead, try some reflective listening: "I hear you're really upset about this. Let's talk about it."
- A lot of drama in a marriage comes from poor communication and confusion. Kindly speak your truth to your husband. It may be harder in the moment, but it can save a lot of heartache in the long run.
- If it's your husband who's emotionally worked up, you can aim for a "neutral" state so his drama doesn't trigger yours. Breathe calmly and tell yourself, "I am safe." You can help defuse his drama by staying centered yourself.

We can all learn from drama; sometimes it seems as though drama just happens to us and we're powerless to stop it.

Fortunately, that's not true.

We create drama. We can learn to create peace and calm instead. If we're used to drama and the chaos that comes with it, peace may initially scare us. If so, we can gradually replace drama with calm and notice how much better our marriage works as a result. Try it and see—you have nothing to lose but your drama.

Alcohol and Marital Conflict

Here are three e-mails I've received recently on a similar theme.

Dear Michael:

I have been with my husband for several years now. Our sex life isn't great, but everything else is good. Last week, I was out of town for work, went to a bar and, after too many drinks, ended up going home with this hot guy. I woke up the next morning in his bed, thinking, "If my husband knew I did this, he'd leave me." What do I do now?

Awfully Unhappy in Austin

Dear Michael:

Everyone thinks of me as this really nice guy, always sweet and patient. And I am—except when I drink. Then, after three or four drinks, I become really mean and cruel to everyone around me, even my husband and our friends. What's wrong with me?

Dual Personality in Baltimore

Dear Michael:

I love my husband and we are good together, except when we go out to the bars. Then, after a few too many drinks, I increasingly want attention from other guys and it makes my husband crazy. Do I need to stop drinking?

Desperately Seeking Attention in Orlando

Many of us love to blame our problems—marital and otherwise—on sources other than ourselves. It's not much fun to take responsibility for our problems, is it? And yet it's really the only way to make changes that last.

Some men decide that they drink too much, so they resolve to drink less. Sounds good, right? Except, it often doesn't work. Why? Because they haven't figured out *why* they drink so much. Like the above drinkers, they think that their "normal" (nonalcohol) life is good—or good enough, anyway—but that, for some reason, when they drink, they become these cheating, mean, attention-seeking guys.

I would say that all of the above three drinkers are kidding themselves in one way or another: they're pretending that their nondrinking life is just fine, when, obviously, it's not. You may be able to kid yourself that

- Your sex life with your husband is okay (when it isn't)
- You really are this nice, sweet person (when you're not)
- You get enough attention from your husband (when you don't)

You are, in essence, lying to yourself. And alcohol, by lowering your inhibitions, shows you the truth. And you don't like it. Sure, you can blame this on alcohol and stop drinking. But that's just putting a bandage on a dirty, deep (psychological) wound. That wound will never heal unless you rip off the bandage and clean out the infection (which, of course, is no fun).

I used to work as a barback when I was putting myself through college and I have clients who bartend in some of the best bars in our city. One of the wisest of them recently told me, "Alcohol is like truth serum: it shows you who people really are beneath their happy, shiny façade."

Wow, that's quite a statement. I don't know if I'd go quite that far, but the man has a point: for most people, alcohol lowers our inhibitions, and—as a result—we allow aspects of our personality to surface that we usually hide, suppress, or deny.

Truth serum, indeed.

So what do we do about this? We could start by admitting to ourselves that we're in denial about parts of our life that really aren't going so well.

Perhaps, as drinker #1 writes, he's not happy with his sex life with his husband, and by pretending he is, he's not doing anyone any favors. If he doesn't address this problem honestly and directly, he's on a path to sabotaging his marriage.

I would imagine that drinker #2 wants to express anger about things in his life that aren't okay with him, but he doesn't know how to—unless his old friend alcohol is there to help.

And drinker #3 may not have worked through his need for attention. He may pretend that he has when he's sober, but when he's not, it leaps out and takes control, much to his (and his husband's) chagrin.

Luckily, this stuff is all very workable. The alcohol is merely showing us the wounds that we're pretending are healed, when, in reality, we've just been changing the bandages. As a wise friend of mine likes to say, "It's not the alcohol; it's you." It's you who can clean out your (unresolved) problems so they don't haunt you and your husband any more. Wouldn't it be nice to be able to have a couple of drinks and not turn into some unpleasant version of yourself?

You can do it. Get help and clean out your old psychological wounds. Your husband will thank you.

CHAPTER THREE

Redefining Gender-Based Roles

As gay men, what dictates the gender-based roles that we play out in our marriages? Does our behavior align with or diverge from traditionally hetero-normative gender roles? In a way, it's easier for us as gay men than it is for straight men. At this point in time, our heterosexual brothers are caught in a gender-role trap: be a man, but not too much so. Be traditional, but don't go too far. Be sensitive, yet masculine. Many straight men are suffering and con-fused; straight women want them to embody an unattainable blend of tough *and* soft, masculine *and* feminine, strong *and* kind.

As gay men, I believe we have it easier: we have *never* fit that mold com-pletely. We've always been adjusting and changing—making it up as we go along. We've been forced to create ourselves as men (powerful and in control) who are gay (not powerful, must hide/adapt). We are used to this paradox, this gender-role balancing act. We're used to balancing our male and female energies: we've been doing it for years. As gay men, we (ideally) have the freedom to be as masculine and/or feminine as we want. We have turned a liability (not being hetero-normative) into an asset; this makes it easier for us to redefine gender-based roles and find our own unique way of being married gay men.

A while back, I went to a terrific workshop, "Gender Roles in the LGBT Community," at the San Diego LGBT Center. Even though both men and women were invited, I was the only guy there (along with about forty very cool women). After the workshop, I spoke with Abby Schwartz, the workshop facilitator, about doing a workshop for both LGBT women and men on the topic of "Moving Beyond Traditional Gender Roles." The people who run the center were very supportive of my idea and I was off and running.

Here are some of the questions I was particularly curious about.

> • What gender roles have you consciously (and unconsciously) settled for?
> • Do they help you or hold you back?
> • How can you move beyond gender roles to define and experience your-
>   self differently?
> • Can you access a new level of personal freedom and inner joy?

I ended up putting together a workshop addressing these questions, and—with my colleague Terri Martin—offered it at the San Diego LGBT Center. I'll talk about and explore some of the material from that workshop in this chapter. Consider this chapter an invitation to examine *your* ideas about gender and gender roles, particularly as they relate to your marriage.

"Why include this topic in a book about gay marriage?" you may be asking. Good question. As married gay men, most of us don't spend much time questioning who we are as "men," we usually do the same-old, same-old, just as we always have. As one client told me, "I'm just like my daddy and he's just like his daddy, only I'm gay."

Exactly: we're gay and, because of that, we can't do it like our daddy did. More to the point of this book, we can't do marriage the same way our daddy did either—because we're married to a man and two men together have to create their own gender roles and their own definition of "husband." A gay husband may be quite different from a straight husband—or not.

As two men together, how will we share our lives? How do we define ourselves as men? Without a woman, how will we decide who does the tasks that are traditionally those of "the wife"? Without a wife, how do we become "the husband"?

As married gay men, we may not be comfortable in being who the straight world thinks we "should" be—but what can we do about it? In heterosexual marriages, gender roles have been pretty clear (if rigid and old-fashioned), even if some of those roles are now changing. In gay marriages, gender roles are usually extremely flexible, maybe even uncomfortably ambiguous: Which of you is more nurturing? More the breadwinner? More the dominant one? Who fixes dinner? Does the laundry? Repairs things that break?

Let's look at some stereotypes commonly associated with heterosexual gender-based roles.

MEN

- Are silent, stoic, emotionally shut down
- Are the authority figures—keeping everyone safe
- Are the primary moneymakers, career-builders
- Defer to the wife in childcare, housework, and cooking
- Are into sports and outdoor activities
- Have few friends ("drinking buddies")—watch sports on TV
- Want to be respected
- Are easily angered; crying is difficult

WOMEN

- Are the communicators
- Are the ones who make things nice/calm/beautiful
- Are the primary homemakers and child caretakers
- Do not consider their careers as important
- Are into shopping and clothes
- Like lunch with "the girls"
- Are focused more on appearances
- Want to feel loved
- Are easily saddened; anger is harder to express

As married gay men, we have a unique opportunity to do it differently from straight folks. We have long been expected to invent ourselves as we go along and we continue to do so legally, psychologically, and spiritually. I encourage you and your husband to not settle for traditional gender roles that box you in and hinder your self-expression.

Do you dare to question the rules and experience yourself in new and powerful ways? I hope so. Answering and discussing the questions in this chapter with your husband is a great way to learn how he sees himself as a man and where that comes from. I guarantee you that talking about these questions with your man will get a good conversation started!

As you go through the questions, notice what emotions come up for you and any physical reactions. Do some questions make you nervous or uncomfortable? Do some questions make you feel free and relaxed, even playful?

I think it's helpful to start off with defining terms, so I offer you and your husband these questions to get you going. Feel free to write down your answers or not, whichever is more useful for the two of you. It might be fun for each of you to write down your answers and, when you're done, read what each other wrote.

- *How would you define "gender"?*
- *How would you define "gender roles"?*

Now let's get more specific. (This is where it gets really interesting.) How would you define "gender roles" for

- *lesbians? bisexual women? transgender women? heterosexual women?*
- *gay men? bisexual men? transgender men? heterosexual men?*

It's helpful to see where we got our original ideas about gender.

- *What were your family's ideas about gender roles?*
- *Which of these ideas have served you and which have not?*

Then let's look at

- *What gender roles have you accepted?*
- *What gender roles have you rejected?*

These next two questions invite you to remember who has inspired you and how you can pass that inspiration on.

- *In your past, who has served as a gender role model for you and how did they inspire you?*
- *In what ways would you like to be a gender role model for others?*

Now we come to my favorite questions. They are designed to help you bring your vision into real life (which, to me, is what my work is all about).

> • Describe what it would like to be totally free of gender role expectations—what if there were no limits to who you could be?
> • What steps in your "real" life could you take to move toward this kind of freedom?

Most of us could be "placed" on a continuum of how we play out gender roles in our marriages, from very conservative, traditional, and rigid on one extreme to extremely flexible, open, and adaptable on the other. Let's look at three gay couples and see where they fall on that continuum.

The 100 Percent Conservatives— A Lot of Conflict and Competition

Simon and Gilberto have been married for one year and together for about five years. They both came from very traditional families: their dads made a good living and their moms were stay-at-home moms. As young men, Simon and Gilberto were raised to be good providers and to not worry about learning "feminine" skills like cooking or cleaning. Simon's dad told him, "You'll have a wife to do all of that stuff, you focus on bringing home the bacon." Gilberto's family also followed very traditional male/female role stereotypes: "My mom would never have considered getting a job; the home was her domain. She and my dad each had their own 'turf,' and everybody was happy."

Simon and Gilberto grew up to not question the masculine roles that they were expected to take on. Both men expected to be the "macho, masculine breadwinner" and to marry a nice girl who would be just like their mom. Not surprisingly, both men came out later in life; Simon was married to a woman for several years before he came out and Gilberto was engaged to a woman for a year until she told him that she thought that he was gay (she was right). For most of his twenties, Gilberto went to his family's house to do his laundry, to let his mom fuss over him and feed him.

By the time these two men came together, each was used to having a woman in his life to take care of him. Neither of them wanted to become this "woman." Not surprisingly, both of them wanted the other to take on the traditionally "wifely" role.

While they were dating, each of them lived alone, had a cleaning person and ate most of their meals out. Once they got married, they assumed they would keep this up, until Simon got laid off from his job. Then the you-know-what hit the fan: Gilberto expected Simon to take on the homemaker duties, as he was now home most of the day. Simon was furious: "Are you crazy?" he yelled at Gilberto, "There's no way I'm gonna do that shit. I'm a man, dammit!"

When two men together each take on extremely conservative gender roles, there's usually a lot of conflict unless the couple can design their marriage so that both of them get to play out the traditional male role. Typically, they find someone else—often, they have to pay this person—to perform the tasks associated with the traditional female role. This system worked out fairly smoothly for Simon and Gilberto until Simon lost his job and the equilibrium shifted.

The 50 Percent–50 Percent Couples— Where Most of Us Are

Tomson and Brian represent the vast majority of gay couples; they aren't as conservative and rigid as Simon and Gilberto, but they aren't as free and easy as our third couple, Tyler and Rick. Let's hear their stories, in their own words.

Tomson: "I was raised pretty middle class; both of my parents have college degrees and worked outside the home. My brother, sister, and I went to day-care and after-school programs until Mom or Dad could pick us up. Mom was a nurse, and had three days off but worked four long days. Dad ran his own printing business, so he had some flexibility in hours. Between the two of them, someone was usually able to take care of us. If not, my Aunt Shelly lived nearby and she usually filled in the childcare gaps. Dad was a better cook than Mom, so we liked it when he cooked, but often, we'd get Mom or Aunt Shelly's food, which was okay. In our house, Dad was clearly 'the husband' and Mom 'the wife,' but they weren't rigid about exactly what that meant. Mom was pretty good at fixing things around the house, as was Dad. Mom liked to garden and

Dad would mow the lawn. They each had equal power in major decision making and got along pretty well most of the time. Dad trained us kids how to cook and Mom taught us how to garden and work outside."

Brian: "My parents had pretty traditional roles: Mom stayed at home with us four kids (two boys and two girls) and Dad worked as a hospital administrator. Mom did the cooking and cleaning and Dad made a good living and taught us baseball, football, and tennis, all sports he enjoyed and liked sharing with us. Even though their roles were traditional, they didn't teach us kids to be that way. Mom taught all four of us how to cook, clean, and do our own laundry and chores. Dad introduced all of us—boys and girls alike—to sports, exercise, being outside, and the importance of going to college so you can make a good living for yourself. As a result, all four of us became pretty good cooks and housekeepers and we all went to college and ended up doing pretty well for ourselves."

It's interesting how we each walk our own paths to the gender roles we eventually grow into. Tomson and Brian were fairly comfortable performing most aspects of traditionally male and female roles when they met. During their dating months, they took turns cooking for each other and initiating getting together for hiking, swimming, fishing, and other activities that both enjoyed.

When they got married, they had to make a few adjustments when they moved in together—neither man liked cleaning much, although they did eventually figure out a schedule that let them alternate the most-dreaded tasks—but overall, they settled into their marital roles without too much strain. Initially, Tomson was a little more bossy and dominant in the home, trying to talk Brian into doing tasks that he (Tomson) didn't want to do. Brian was willing to give these tasks a try, but when he realized that Tomson expected him to permanently take these tasks as "his," he bridled. They argued. They complained. They pouted and, eventually, they compromised.

The 100 percent Rule/Role Breakers— Especially Common for Gay Men in Their Twenties and Early Thirties

Tyler and Rick met in a gay hiking club when they were in their mid-twenties. Each of them is described by friends as "very mellow" and "easygoing." Tyler's dad worked in construction (on the crew) and his mom worked in the construction company office. But that's where the predictable gender roles end.

> Tyler: "When I was born, my mom took a leave from her job to stay home with me and Dad continued to work. But Mom didn't like being home all day and Dad missed spending time with me, so they switched. Mom went back to her job (happily) and Dad stayed home with me. He got a lot of kidding from the guys on the construction crew, but he didn't care. He said he loved staying home with me."

Tyler said that his dad stayed home and provided most of the childcare until he was about a year old. At that time, his mom felt guilty that she wasn't spending more time with him, so Tyler's parents once again made a job/childcare trade.

> Tyler: "The only way they could get away with this was because they both worked for a small construction company where they were each much-loved and highly valued employees. Although their bosses weren't thrilled with them switching around like this, my parents basically told them, 'This is what we need to do; we hope you can work with us. If not, we'll need to look elsewhere for a place that will.'"

When Tyler was about eighteen months old, his mom became pregnant again. This time, his parents decided that his mom would continue to stay home and provide childcare for Tyler (and his soon-to-be-born little brother) and Dad would stay at work. Tyler's parents continued this arrangement for several years until he and his brother were both in school; at that time, his mom went back to work for the construction company.

> Tyler: "It was so amazing to have a year 'alone' with my dad, a year alone with my mom and then the rest of my preschool life 'sharing' my mom with my brother. I am still extremely close to my dad, who I'll always feel a special bond with. And I'm close to my mom too, although my brother seems a little more bonded with her, and that's okay."

It's not hard to see where Tyler gets his gender-role openness. Rick's story is quite different, but he too was raised to see male and female childcare/work roles as fairly interchangeable. Rick's parents both worked from home: his mom was an IT consultant and his dad sold software. He grew up with both of his parents taking care of him at home.

> Rick: My mom liked her job a whole lot more than my dad liked his, so when Mom became pregnant, she kept working until I was born. Then, Mom and Dad shared childcare and money-making duties pretty much equally. Mom would spend the morning with me while Dad worked and Dad took care of me in the afternoon while Mom worked. They were both there to cover for each other if either one of them had a special project or something. We all spent evenings together and then, once I went to bed, Mom and Dad both went back to work for a few hours."

Rick told me that this childcare/work arrangement between his parents usually worked out quite smoothly. He said he was lucky to grow up with both of his parents around most of the time. However, he said that a few gender role stereotypes did play out in his family.

> Rick: "My mom did most of the cooking because Dad didn't like to and Dad usually made more money than Mom did. In that way, I guess they were stereotypical. Mom and Dad both liked to garden, but Mom was into her flower and vegetable beds and Dad was more into moving rocks and landscaping."

It probably won't surprise you to know that Tyler and Rick have a marriage where neither of them is "expected" to do any particular task. Instead, they do the things they each enjoy and negotiate to divide up the tasks that neither of them likes.

If you and your husband are more like Tyler and Rick, you probably are very flexible and fluid in how you've set up your home and life together. On the upside, you have a lot of options: you literally get to make it up without much baggage as to what is "right" or "wrong."

It's not all sunshine and happiness, however; it can be very disorienting for a gay couple to have to make it all up. It's natural to (unconsciously) follow the patterns we were raised with. This is great if the patterns are a good fit for you and your husband. But if these familiar patterns aren't a good fit, don't be surprised if you and your man experience competition and conflict as you define (and redefine) gender-based roles for yourselves.

I'd like to share with you one of the tools that the two of you could use to help determine who does what tasks around your home.

1. Together, make a list of all the household tasks that need to be done.
2. Pick one of these tasks that you are willing to do. Write your name by it.
3. Have your husband do the same.
4. Repeat steps 2 and 3 until all the tasks are assigned.

You might want to try this once a week, at the beginning, just to see how it goes.

I've been using this exercise with couples for many years now and I've observed that there is a pattern for how it usually goes: there are always tasks that each of you is happy to do; that part's all good. Then you get to the tasks that are "okay" to do, and the two of you are probably getting a little uneasy. Eventually, you get to the stuff that neither one of you wants to do. This is where the exercise really comes in handy. By repeating steps 2 and 3 until all the tasks are assigned, you're dividing them up as equally as it is possible to do. Both of you will get to do things you enjoy and both of you will have to do some tasks that you don't.

Most couples only need to do this a few times before they see a pattern. At that point, there are usually only a few things that both of you really hate doing. If that's true for you and your husband, alternate *these* tasks on a regular basis, so at least you have some variety and no one gets stuck doing the same dreaded task for very long. Ironically, when you both share the unpleasant stuff, it's actually a bonding experience and it's a really good way to not get stuck in gender-based roles.

Gender-based roles may also play out in your sexual relationship(s). Consider these stereotypes.

Husband #1—This man can easily separate sex and love: "sex is just sex: nothing more," a traditional male gender-based point of view.
Husband #2—This man does not easily separate sex and love. For him, they need to go together. This is a less traditional gender-based point of view and is often associated with the female gender role.

Of course, these two types of "husbands" are extreme examples. Most of us are somewhere in the middle.

> Noah: "My husband and I have never been monogamous. From the very beginning, we talked about how much we like having sex with different guys and that no matter how much we love each other and want to be together, we enjoy our Grindr and Scruff adventures too much to give them up. Neither of us has any problem with this emotionally. Sure, we like some of our FWBs (friends with benefits) better than others. Some of our FWBs we hang around with socially, but we don't have romantic feelings toward any of them. It's easy for us to separate the love and affection we have for each other from the sexual desire we have for other men."

> Liam: "I've been with Dave [his husband] for seven years now, and our relationship goes through open and closed periods. We started out in an open relationship, because Dave wanted it that way. It was okay with me, but I wasn't thrilled about it. Once I got to know Dave, I could see that he could easily separate his love for me from his sex with other guys. One-night stands are easy for him, particularly since he travels a lot for his job. This isn't the case for me. Dave and I have had some three-ways, which I liked, but I need to have some emotional connection with a guy to have sex with him. I don't need to be in love with him, but I at least have to *like* him as a person."

> Mason: "Micah [his husband] and I are monogamous and we like it that way. For us, sex and love go together. The best sex I've ever had is with him, because I know and trust him. Even though our sex lives are pretty predictable—we've been together for ten years now—the level of intimacy we have is what I've always wanted—him too. If either of us had sex with someone else, it would be a real threat to our marriage, because neither of us could have sex with someone we didn't love."

It's clear how, for these three guys, gender-based roles play out in their sexual relationship(s). Noah is a Husband #1 kind of guy; Mason is a Husband #2 type, and Liam is somewhere in the middle (although he's married to a #1 type). It might be interesting for you and your husband to consider where you are compared to the above three couples.

Questions for Consideration

- Which of the above three couples do you most identify with? In what way(s)?
- Can you easily separate sex from love? Can your husband?
- How does this affect your relationship?
  Are you both happy with this arrangement or would you like to change it?

Internalized Homophobia
and Gender Role Rigidity

Homophobia encourages us to adhere to and follow traditional male roles and to deny our own individual talents and abilities when they don't align with the stereotypes. Did you try to act more masculine when you were struggling with coming out? Did you downplay qualities that would have been considered "feminine" by those people you were trying to impress (parents, bosses, teachers, colleagues, etc.)?

Randy: "When Kirk and I were first married, I was coming from a relationship where my ex—Andy—was not 'out' at work or to his family, so I was in the habit of 'acting' as straight as possible. I didn't realize how doing this for eight years had affected me; but it did. I was always trying to 'not' act gay. Andy had a lot of internalized homophobia that he hadn't dealt with and looking at his family, it's not surprising. It took me several years of being with Kirk to be able to 'relax' and be myself."

Frank: "When I met David's family, I was so freaked out. His dad is like Robert DeNiro in all those 'Meet the Focker' movies. Although David never told me to act more butch, I found myself doing it to please his dad. I thought I had worked through my internalized homophobia, but I got a big surprise. Later, David and I talked about it. He told me that he's never felt butch enough to make his dad happy either, but he let it go years ago. He encouraged me to be myself with all his friends and family. When we had our wedding, this was hard for me, but he kept reminding me, 'I love you just as you are; don't butch it up for me, please.' What a relief."

Oscar: "I work in a very conservative corporate environment. I want to be successful there, but don't want to pretend I don't spend my life with my husband Krenar. It took me a while to put a wedding picture (of us) on my desk. I knew people would ask me about it, since few of my work colleagues were invited to our wedding. Krenar and I talked about how to handle this macho man/aggressive corporate culture in my office. I decided, with his help, to gradually come out at work to people who seem gay-friendly. But in all truth, it's quite a slow process for me. I don't want to alienate the people who have the power to promote me and determine my salary."

If you're reading the above vignettes and thinking, "I feel sorry for those guys. I don't have any internalized homophobia," I invite you to think again. The other day I was talking with a new client, a well-adjusted, happily married gay man, who told me, "I don't think I'm homophobic anymore. I think I've worked all that through."

My response was, "Really? Do you think that's possible?"

He was pretty surprised to hear me say that. And that led us to a discussion of what homophobia really is. Internalized homophobia is based on fear—a fear that who we are is not okay and that if we allowed how we feel inside to show outside, we will never fit in.

Ironically, for many of us, this fear encourages us to act as if we are superior to others. It combines—unfortunately—with racism, misogyny, and ageism to manifest in a variety of subtle and not-so-subtle ways in our community: men feel superior to women; white people feel superior to people of color; gay men and lesbians feel superior to bisexual and transgender men and women; young people feel superior to older people; wealthy people feel superior to poorer people—and young, middle-class gay white men feel superior to everyone else in the LGBT community (but still feel inferior to their straight counterparts).

To me, internalized homophobia is the process of how we take negative stereotypes, beliefs, and prejudice about being gay and use them against ourselves, like Randy, Frank, and Oscar described above.

The intensity of our internalized homophobia depends on how much self-hatred we have consciously and subconsciously internalized. Growing up in a conservative, Republican family in a small Ohio farm town, I was filled to the brim with internalized homophobia. I had so few allies and so little support that I didn't come out until my early thirties when—in a men's support group in New York City—I burst out with: "I don't want to be gay, but I am."

I did so *not* want to be gay that I struggled hard for years *not* to be. Or, more accurately, not to admit it to myself.

Internalized homophobia also applies to the things we do and the ways we act (or try to act) to conform to hetero-normativity. Have you ever seen profiles on Grindr, Scruff, and OK Cupid that stress how "masculine" the guy is? Or all those "No femmes, no fats, no old guys" statements?

No internalized homophobia there, right?

Behind most internalized homophobia is fear: we want to fit in and be accepted. It's scary to feel alone, isolated, and "weird." So we hide the parts of ourselves that may not be acceptable to our friends/community/work colleagues/family—maybe even to our husband—and work hard to promote and parade the parts of ourselves that everybody seems to like. Let me introduce you to a psychological term: "ego-dystonic homophobia" refers to a sexual orientation that is at odds with your idealized self-image. In essence, who you are is a bad fit with who you think you have to be (at work, with your in-laws, in gay-hostile environments, etc.).

The result is depression, fear, shame, and—in the most extreme cases —suicide.

I can honestly say that in my early twenties, I felt such self-hatred for my same-sex attractions that I occasionally thought about suicide. Luckily, it never went further than that. But not every gay man is so fortunate. Internalized homophobia is strongly correlated with suicidal thoughts and acts among gay youth.

What can we do? We can start by telling ourselves the truth about the parts of ourselves that as gay men we hide and are ashamed of and getting support to address them. We can tell the truth to our husband, friends, counselors, mentors, and family. We can notice when we feel shame and ask ourselves, "What is going on with me right now?" and "Where does that come from?"

This is the first step on the path to freedom: we stop fooling ourselves. Even if we convince others we're cool, what really matters is what we say to ourselves. Our own self-opinion is much more powerful than what others think of us.

If you feel bad about your sexual orientation, you probably find lots of ways to subconsciously sabotage yourself and your marriage. You may attempt to hide the ego-dystonic parts of yourself from your husband. This is a severe impediment to marital emotional and sexual intimacy: you don't want your husband to see those sides of you that you're embarrassed about, so you pretend to be slightly (or largely) different from whom you really are. And you wonder why you feel depressed and alienated from your husband.

It may even impact your sex life and who you allow yourself to be in bed. How many "top" guys have wanted to try bottoming, but their masculine identity was so tied up in being the "top" that they were unable to admit what they really wanted? You may think that this is unusual, but sitting in my therapist's chair, it is not. If you think that you have to be and act a certain way to be a "real" man, then the gender-based masculine role that you've taken on is in control of you.

Luckily, you're not stuck.

To be free and happy, I invite you to explore the parts of your personality that have long been "missing" or embarrass you. How will you recognize them?

1. Just notice the times in your life when you're embarrassed to let people see who you really are.
2. Just notice the types of people in the gay community that make you uncomfortable—and be grateful to them: they are truly your best teachers.

Questions to Consider

- What situations make you feel uncomfortable being gay?
- How have you navigated these situations in the past?
- Where do you see internalized homophobia in your life? Where do you see it in your marriage?

Gender Roles and Happiness

As married gay men, I wonder if we have different expectations of happiness than straight folks do and if it's smart for us to buy into hetero-normative definitions of happiness. You may not think of gender roles as related to your happiness, but to me, there's a definite correlation: if we expect the same of ourselves as straight men do, it's my experience that our marital and individual happiness will suffer.

For example, let's look at money: at this point in time, gay couples typically don't have as many children as heterosexuals do. Therefore, let's ask ourselves: Do we really need to make as much money as heterosexuals with children, who typically have lifelong obligations to support them? If not, let's reexamine whether our money/income/job is making us happy. Perhaps we don't need to work as hard/long/much. Perhaps working less would make us—and our marriages—a whole lot happier.

And what about our homes: Do you and your husband really need a big home? So much space? So many rooms? Straight folks with kids may need all those rooms. Do we? If not, why are we paying such expensive rent/mortgages? This financial pressure may be a big drain on your marital happiness. Would you and your husband's life be more relaxed and pleasant with a smaller residence that costs you less and allows you have a good life with less money and have fewer financial pressures?

Just asking.

I know that this goes against the stereotypical male image of success: big house, fancy cars, summer home, big yard, gardener, housekeeper, eating out at fancy restaurants, designer clothes, expensive vacations, etc. But as gay men, we don't have to buy into that gender-based stereotype. If you and your husband are working like crazy to pay for things that you really don't need, wouldn't it be helpful to question whether following these male gender-based expectations is really working for you? Could a satisfying gay marriage be simpler than we'd thought?

I know, shocking, isn't it?

From my years as a psychotherapist, I've observed that when we, as gay men, do what hetero-normative society says will make us happy (e.g., have a big house, work at a high-pressure job with a big paycheck, work out like a crazy man to get a body that's admired) and these actions don't bring us happiness, then we think there's something wrong with *us*. We criticize ourselves and think that *we* are doing it wrong, rather than questioning straight men's assumptions about happiness.

I encourage you and your husband to start questioning traditional gender-based roles and take the chance to discover what honestly makes the two of you happy. Isn't this a better strategy for marital satisfaction than blindly imitating straight marriages and hoping for the best?

> ## Questions to Consider
>
> - What heterosexual ideas of happiness have you assumed were true for you? Were they?
> - What do you and your husband do differently than straight couples?
> - What could you do (e.g., make less money, be content with a simpler life) to have a happier marriage?

Talk about this with your husband. Keep an open mind about this stuff; you may be surprised by what you hear, from him and yourself.

Parenting

Is it true that every child needs someone to play the (up-until-now) traditional "dad" and "mom" roles? The traditional dad's role is to encourage, coach, and be a role model for what is possible—to focus on achievement, give mostly nonverbal praise, and offer a strong masculine "presence." Mom's role, according to gender-based stereotypes, is to comfort, nurture, and hug. She is a role model for communication, empathy, and understanding. She offers verbal praise, empathy, and a soothing, gentle presence.

In a household with two dads, how are these "roles" divided up?

Tanner: "My husband Auggie and I are the parents of three kids, all adopted, all with special needs. I tend to be more of a communicator and nurturer, so I play more of the 'mom' role. However, Auggie and I can both be pretty good comforters and nurturers when we have to. We just have different styles; he's quieter, I talk more. When we have parent-teacher conferences, I tend to say more and he fills in the blanks if I leave anything out. We both have a lot to do being dads to these three active, demanding kids. Auggie and I like to be outdoors whenever we can, so we take the kids hiking and camping and swimming a lot. Auggie likes to read more than I do, so he usually does the bedtime reading. We take turns giving the little ones baths (because neither of us likes it very much)."

Hank: "Daniel, my husband, and I recently adopted a baby, so we're kind of going crazy figuring out how to be a family of three. We both went to parenting classes, and our moms and sisters gave us a lot of well-intended advice, but once Sean arrived, we both panicked: 'Omigod, what do we do now?' was pretty much our initial reaction. But things are settling down and we're all muddling through together. We alternate who gets up in the middle of the night, who changes diapers, who feeds Sean—we both like to learn how to do all this stuff, so we good-naturedly 'fight' over gets to do what. This will probably change (laughs), but for now, we're really loving it and it sure has brought Daniel and me even closer than before—we both *love* being dads!"

Paul: "My husband Jess was married before and he has two kids with his ex-wife: Jackson (age seven) and Jennifer (age nine). When Jess and I were dating, the kids were pretty much in the background; they came for visits occasionally. At that time, his ex was really angry at him, so the kids weren't around much. Now that he and his ex get along better, the kids are with us every other weekend. I gotta be honest: it's a challenge. They're still mad at their dad for leaving their mom and they're not too happy with me as the one who 'took him away' from them. When he was married to his ex, Jess was the traditional 'work long hours' kind of father, but lately he's making more of an effort to spend time with the kids. I'm finding myself acting like the 'good step-mom,' being emotionally warm and available, but not pushing myself at them. They're very slowly coming around."

While I'm sharing gay parenting stories—and redefining what it means to be a dad—I'd like to share with you an e-mail I recently received from two very surprised dads.

Dear Michael:

We are two formerly happy and carefree gay men. Last month, my husband's ex-wife essentially gave us custody of their three kids. They've visited us off and on for the past six years we've been together, but the kids have lived most of their lives with their mom, her new husband, and his kids. But now their mom can't handle them, so guess who's stuck with them now? Help! We are miserable and need some suggestions on how to relocate our sanity.

P.S. The kids are eleven, thirteen, and sixteen (two boys and a girl, in that order).

Pathetic New Parents in Philadelphia

Dear Pathetic:

What an alliterative sign-off you have. Well done! You will need this same creativity with these three kids. Kids? You've got teenagers! I was (in another life) a middle school counselor before I went into private practice as a psychotherapist, so let me share some suggestions for your consideration.

Many parents (and stepparents, yes, that's you!) mistakenly believe that by the time their kids are teenagers it's too late to have much effect on them. Wrong! Despite rap music, baggy clothes, piercings, tattoos, and other accoutrements of the young, survey after survey shows that teenagers look up to and respect their parents *more* than rappers, movie stars, and even self-appointed role models like Justin Bieber and Selena Gomez. So don't give up on these kids; you and your husband are their most powerful role models, even if you can barely get two words out of them (which is typical, by the way).

I know it's corny, but you can't be too loving with teenagers. Surprised? Many adults are. Oh sure, the kids will say "oh yuck" and "oh grow up" if you hug them in public, but in private, they need lots of hugs, encouragement, and even a bedside chat now and then. They may not ask for it, but they need it.

It may be helpful to remember your own teenage years, for example, how nerve-wracking they were and how insecure you felt. (You didn't? Liar!) Well, the *rest* of us found those teenage years to be awkward, uncomfortable, and just plain *awful*. Therefore, any parental (or stepparental) love and encouragement is powerful indeed. Just don't expect to be thanked for it—because you won't be.

You and your husband are likely to be challenged by these three: teenagers typically ask "why can't I do that? and "how come other kids get to do this?" Their ability to reason may be quite impressive, and they are likely to challenge you if you ask them to do something that doesn't make sense.

As the stepdad, I strongly recommend that you avoid taking on a major disciplinarian role. Eventually, however, you'll get dragged into it despite your best intentions, so be prepared to talk about why you and your husband have house rules (you do, don't you?) and chores for them to do (right?) and a reward system to encourage them to act wisely and skillfully (don't just punish them!).

Be willing to set reasonable limits, and have these limits (and all other rules) clearly known by all. Teenagers will complain for hours about your rules, but the dirty secret is they love structure, security, and predictability and they'll count on you to provide it and to withstand their whining and moaning about it.

All teenagers need fair and firm rules and limits. You can always relax the rules little by little as you, your husband, and the kids all get used to each other, but it is harder than hell to *tighten* up rules when you've started off too loose. When in doubt, err on the side of too much structure: then—later on—when you ease up, you're the heroes (not the zeroes).

As dad and stepdad, encourage the kids' independence: rebelling against your parents and pushing hard for your autonomy is *normal* for teenagers. They are not out to get you (repeat this over and over, like a mantra). Give these kids some psychological space, help them to be self-reliant, let them learn from their own mistakes (without embarrassing or belittling them), and keep remembering how *you* were at that age.

Pick your battles. Like a good marriage, it's good to cut them some slack. Decide what matters (e.g., grades) and what doesn't (e.g., hairstyles).

Be mature enough to apologize when you're wrong, explain things when you're asked, and give comfort when it's needed. We're the grown-ups, they're the kids. We can do this, and we can get help in doing it. Call the nearest LGBT Center (or go online) for excellent referrals to LGBT parenting groups, family-oriented events, and organizations. There is a wealth of resources on the Internet and in most urban areas. Get support. Don't do it alone.

Because these children have come to live with you, they're probably disoriented: they may be away from their close friends, their old school(s), and their old neighborhood. They need your and your husband's involvement with their lives. It is particularly helpful to get to know their friends. Observe these friends; don't judge them prematurely. Verbally criticize their friends and they probably won't talk about them to you again (bad move). Try to *stay neutral* and you'll get *a lot* more useful information. As the stepdad, you have an advantage of distance and perspective. Once the kids realize you're not the "wicked stepdad" type (or are you?) they may talk more to you than to their dad. You may be a safe oasis in their new life.

Be available but not intrusive. Stepdads typically have thankless roles; they usually do best when they let the stepkids come to *them*, not vice versa. Stay as neutral as possible, keep your judgments and criticisms to yourself, and see who these young people really are. They might just surprise you with their wit, intelligence, and compassion.

Make sure that you and your husband take time away from the kids to nurture *your* relationship. It is likely to be pushed, prodded, and tested by these kids on a daily basis. That's all the more reason to take really good care of yourself and each other.

Are Two Dads Better—or Worse—than One?

Traditional gender-based roles say that you need a mom and a dad, and that anything else is a poor substitute. Fortunately, that's an old wives' tale (sorry, I couldn't resist). I read a lot of research studies when writing this section, and, overwhelmingly, the research does *not* validate those outdated stereotypes.

I could give you a list of all the studies that confirm that two dads are as "good" as a mom and a dad, but to spare you the boredom of reading through a lot of research studies, allow me to cite one study[1] as an example.

Households with same-sex parents show no differences from those with heterosexual parents according to researchers affiliated with the Williams Institute at UCLA School of Law, the University of Amsterdam, and Columbia University.

This study found that with regard to spouse or partner relationships, parent-child relationships, or children's general health, emotional difficulties, and coping and learning behavior, there were no differences.

Titled "Same-sex and Different-sex Parent Households and Child Health Outcomes: Findings from the National Survey of Children's Health," the study compared family relationships, parenting stress, and child outcomes in households with same-sex parents versus different-sex parents.

Ninety-five same-sex households were matched with ninety-five different-sex parents based on eight demographic characteristics: parental age, education, U.S. birth status, and current geographic location, and the child's age, gender, race/ethnicity, and U.S. birth status.

Here is a direct quote from the study:[2]

In recent years, several courts have thrown out the testimony of witnesses who have attempted to draw conclusions by comparing children of same-sex parents who were not continuously coupled, and whose children had experienced family transitions (parental separation, adoption, foster care, etc.), with children of different-sex parents in stable families. In these cases, courts have either rejected these comparisons as invalid research or rejected the expertise of the witness trying to make such comparisons.

—Douglas NeJaime, UCLA Professor of Law and
Faculty Director at the Williams Institute

From 1995 through 1997, while at San Francisco State University's School of Social Work, I wrote my master's thesis ("Working With Gay and Lesbian Families: Selected Issues for Social Workers") on possible psychological differences between children of same-sex parents and those of opposite-sex parents. While it was a small sample (certainly not what the UCLA/Williams Institute Study had to work with), I came up with similar conclusions: children of same-sex parents showed no emotional or developmental differences from those with heterosexual parents.

In some ways, I think our children actually have *advantages* that children of heterosexual parents typically lack. As gay men, we usually have to do a whole lot of research before deciding to become fathers. When we make the decision to create a family, it's with a heightened awareness of possible problems and difficulties. Gay parents are *not* naïve parents: we are aware of what we're up against and have faith and confidence in ourselves that we are up to the challenge. What children wouldn't benefit from parents like that?

Gay families rarely happen without much thinking and weighing the consequences of what both parents and children will have to deal with. Gay parents are typically very concerned, aware, and involved parents. My research showed that my small sample of gay parents were actively involved with their children's schools and regularly volunteered in the schools, often as a method of monitoring the teachers' and administration's attitudes toward gay families.

I finished my thesis in 1997. In terms of what's changed in the world of gay parenting and gay marriage, that was eons ago. There has been a mountain of research published in the past twenty years that illustrate the strengths of gay families, or, as I prefer to ask: "How are our families wonderful and special?" and "What unique gifts do we, as gay fathers, bring to our children?"

And, at the risk of being just a little bit anarchistic: we don't need to settle for "normal" children, at least, by hetero-normative standards. Here are two ways that our children are often above and beyond the norms of children of opposite-sex parents.

It is my experience, as a psychotherapist, that children of gay parents

1. Are more empathic to others. These children come from families that are not traditional and have increased tolerance for viewpoints other than their own. The flip side of being teased for having two dads is the inner strength that these children typically develop, as well as an ability to identify with a wide variety of people and family structures.

2. Have higher self-esteem. The majority of these children *knew* they were wanted and loved. Unlike heterosexual parents, same-sex parents usually have to go through a lot of work to become parents. Gay men particularly have to jump through many hoops to become fathers. The children of these fathers *knew* how much they were wanted; this was really, really good for their self-esteem.

So, aspiring gay fathers, have no fears that you are messing up your child's psyche or saddling them with emotional impairments as a result of having two gay dads. Instead, know that there are many *benefits* to having two wonderful gay fathers—many, I believe, are yet to be documented. But now that legal same-sex marriage has been around for a little while, I expect a lot more studies to be done on gay families. We've only just begun . . .

I'd like to conclude this chapter with quotes from four happily married gay men. I read a lot of research studies when I was writing this chapter. After digesting them all, it seemed that the bottom line question (for most of them) was: What happens when two married gay men have both been brought up to play the same gender-based male role?

Ned: "On our anniversary, I brought a dozen red roses to Pete's [his husband's] office, but he took care of the check at dinner. Neither of us did this out of any sense of obligation. We just wanted to make each other feel special."

Tommy: "It feels so good to me to do things for Marcel [his husband] because I want to instead of feeling that I 'should' do them. Our sense of taking care of each other sometimes falls in line with traditional gender roles, and sometimes it doesn't. Sometimes I open the door for him and am super-protective of him. Other times, he does this for me. It's great to be able to play both 'roles' whenever we feel like it."

Flynn: "I get so sick of all this 'guy' stuff and 'girl' stuff: Can't we all just take care of each other however it happens to play out? Instead of worrying about who's paying for this or that, opening doors, pulling out chairs, and that kind of stuff, Thomas [his husband] and I try to have a marriage of equals. We both end up playing all the 'parts' over time, and it works well for us."

Kenton: "To me, marriage is an institution whose purpose is to encourage the two married men to support and protect each other financially, emotionally, or spiritually. It doesn't matter if I act like the 'man' or Luis [his husband] does. Who does what for whom varies from day to day, moment to moment. We like it."

I couldn't say it better myself.

CHAPTER FOUR

Soul Mates, Family, and Community Support

Dear Michael:

I've been in several important romantic relationships; I was married and divorced and am now married to my second husband. I *really* want it to work this time. However, I wonder if I'm setting myself up for failure by searching for something special, something my friends call a "soul mate." Do you believe in such a relationship? If such a man exists, how the hell would I recognize him?

Perplexed in Providence

Dear Perplexed:

It sounds like you've realized by now—from your past relationships and marriage—that what you are initially attracted to in a potential husband isn't the person that you ultimately end up making a life with. (If you haven't realized this, perhaps *that's* your next step.)

After the honeymoon phase is over—I call it "when the glitter wears off"— you are left with a real person, not the idealized image of your perfect soul mate. Some gay men don't like to hear this, so they keep moving from one man to the next, searching for their (mythical) soul mate. Eventually, if you're lucky, you realize that when you trade in one man for another, you still have the same work to do. You're going to have to do it sooner or later, once that glitter wears off.

And it will. It must.

The wiser you get, the less you'll romanticize your marriage. It's very tempting, though. You hear about this idealized kind of love in every love song, see it in most movies and read it in all those touchy-feely greeting cards. It's an essential part of consumer culture: romanticizing marriage is a great way to sell products, ideas, and illusions. And, Mr. Perplexed, none of them is free, literally or metaphorically. The wisdom born of experience will show you the emptiness of that approach and, hopefully, in your current marriage, you're going for something deeper.

Romanticizing marriage is a great way to encourage illusions and delusions. The idea is usually some version of "Once I meet my soul mate, it will be so special, good, and easy. We'll go for romantic walks on the beach (or wherever) and we'll just magically 'get' each other."

This is not reality. Reality has bad breath and farts; reality is often boring; reality doesn't load the dishwasher the way you like; reality gets angry and irrational. So what can you do? It's usually best to hang in, keep working with it and learning from it, opening to your fears, becoming more vulnerable and insightful. Marriage can be the ultimate learning experience.

But that doesn't mean it's easy, romantic, or "soul mate city."

Every time you trade in a partner, you end up back with yourself. Yes, it's *you* that's the magic ingredient. You, not some imaginary perfect soul mate. It's very tempting, I admit, to end a marriage, dump the man, and run away from a relationship when it somehow—through intimacy or revelation—takes you to a vulnerability that's both new and terrifying.

So, instead of realizing the amazing, yet scary, opportunity before you, you start to judge and push your husband away and—eventually—move on to the next one. And then the whole damn thing starts all over again.

Des: "I went through man after man after man, looking for the 'right' one. I always found something wrong with each of them, so I could justify leaving them and moving on. Eventually, one of my friends told me, 'The problem isn't them, Des, the problem is you.' I started to see how afraid I was of letting some man love me, really love me. I was afraid that once someone got to know me, he would see what a phony I was and leave me, and there was no way I was going to let that happen."

Jim: "I lived with a few guys before meeting my husband, Peter. These guys were great guys, but I kept thinking that something was missing. We'd do really well the first couple of months, and then I'd start to feel bored with them, like, 'How can I be with this guy if he's so boring?' so I'd leave and look for someone who didn't bore me. After going through quite a few guys, I went to a therapist and said, 'Why are all the men I meet so boring?' It took me a while to see that *they* weren't boring, I was bored and dissatisfied with myself and used them as a diversion."

Christopher: "I have always been a very judgmental person. My whole family's that way. I look at someone and see what's wrong with them before I see what's right. So, of course, I could never find any man 'good enough' to marry. Then Charlie came along. He was totally wrong for me: he looked wrong, acted wrong, had the wrong kind of job, car, clothes—but somehow he got through my defenses and I found myself beginning to love him. He didn't fit my pictures, but we sure are happy together."

Do you believe in soul mates? Because, if you do, recent psychological research shows that you're going to have a very hard time in your marriage.

New research[1] suggests that believing in the concept of soul mates tends to make people more dissatisfied in their relationships. If your husband must be your soul mate, it implies that the two of you should have perfect harmony and no conflict. As a result, when you and your alleged soul mate end up arguing—as you inevitably will—it hurts even more.

Instead of yearning for a soul mate, why don't you and your husband view your relationship as a journey, a process that unfolds over time, for example, "our marriage is an ongoing adventure" and "look how far we've come."

Viewing love as a journey—not the magical stuff of soul mates—is guaranteed to bring you and your man more marital satisfaction. When you expect occasional conflict (remember chapter 2?) and hard times in your relationship, your marriage is much more likely to be resilient and happier. Believing in soul mates, destiny, or the idea that there is exactly one man you are meant to be with results in relationships where couples put less effort into working through conflict.

Soul mate believers expect that nothing should go wrong in their relationship; that it will be easy. When conflict happens, Mr. Soul Mate is likely to question whether his husband is really *the* one, so he's likely to give up on working it out.

Think Friendship; not Soul Mate

Okay, we've let go of the soul mate cliché. Right? One research study I read found that there's one relationship cliché that may actually be helpful: thinking of your husband as a good friend. Valuing the friendship aspect of your relationship might be the most important thing you can do.[2]

This study found that couples who are, at their core, very good friends are more likely to be more in love and more committed to each other, and even have better sex than couples who value their friendship less. All that good stuff keeps growing over time, the research suggests, and these couples are also less likely to split up.

Why is friendship so important to a loving relationship? I think that the core of friendship is the core of a good marriage: kindness, mutual respect, enjoying each other's company, common interests/values, and acceptance (even when there are major differences of opinion). These qualities make both friendships and marriages strong.

What about sex, you might say? Well, great sex is a wonderful thing, yet in most marriages, the sex continues, but is often less important than the emotional bond and the physical intimacy—touching, kissing, lying on the couch together watching a movie—that may not lead to orgasm. Friendship-based love will grow stronger as the (inevitable) repetitive nature of sex with someone you love—over time—becomes less exciting and novel, but deeper and more fulfilling.

When I was younger, I loved the idea of soul mates and was determined to find mine. I was idealistic and went through quite a few men (and women) in my search. Alas, none measured up: they were all too fallible, like me. It took me a long time to learn that there is *no* perfect man destined for me, you or any one.

A belief in soul mates may sound very romantic and spiritual, but is neither helpful nor accurate. A great relationship is less about magic or destiny than about finding someone who is both friend and lover, fellow adventurer and faithful companion.

"I've Got My Soul Mate, But No Friends"

Dear Michael:

I'm a married gay man who isn't very good at making—or keeping—friends. I'm kind of a loner and always have been, but I'd like a friend to hang around with. My husband has a lot of friends (he calls them, "our" friends, but really they're "his") while I have none. I've got my soul mate, but no friends.

To be honest with you, I've not been a very good friend in the past: I get impatient easily, frequently get annoyed with people, and don't like talking on the phone. What would you recommend?
Friendless in San Francisco

Dear Mr. Friendless:

Isn't it funny how so many people think that once you've found your perfect husband/soul mate/ideal guy that you don't need friends anymore? Lonely guys think that marriage to an amazing guy will "cure" their loneliness and men with friends often believe that they won't need them anymore once they're happily married.

It doesn't work that way. So let's talk about how to make friends when you're happily married.

Years ago, I facilitated a group that helped gay men develop and fine-tune their social skills. Yes, Mr. Friendless, making and keeping friends is a *skill*. Fortunately, like any skill, it can be learned.

Friendships take time, energy, and commitment. If you're not good with communication or understanding social cues (what is often called "emotional intelligence"), relax. You can, with some focus and effort, become better at being a good friend and attracting quality people into your life.

From years of helping clients go from friendless to friend-full, here are some ideas on how to master the skills of friendship:

Loneliness: We want friends so we won't feel lonely. Loneliness is an emotional response to not feeling connected to other people; it can be experienced even when we're happily married to the greatest man on earth. As a psychotherapist, I see loneliness as an emotional "alarm clock" that lets us know when we are drifting toward isolation and we need more human interaction (and not just with our husband).

Impatience: Many of us lack patience when it comes to making new friends. We want great friends and we want them *now*. Unfortunately, it rarely works that way. Another form of impatience: Are you the kind of guy who gets impatient with the friends you already have? Do you typically interrupt your friends with some version of "Get to the point, already"? If this has been a problem in your friendships, try this the next time you get impatient: (1) take a deep breath, (2) make eye contact with your friend, and (3) repeat something that they said (to encourage yourself to really listen). If you typically find yourself rehearsing what you're going to say when a friend is talking, bring your attention back to your friend and tell yourself "My turn will come. Let me listen to him/her as I want him/her to listen to me."

Forgiveness and Flexibility: Every friend, no matter how great they are, is going to mess up. Can you forgive them, or do you hold a grudge and try to "make them pay"? It's got to be okay for *you* to mess up and for *them* to do the same; otherwise, your friendships will be very short-lived.

Enjoying Your Own Company: What makes you attractive to potential friends? It's hard to be attractive when you're miserable. So, how can you enjoy your own company more and be better friendship "bait"? Do things on your own—yes, Mr. Friendless, break that dependence on your wonderful husband to do it all for you—or, when you go somewhere with your husband, use him as your emotional "base" and be like a satellite, orbiting around him, walking around, talking to people and then coming back to him as your touchstone to feeling safe. Don't cling to him and let him do all the talking; start to go off on your own, enjoy your own company and get better at meeting new people.

Finding Friends: How do you meet like-minded people? Well, what do you enjoy doing? Don't put yourself in situations that you don't enjoy, unless it's a dinner to meet your husband's boss. Do things you enjoy, alone or with your man: you're much more likely to be relaxed and happy, which makes it much easier to meet new people and talk to people that you already know.

Phone Challenges: Lots of people don't like talking on the phone. Texting is a good backup. Some people don't like phone calls because they feel put on the spot when the phone rings—they don't know what to say. In that case, use caller ID so you can decide whether you are in a good place to talk to the person calling. If not, you can listen to their voice message and call (or text) them after you've thought about what you want to say/ask/share. If you do want to talk with them, take a deep breath before you pick up and greet them with some neutral phrase like: "Hi Chris, how's your day going?" or something equally friendly and benign.

Give some of these ideas a try and soon you won't be friendless anymore. Also, let your husband know that you want to make friends and get his support. If he's really good at making friends, he might be your best adviser. It's great to have friends as a couple ("our friends") and it's even better to have some friends of your own.

When Your Family and Community Don't Support You

Now that you have friends (right?), let's take a good look at what you can do if your friends, family, or community don't support the marriage you and your husband have "designed" back in chapter 1.

If Your Marriage is Open

If you and your husband have chosen to have an open (nonmonogamous) marriage, obviously not everyone in your life is going to be as excited about this as the two of you. In my experience, few of us have families that will "whoop!" with joy about this. (I'm from a small town in Ohio, remember, and we "whoop" with joy there.)

In my experience of working with nonmonogamous married gay couples, if you want marital support from your friends, family, and community, there are three critical questions to consider.

1. *Who to tell:* Can you tell all your friends or just some of them? Are there any family members that you're comfortable sharing this with? Is the community you live in supportive of an open marriage?
2. *When:* Timing is very important. Some people, like your friends, probably know already. On the other hand, there may *never* be an optimum time to tell your family. Is there a need to share this with your community?
3. *How much to tell:* This is the hardest question. Do you tell your closest friends everything (including details of your sexual escapades)? Do you tell other friends some details, but keep most things purposely vague? Do friends in the first group talk with friends in the second group? If so, all of your friends may soon know a lot more than you'd planned for. Is there anything that your family members would *want* to know or be comfortable knowing? Sometimes, our siblings are able to handle limited amounts of information. Again, the challenge is that one sibling could

tell another and that person could end up sharing it with your whole family. There's no controlling information once it's shared.

Many of my clients have friends, family, and work colleagues who don't approve of their open marriage. Let's hear from two guys who are dealing with marriage disapproval from their friends. Greg and Theo are a binational couple (USA and France) who have lived in the States for the past eighteen months, after living together in Paris for about three years.

> Greg: "Theo and I have never been monogamous, even when we first started dating in Paris. His French friends didn't like me at first, but they eventually came around. Most of Theo's American friends are single or dating and I thought they'd be okay with open relationships, but they are astonishingly conservative. I don't really talk with my friends much about my sex life. They know that Theo and I aren't monogamous, but I don't go into detail with anyone. My closest friend is a straight woman who thinks I should be like her: married, monogamous, and bored out of my mind. No thanks!"

> Theo: "I lived with Greg in Paris, where none of my friends cared if anyone's marriage was monogamous or not. Here in the States, there is such a puritanical undercoating to everything, but no one talks about it. My friends here are mostly in committed gay relationships, not marriage, and think that monogamous relationships—marriage, particularly—are the ultimate goal. When gay marriage was legalized, they all said to Greg and me, 'When are you two gonna get married?' I wanted to say, 'Never.' But it seemed important to Greg, so, why not? We just don't talk with our friends about the men we have sex with. It's really none of their business."

It's naïve to expect that all gay men are open-minded regarding the "monogamy or open marriage?" question. Many—if not most—of us have a variety of friends: male, female, LGBT, straight, younger, older; it's highly unlikely that *all* of our friends are going to be big fans of open marriage. And what about our family? Isn't that an even more difficult group of people to get approval from?

In my experience, very few men in open gay marriages talk about it with their family members. Perhaps it's like Theo said, there is a "puritanical under-coating" (such a great phrase) to sexual relationships and marriage. Marriage, so long a heterosexual privilege, is, in the eyes of most people's family and relatives, "supposed" to be monogamous. Maybe it's wise to assume that your family (or your husband's) won't approve of your open marriage, but then, does that mean that you have to keep it a secret from them? Or, do you risk sharing it and the possible ostracism that may result?

It sounds like a *Sophie's Choice* situation to me . . .

Pedro and Thomas both grew up in middle-class Ohio families—Pedro in Cincinnati, Thomas in Columbus—who expected them to end up happily married to nice girls in monogamous relationships much like those of their siblings and other relatives. Surprise!

> Pedro: "Our family wasn't very religious; we went to church on Easter and Christmas, the 'dress-up' holidays. So I didn't get much guilt over being gay. When I told my family that Thomas and I were getting married, they were all so excited. They just 'assumed' that we were going to follow their example and live the gay version of their monogamous marriages. I never once thought about telling them that we had no plans to be monogamous. They would have freaked."
>
> Thomas: "Sex was never talked about when I was a kid, so I didn't expect to talk about my sex life [with Pedro] with my family. When we started dating, my mother wasn't sure how she felt about it, she was still hoping that I'd settle down with a 'nice' girl and kept asking me why I hadn't met one. Finally, one day, I told her, 'I've met a nice guy, would you like to know about him?' She was speechless. When she finally found her voice, she turned to me and said, 'Okay, tell me about him.' Although she seemed to accept Pedro, she actually *didn't* want us to get married. She was hoping I'd leave him and go back to dating girls. When we got married, the reality of it hit her hard. Before the wedding, she and my Dad sat me down and we had 'the talk': Are you sure this is a good idea? What will people say? Isn't it unnatural for two men to be married? Who will do the cooking and cleaning?'"

It is my observation that married gay men in open marriages rarely share it with their families. Oh sure, there's the occasional "cool" sister or cousin who's okay with it all, but most of our family members are not.

Where does this leave us? What are our options?

Well, why not think of it from another point of view: if you were marrying a woman, no one would ask you about your sex life with her. No sibling, aunt, or grandma would sidle up to you at family gatherings and say, "Hey Michael, how's your sex life with Julia? Is it good? Are you monogamous? Do you have sex with other women? Does she have sex with other men? Do you have three-ways?"

Not gonna happen. Then again, most people wouldn't necessarily approve of open heterosexual marriage, either.

So, perhaps that's the path that we can choose to take with our families: keep our marital sex life to ourselves. Other options? If any family members are sympathetic, maybe we can honestly share with them. The downside? They may talk with unsympathetic family members and then the cat is out of the bag. This may be okay with you and your husband, or not.

What I see as the biggest mental health challenge in sharing or not sharing about your open relationship to your family is the idea that it has to be "secret." Secrets always, *always* mean shame. So how can you not talk about your open marriage with your family *and* be proud of it? It takes conscious work to balance these two. It helps to talk with your husband about this. You can help each other and get the support of your (open marriage–friendly) friends.

The Double Standard in Our Community

As married gay men, we embody two (potentially conflicting) paradigms: we are gay men (and enjoy our sex lives tremendously, thank you very much) and we are married (which brings with it the hundreds of years of marital expectations from the heterosexual world).

Attention Mission Control: we have a problem here.

Yep, we've got a major conflict: as a community, we like to have sex (and lots of it), yet, as married men, we want to "do" marriage right. What a paradox. And it gets even more perplexing: as gay men in open marriages, we hope that our community has our backs. But do they?

Before we go further, let's define "community," a term that gets thrown about awfully loosely. My definition: a community is a group of interdependent people who share common attitudes, interests, and goals. We are interdependent people who depend and rely on each other. This doesn't mean that we approve of everything our brothers (and sisters) are doing, but we know we can depend and rely on them. A real community does not sabotage each other's happiness, whether out of jealousy or some other form of animosity.

That being said, what, then, does the gay community want? Do we want to have it all? Do we want to have all the options: Marriage, not marriage, monogamy, not monogamy, singlehood, not singlehood? Ideally, you would hope "yes," wouldn't you? But let's talk reality.

In reality, all options are not and cannot be seen as equal. Some gay men are going to value sex more and find monogamy not their cup of tea. Some gay men are going to want to be married in a more traditional (read: heteronormative) way and are willing to give up a sex life full of variety (if, that is, they ever had it) and embrace monogamy.

In my experience, there is no one point of view that the gay community is solidly behind. It's usually "monogamous gay marriage is the best thing ever" for the television cameras and morning news shows, while it's "Oh hell no, I'm not going to have sex with only one man for the rest of my life," in private conversations with our closest friends. Our private and public faces are often at odds; that's one of the reasons I've written this book—to bring both "faces" to light and eradicate the shame typically associated with the private face.

There is no one, monolithic, unified voice in our "community." As gay men, our community is typically made up of many smaller subsets, each with its own mores and expectations. Every city and town is different, every neighborhood a subset of that.

As gay men in open marriages, we can't necessarily expect the gay community to have our backs. If you live in New York City, you may get the support. If you live in El Paso, you may not. (I could be wrong about both of those, by the way.) Let's hear from two gay men and the support—or lack of it—they received from their communities.

Jason: "When I was single, I was a wild child: I had lots of fun and lots of sex with both men and women. When I hit my twenties, I realized I was gay and focused on the boys. I traveled the world, hitchhiking my way around Europe, doing odd jobs and having sex with men in many countries. It was great. In my thirties, I came back to the States and went to grad school. I graduated and got a job in my field. Then I met Hale. What a guy: funny, sexy, and just as much of an adventurer as I was. We were *never* monogamous. Never even considered it. When he proposed to me, I was shocked. 'Really?' I said. 'You want to get married. Why?'

He told me that I was the one for him and he thought that marriage could be 'a new adventure' for us. I liked that point of view, so we got married. A year later, he got a great job offer, so we moved from Chicago to a much smaller city. The gay community here is pretty conservative. Everyone pretends that their relationships are monogamous, but really, they're lying. No one is willing to admit that they're having sex with lots of guys, even though most marriages we know are definitely *not* monogamous. It's really pretty funny!"

Hale: "Jason and I like to push boundaries, our own and other people's. I never considered marriage when I first got to know him, but eventually, it was clear to me that marriage was *the* great adventure. Two guys like us are way too uninhibited to ever 'settle down,' so experimenting with settling down was more radical for us than just about anything else! Ironically, I love being married to him: I love cuddling with him every night and knowing that he's my man. We never considered having a monogamous marriage: it's just not us. This worked just fine when we lived in Chicago, but now, in a smaller, more conservative city, most people we know—LGBT and straight—are all about monogamy. Ugh. Not my style. So we just do our thing and don't really talk about having an open marriage. We don't feel ashamed about it, though. We just don't live in a community that's okay with it, so we keep it to ourselves."

It's probably a good coping strategy to *not* expect the gay community to embrace your open marriage. Then, if they do, it's a terrific surprise. This may sound depressing, but it's not; it's just the reality of the big picture. While it's true that there were lots of gay men on the legal/moral/ethical front lines of same-sex marriage, fighting for the right to marry the men we love, it's also true that there were lots of gay men who were very *ambivalent* about gay marriage, not sure it was for them and, if it was for them, not sure how it would "work."

Indeed, this is one of the issues that generated the book that you hold in your hands (or on your tablet).

The Hetero-Normative Culture at Large

"If you ever want to upset a bunch of straight people, start talking about your nonmonogamous marriage." Guess who said that? No, it wasn't a gay man; it was a polyamorous bisexual female former client of mine. She and her husband rarely talked about their open marriage with people they didn't know. Let's call her "Cassie" and let her tell her own story.

Cassie: "I am bisexual and am currently married to a mostly heterosexual man (but I'm working on him!) I was previously married to a lesbian. I have a very conservative job in a large corporation and I look like the All-American Girl Next Door (I'm thirty-two). My husband and I have found that one of the easiest ways to upset people is to start talking about polyamory and one of the biggest ways to upset straight men is to talk about bisexual polyamory. The polyamorous community is huge, but unfortunately, there is so much secrecy and shame about our (nonmonogamous) sexual lives that we can't seem to shake off."

Sound familiar, gay men? The shame, the secrecy, the way it easily upsets hetero-normative society? We are not alone in our struggle. In fact, I've had a lot of straight friends, colleagues, and clients tell me that they want to read this book. As I was in the process of writing it, straight, gay, lesbian, and trans folks told me things such as, "I want to read a book that opens up the conversation about marriage and monogamy" and "I'm interested in reading a book that questions things (like traditional marriage) that we've all taken for granted but that don't work very well for *anybody*."

Now that we've seen how open gay marriages often lack support from friends, family, and community, let's look at how monogamous marriages fare. Do they get more support from friends and family? Is the gay community more supportive of their monogamous relationships?

Let's see.

If Your Marriage Is Monogamous

With all the excitement about legal gay marriage, you'd think that the gay community would be totally supportive of yours, right? Well, it ain't necessarily so. Surprised? So was I. Here are three e-mails that I've received from happily married (as far as I can tell) monogamous gay men. They tell the tale much better than I.

Dear Michael:

I am so disgusted with our community. It seems that nobody is faithful to their partner or husband anymore. I was in a ten-year relationship that recently ended. I was faithful to my boyfriend and (to my knowledge) he was faithful to me. Now that I'm single, I am meeting all these gay men in "committed" relationships who want to fool around with me "on the side." At first I thought it was just a fluke, but it keeps happening over and over again. I'm not looking to rush right into another relationship, but I don't want to be someone's "piece on the side" either. Why isn't anyone faithful anymore?

Fed Up in Phoenix

Dear Michael:

Is it me or are gay men only interested in what we can't have? When I was single, I wasn't particularly popular, but I did okay. Now that I'm married, all these guys I've known for a long time are hitting on me at the gym and anytime I'm out without my husband. What's going on here?

Just Curious in Los Angeles

Dear Michael:

A few years ago, a straight friend of mine told me that, when he got married, single women started paying him a lot more attention. He asked me if this is true for gay guys. At the time, I wasn't sure. Well, now I know: it's true. My husband and I got married about a year ago and ever since then, guys have started asking me if I want to "hook up" with them, alone or with my husband. Some of these guys are in relationships and some are single. Why does that ring make you so much more desirable?

Suddenly Popular in Salt Lake City

After reading these e-mails—and others like them—my response was: gulp. Are we really so disrespectful of each other that we don't honor and respect another gay man's marriage? We don't have to be "rah-rah, sis-boom-bah" about monogamy, but do we need to actively test and mess with someone else's marriage?

Luckily, not every gay couple is going to run into this, but not everyone in the gay community is going to think that your monogamous marriage is such a wonderful idea and some folks are even mean/unkind/jealous enough to want to jeopardize it.

We may also have family, friends and coworkers who don't believe that we, as gay men, should be married. The fact that it's legal doesn't mean that the straight world is happy about it. I've had clients whose (heterosexual) parents, siblings, friends, and work colleagues have overtly and covertly let them know that they did *not* approve of gay marriage and *their* gay marriage in particular.

Let's look more closely at what happens when our friends don't support our (monogamous) gay marriage. Jeremy and Paul are a couple I've recently been working with. They aren't very close to their families, who live thousands of miles away, so their friends are basically their chosen family.

> Jeremy: "I love my friends, which is good because my family members are a total pain in the ass and super-conservative. It's hard though, because most of my friends are single and really into hooking up on Grindr and Scruff. They don't really 'get' our monogamy, and keep asking us, 'How long do you think you guys can keep this up?' The coupled friends we do have are in open relationships, so they're not very supportive either."
>
> Paul: "I have more married friends than Jeremy, because I'm older, but most of my married gay friends are not 100 percent monogamous, so they think that we're kidding ourselves about pulling this off in the long run. Sometimes I doubt myself and wonder if they're right."

It's awfully hard to hold onto your idea of monogamous, romantic love when the friends you're closest to think you're foolish and naïve. And yet, that's just what Jeremy and Paul are trying to pull off—with difficulty.

And what can you do when your family (or your husband's) doesn't approve of your marriage?

Mack and Ramon both come from conservative, Catholic families. Although they are no longer active in the church, both went to Catholic schools and are close to their families, emotionally and geographically. They spend a great deal of time—mostly together—with their parents, grandparents, brothers, sisters, nieces, and nephews.

> Mack: "You can call yourself a 'Catholic in recovery,' but basically that means that you still feel guilty a lot. I am really tight with my family, but they drive me crazy. It took them forever to decide to come to our wedding, and then they let us know that they really didn't approve of gay marriage. They are still really uncomfortable referring to Ramon and me as a married couple, even though we've been together for over three years now."
>
> Ramon: "I love my family; I am so close to them and would do nothing to hurt them. But their values are so conservative and rigid. There is no way that Mack and I could ever live up to their expectations, so they're

constantly letting us know that they're disappointed in us. It's not overt, but consistently covert. We just feel like we will never be married 'the right way,' aka 'their way.' It's crazy-making."

Mack and Ramon have the opposite problem of Jeremy and Paul: their families don't think they are conservative enough, while Jeremy and Paul's friends think they are too conservative and naive. Ironic, isn't it?

In some ways, married gay men are damned if we do (stay monogamous) and damned if we don't. Often, our "community" doesn't support nonmonogamous marriage because, as the public "face" of the community, it's not politically correct. Okay, you might say, after fighting so hard for same-sex marriage, we need to present a good community image on those morning news programs.

However, the community doesn't—in private—support monogamous gay marriage either. Not everyone is happy for you when you get married, nor will they necessarily be impressed by your monogamy. I have heard single gay men—and gay men in open relationships—describe monogamy as "naive" and "regressively hetero."

And what do you do if one of the communities you belong to is strongly hetero-normative and doesn't support gay marriage at all?

Alfonso and Johnny put it quite well.

Alfonso: "I work at a nonprofit in the gay community. Everyone thinks that Johnny and I have this perfect, happy marriage. We seem to be the envy of most of my friends and colleagues, yet they have no idea how hard it is to be married, especially working in the heart of the gay community here. You'd think that everyone in the LGBT community would be supportive, since we all worked so hard to get same-sex marriage legalized. But hell no! Not only is the community *not* very supportive, but ever since Johnny and I got married, guys who, a few months ago, congratulated me on our marriage are now hitting on me. There seems to be a veneer of valuing marriage, but you scratch the surface and everyone just wants to have sex with you. What's up with that?"

Johnny: "I work in a very straight, corporate accounting firm. Almost everyone there is married and has pictures of spouses and kids on their desks. I am afraid to totally come out there. I've just started wearing my wedding ring, but no one's asked me about it. Not only am I *not* comfortable being gay here, I would be *super* uncomfortable being married and gay here. I really feel trapped, because I like my job and am well compensated, but I'd face a lot of mostly silent disapproval if I put a photo of Alfonso and me on my desk. Once, at an office party, someone asked me, 'Do you think gay people really know how to love, or is it mostly about sex?' I was so angry I didn't know what to say."

These guys have two very different communities—yes, the people you work with constitute a community—yet each is unsupportive in its own unique way.

Heterosexual Culture at Large

We live in a hetero-normative world. While the gay community has made great strides in recent years, we live smack dab in the middle of a 90–95 percent straight world (if statistics are to believed and we constitute 5–10 percent of the population). Let's not underestimate the effect this may have on our marriages.

While monogamous, heterosexual marriage is, by far, the cultural norm, it hasn't been doing too well, at least from a numbers point of view. When almost half of all straight marriages end in divorce, you can't say that marriage, as a cultural institution, is a totally successful, rewarding phenomenon for our heterosexual brothers and sisters.

Perhaps by questioning marriage and exploring its possibilities, we can support our straight brothers and sisters to do the same. Wouldn't it be great if all people everywhere decided that it was time to examine and critique the institution of marriage and use that information to design a marriage that really works for them, monogamous or open, gay or straight, young or old? I admit that this is one of the intentions for this book.

As a sixty-three-year-old gay man and psychotherapist, I've had a lifetime of hearing—personally and professionally—why some straight people hate gay marriage. Here are some of the reasons I've heard most often.

Envy: Straight men often envy the ability of married gay men to have sex with a variety of men; this is true for more than a few heterosexual women too.

Fear: Straight people may believe that—somehow—our marriages will harm or cheapen theirs. This is especially likely to be true if they don't like gay people in general and think of us as "second-class citizens."

Anger: Fear often manifests as anger. A client once told me that, when traveling in a rural area with his husband, someone said to him, "How dare you dirty homosexuals spread your filth and diseases to a sacred institution like marriage." Yikes!

Unresolved same-sex desires: A lot of homophobia is the result of the fear of same-sex attraction. It's a lot easier to hate us and our marriages than it is to admit that you're attracted to us.

Biblical references: I am certainly not a Bible scholar, but I have heard so-called religious people throw around any number of alleged Bible quotes condemning us homosexuals to all sorts of awful places. As a recent client told me (his father is an evangelical minister): "Anyone up for the fiery lakes of Hell?"

What do we do when our marriages—monogamous or open—aren't supported by the world we live in? How do we hold to our hopes and dreams for our marriage and not be discouraged or dissuaded?

It's easy when your desires align with those of your friends, family, and community. But when they don't, there is often dissonance and doubt.

You can surround yourself with like-minded people, but not all the time. And even if you could, would it be a good idea to be so insular? Some places are lucky enough to have married gay couples' groups, but even then, that can't be your whole world, can it?

Isn't it healthy to experience people with different ideas/beliefs? Isn't this how we learn and grow? Isn't "preaching to the choir" pretty pointless?

And isn't this how new ideas are shared? Others may need/want to hear what you and your husband have to say about marriage—it might open their minds. It might even normalize what they've been secretly thinking but may be afraid to speak aloud.

This is how we grow, my brothers, not by insulating ourselves into gay ghettos (that's so twentieth century), but by sharing our experience with the larger world and seeing what happens.

PART II

EXPLORING OPEN MARRIAGE

CHAPTER FIVE

Sexual Freedom and Expression

What I love most about this chapter is that it helps you and your husband to talk more easily about your sex life. This is not a small thing! Despite the popularity—and ubiquity—of gay porn in our community, there is very little honest talk about sex.

I see this in my private practice all the time: so many gay men tell me that they have no one to calmly, rationally explore their sexual lives with. I encourage my clients to talk about their sexual lives as an integral part of their relationships and marriages. Much of traditional psychotherapy has not been very good at this, but happily, that's changing. And it is my hope that this book will help the process along.

A big part of mental health is having a healthy sex life, but for some reason, our sexual selves are often left out of any discussion about our mental and physical health. Maybe it's because it makes some doctors or therapists—or us—nervous. Well, it's time to get over those old taboos and welcome our sexual expression as a wonderful and essential part of who we are. So, let's talk about sex . . .

We have a lot to celebrate as gay men alive today. There have never been gay men like us. This is due to (1) longer lifespans, (2) overall increased physical health, and (3) the mental health of being able to be *out* (as our forefathers never could).

Whether you're single or married, it's all too easy (and popular) to focus on what's wrong with our sexual lives. There are many articles about HIV, STDs, impersonal hookups, sex addiction, PNP (party 'n' play), the pros and cons of PrEP,[1] sex on crystal meth, etc. But how often do we focus on what's *right* with our sexual lives? How often do we let ourselves *celebrate* sex and acknowledge how much we enjoy it? Specifically, I'm talking about how vibrant, healthy sexual expression in our marriages can help heal us emotionally and physically.

To do this, it helps to let go of old ideas about sex. Regardless of our age, most of us have a lot of long-held negative beliefs about our sexual selves and embarrassment about some of our sexual histories and fantasies. However, it's not so easy to give up these old beliefs about sex. So let's start right there . . .

I'd like to include, in this chapter, some of the most helpful questions that I've used with clients over the years to facilitate open and honest discussions about their sexual lives. I've used these questions with individuals, couples, and in workshops. I offer them here as vehicles that you and your husband can use as starting points for conversations about your sex lives.

Let's start by looking at your family beliefs about sex and your previous sexual experiences.

- *What are my family beliefs about sex?*
- *How have these beliefs helped me? How have they held me back?*
- *What are some of the most wonderful sexual experiences I've had?*
- *How have these experiences changed me?*

Are there any obstacles to celebrating your sexual self?

- *What stands in my way of enjoying a terrific sex life?*
- *Am I holding onto any old ideas that hold me back sexually?*
- *Do I have any physical challenges that hold me back sexually?*

Celebrating your sexual fantasies: Can you enjoy them without guilt and shame?

- *Do I let myself have sexual fantasies? If so, can I enjoy them?*
- *What are some of my fantasies about sex?*
- *Have I ever fulfilled a sexual fantasy? When and how?*
- *Are there any sexual fantasies that I would really like to experience? If so, how could I make them a reality?*

A well-balanced sexual life involves our head and heart, not just our genitals.

> - *What role does your head (thinking) play in your sexual life? Do you want it to be more or less involved?*
> - *What role does your heart (feeling) play in your sexual life? Do you want it to be more or less involved?*
> - *What role do your genitals (libido) play in your sexual life? Do you want them to be more or less involved?*
> - *How can you balance your head, heart, and genitals to make your sexual life really alive?*

I recommend that you and you husband answer these questions individually and then, collectively, share them. In my experience, the sharing phase is often one of surprise and discovery. It is typical to hear some version of "Really? I had no idea you felt that way/liked to do that/wanted more of that. Why didn't you tell me?" These questions open the doors to information that you may never have shared with anyone before. It can be very eye-opening to share them with your husband! If we are willing to see our sexual expression as a wonderful and essential part of our marriages, we can explore sex with our husband and/or with others, allowing our sexual expression as married men to heal us emotionally, spiritually, and physically.

Now that you and your husband have explored some of your ideas about sex, your sexual histories, and your sexual fantasies, let's talk about sexual freedom. In my experience, this is one way that gay marriages typically differ from straight ones. After all, we are so all about sex, aren't we? At least, that's a stereotype that the straight world has held onto for years. But is there some truth there? Are we more about sex than straight men? If so, why?

For some of us, sexual freedom and expression differ vastly from the heterosexual model. Most married straight men—if they're honest—will admit that they would love to have sex with more than one woman (i.e., their wife), but that most married women won't have it.

Many of my gay clients value their sexual freedom in a way that straight men cannot imagine. Look at our history: for so long, being gay meant being sexual with lots of guys. We were ostracized by straight society, called "deviants" and "perverts." While it seemed that so-called legitimate society had no use for us, at least we could have some small revenge on them—we could have all the sex we wanted!

This appeared, for a time, to be a real boon: one of my clients said that, in the 1970s, he used to tell his straight friends, "I feel sorry for you married straight guys; you can only have sex with your wives, while we can have sex with whoever we want, whenever we want."

If, historically, an important part of being gay was the freedom to have sex with whomever we choose, whenever we choose, and however we choose, now that we can get married, this begs the question, if being gay isn't primarily about sex, then what does it mean to be gay? What is our primary focus? If our purpose is to be like straight folks, then we should mime their lives and imitate their marriage structure.

But what if our purpose is to find our own paths to happiness? What if our own ways of relationships are different? I believe that, as gay men, we have a special gift, and, as with all gifts comes responsibility for that gift. Since we are able to love other men, we have the responsibility for creating a different kind of life, and, in turn, a different kind of relationship/marriage for ourselves.

Questions to Consider (do these with your husband)

- How important is sex to you (on a scale of 1 to 10)?
- Are you comfortable with monogamy? What about it do you like? What about it bothers you?
- Would you prefer a sexually open marriage? Why? How do you see that playing out?

Sex as Sport?

There's talk in the air—particularly among my younger gay clients—of "sex as sport." What does this mean? From what I hear, it's about sex as an activity, like tennis or baseball—just for fun, good for exercise—no muss, no fuss—and no emotional drama. This is what I call "sex lite": sex without commitment, emotional drama, and seriousness.

Sex as sport is what a lot of married gay men want from their sex buddies. Is this a good thing, or a step down into unhealthy relationships? I think neither. Let's not oversimplify sex; it's a supremely rich, deep, and complicated activity involving three key aspects of yourself: your mind (thoughts), heart (emotions), and genitals (libido). Each of us has his unique way of "mixing" these three together in our sex life with our husband and other men.

Instead of judging and condemning sex as sport, why not be curious about it. (Of course, I am assuming that all sex as sport is safe sex. Otherwise, that's "sex as stupidity.") For example, here are some ways it might work for you.

Sex as Playful

> Evan: "I'm an industrial engineer—very linear and methodical in my thinking. I have a good sex life with my husband, but he's a lot like me, another 'Mr. Rational.' I have a different kind of sex with my fuck buddies; it helps get me out of my ultra-logical side and let myself go, be a bit uninhibited."

Playfulness is an aspect of being childlike (not childish); playfulness helps keep us youthful, spontaneous, and carefree. It's a good antidote to stress, anxiety, and panic. When life gets too serious and you feel "boxed in," some playful, light-hearted, adventurous sex may be just what you need. Even better: try to integrate some of this playfulness into your marriage, if your husband is open to it.

Sex as an Escape from Reality

> Gerhard: "Sometimes, when things really suck, it's good to have an escape. Sex is sometimes a good temporary escape from my problems."

Sex can certainly be a temporary distraction or diversion from a rough day or week. If you notice that this is becoming a pattern, however, you may be avoiding something that needs your attention. I recommend that you use sex as an escape sparingly, for best results.

Sex as Conquest

> Corey: "I like the thrill of the chase and the excitement of 'conquering' someone—it makes me feel very masculine, powerful and sexy."

When your life feels out of control, being the "dominant" person in sex can help you feel more in control, even if it's just for an hour or two. When things just don't seem to go your way and you feel a sense of "What do I do now?" this kind of sex can help you "rebalance." Be careful, though; it also has its "dark" side: a need to exert control over others.

Sex as a Boredom Filler

Nate: "Sometimes life just gets a bit too routine for me, so I'll look to have sex with some hot guy who isn't my usual 'type.' And since I'm usually a bottom with my husband, I might want to change it up and top this new guy."

Who among us hasn't been bored and considered sex as an option? In some ways, sex is right up there with food in this department. The downside? It's a temporary fix for what might be a more permanent problem. If you find yourself frequently bored, don't use sex as an avoidance mechanism; instead, take a look at what you're avoiding and do something about it. Ongoing boredom is usually about avoiding something in your life that you hope will just go away (but rarely does).

Sex as a Self-Esteem Boost

Jacob: "I was chatting online with this handsome dude and he told me I was hot—it was just what I needed, 'cause I sure wasn't feeling it."

Again, the main problem with this is that once the sex is over, where is your self-esteem now?

Sex as a Reward

Rory: "Lately, I've been working way too hard, way too many hours, so tonight I'm gonna have myself a cute little twink. I deserve it."

And he did feel good, for a while. Even better: don't be so ultra-good, so hyper-responsible and you may not need sex as a reward!

While sex as sport can give you short-term relief for a variety of life's problems, these problems don't go away just from having great sex. There is nothing intrinsically "bad" about sex as sport: you can use it to make your life more stimulating or you can use it to avoid emotionally connecting with people, like your husband. If you're afraid to make love with the man you know (and love) best, then sex as sport with the newest hot guy on your radar may be a diversion from working through your obstacles to a deep, rewarding, long-term relationship with your main man.

Let's take a look at the concept of emotional monogamy: your husband is your primary commitment and your relationship with each other is—by far—the most important relationship in your life, but you may have the option to have "sex as sport" outside of your relationship. Is this a good thing, or a step down into unhealthy relationships?

I think neither.

In my experience, there is nothing intrinsically "bad" about sex as sport; you can use it to make your married sex life more stimulating *or* you can use it to avoid emotionally connecting with your husband. If you're avoiding making love with your man, then sex as sport with the newest hot guy on your radar may be a diversion from working through your obstacles to a deep, rewarding marriage.

I admit to a bias: I believe that the absolute best sex with your husband—or anyone, really—involves your mind (psychological arousal), your heart (emotional connection), and your genitals (sexual energy). When you get all three working together, the possibilities for deep, amazing, mind-blowing sex are amazing. While sex as sport can be great fun, there's a lot it doesn't offer. Many of us choose marriage because we want someone to cuddle with at night, wake up in his arms, laugh with him over breakfast, and kiss him goodbye before we leave for work.

If you like the idea of sex as sport, consider it a rich, calorie-laden dessert to be enjoyed now and then. However, if it becomes the "main course" of your sex life, you may be using it to avoid the vulnerability of your marital relationship. If that's the case, try having "dessert" a little less often and explore bringing more of your heart into your sex life with your husband. Perhaps then, sex as sport can evolve into something even better.

Since this chapter is about sexual freedom and expression, let's talk about testosterone: when you put two gay men together, you've got lots of it. In any meaningful man-to-man relationship or marriage, we need to balance the desires and demands of our heart, mind, and genitals. For example, when you met your husband and felt an attraction, how and when did you decide to have sex with him? Was it right off the bat, when your heart and mind barely know him? Or was it later on, when your libido had been moderated by the wisdom of your mind and the feelings in your heart?

I'm not here to tell you that there's one *right* way to do it. One couple I worked with—Chad and Mark—met in a rather unusual way. I'll let Mark tell it.

> "I met Chad at a bathhouse, had great sex with him, exchanged numbers, you know. Then, the next day, I thought about this guy and wondered if there might be much more possible with him. Initially, my dick called the shots, but then my thoughts and feelings kicked in. I asked myself, 'Can I turn a hot hookup into a possible relationship?'"

Chad and Mark have now been together for three years and married last year.

Another way to summarize what Mark experienced is: How can I have a relationship where my mind, heart, and libido are all working together? Isn't this the ultimate goal of sexual expression? And won't this be the best sex ever?

It's pretty common for couples who've been together for years to report a drop-off in the *frequency* of their sex life. While this is understandable, let's focus on the *quality* of your sex life, and how you can maintain that, whether you're having sex with your husband or another desirable man.

Let's use our case study couple, Tomas and Larry, as an example: when they began their marriage, they decided to be monogamous. However, over time, differences in their sexual expression and preferences become clear. Larry wanted sex more often than Tomas. Larry worked at home and liked having sex in the middle of the day—a "sex break," he called it—while Tomas worked in management for a large corporation and frequently worked ten-to-twelve-hour days. This is another reason he was less interested in sex than Larry; he was usually too tired after these long workdays to be interested in sex. For him, sex had to wait until the weekend when he could "recover my energy," as he said. Over time, Tomas became interested in sexual activities—leather and bondage—that Larry didn't share. Larry was comfortable with Tomas exploring his new sexual interests, but Larry wasn't interested in participating.

Given these differences, how is this couple going to negotiate their own sexual freedom and expression?

In this case, they came to therapy and began to talk about what they wanted when they got married and what they wanted now; this had changed over time and, while their love for each other had deepened, their sexual desires had shifted.

Tomas became involved with the leather community in the city where they lived. He began to go to weekend "play parties" where he and other men experimented with leather, bondage, flogging, and other fetish activities. Tomas was a little sad that Larry didn't want to participate, but he was surprised to find that many other men in the group also had partners that did not share their interests. Tomas began to form friends in the leather community and to feel more comfortable there.

Larry—as you might remember—wanted to have sex at lunch, but Tomas wasn't available, due to his work. Larry asked Tomas how he felt about Larry using Grindr to meet other guys "just for lunchtime sex," as he put it. Initially, Tomas wasn't okay with it, so Larry acquiesced. However, as Tomas became more involved with the leather community, he began to see that "Larry and I don't have to share everything sexual; in fact, it's nice to have something that's just mine. Plus, Larry likes to hear me tell him about the 'play parties' I go to. He's not jealous, he said it kind of turns him on."

Progression from monogamy to an open relationship is an individual and unique path for every couple. Initially, Larry was more comfortable opening up the relationship than Tomas, so he waited for his husband to be "ready." Tomas's exploring the leather community was his entrée into exploring sex without Larry; their timing is pretty typical. For most couples, the timing isn't synchronistic; one man is ready and willing before his husband. Usually, if the eager-beaver guy is willing to be patient and wait for his man to join him, it works out well.

The key to making this work is being able to talk about it all along the way. An open relationship won't work without good communication between the partners.

In this case, Larry told Tomas "I feel a bit frustrated—emotionally and sexually—but I don't want to do anything you're not comfortable with." This put a bit of pressure on Tomas, who was tempted to emotionally cave in, but in couple's work, Tomas learned to speak his truth to Larry, even though he was afraid Larry might not like it.

Negotiating an open relationship can actually be *constructive* for a marriage; it forces you to talk about things that you may hesitate to bring up with your man, and it encourages you to speak your truth in a loving, respectful way as you and your husband work through difficult emotions *together*. As Larry and

Tomas told me recently, "It was awkward and uncomfortable talking about what we both wanted, but honestly, it was so good for our relationship. we now know each other better than almost any other couple we know."

Talking about sexual freedom and how you will each express it can be really great for you and your husband. All you have to do is get through the (temporary) awkwardness.

Questions to Consider

- Is there anything that you're hesitant to tell your husband about your sex life together?
- How has your sex life changed since you've been together?
- What's missing? What's better than you expected? What's not as good as what you expected?

In the next chapter, we'll look at two of the biggest challenges to an open marriage: negotiating jealousy and insecurity.

CHAPTER SIX

Negotiating Jealousy and Insecurity

It is inevitable that jealousy and insecurity are going to rear their ugly heads in your marriage. As human beings, no matter how wise or sophisticated we are, there are still aspects of our personalities that want security and predictability. Fear is often associated with uncertainty. And yet, an open marriage invites uncertainty (which also can feel like excitement). Excitement and fear are two sides of the same coin. You can't have one without the other. So how can you and your husband navigate jealousy and insecurity in your open marriage?

Jealousy and insecurity can drive us to do foolish and desperate things. I'll bet you know someone who hasn't been able to get a handle on his jealousy, and ended up really messing up his relationship.

Pretending jealousy and insecurity don't exist is one way that some married men deal with—or avoid dealing with—these challenges. Don't go there! It doesn't work. If you want an open marriage, being able to talk about this stuff is crucial. If you and your husband can't have honest, respectful conversations about your jealousies and insecurities, I seriously encourage you to question the feasibility of an open marriage.

Why? Because maintaining a happy, successful open marriage is just too hard if you can't talk about it.

Sometimes, talking about it looks like negotiating. Each of you may want different things from your marriage, and they may not easily coexist. In that case, respectful, calm negotiation is definitely the way to go. Some couples avoid discussing this stuff, waiting instead for a crisis to blow up so that they *have* to talk about it. This is a very high-stress way to do it. It's likely to wear you both down and make you wonder whether it's worth it. Instead, begin to talk with your husband about your possible jealousy and insecurity *before* something dramatic happens.

Questions to Consider

- What does your jealousy look like?
- How does insecurity manifest itself in your life?
- How have you worked with these feelings in the past? What worked or didn't work?
- What is the best way for you and your husband to talk about this stuff?

Tomas and Larry have struggled with jealousy and insecurity. When they began their marriage, they chose to be monogamous. However, over time, differences in their sexual expression and preferences became clear. Initially, Larry was more comfortable opening up the relationship than Tomas, so he waited for his husband to be "ready." Tomas's experiences in the leather community were his entrée into exploring sex without Larry.

Tomas began to deal with his insecurities and jealousies and—encouraged by his friends in the leather community—stopped being so docile with Larry. He began to be more honest and direct in talking about what he wanted and didn't want, even though he was afraid Larry might not like it. Tomas constructively used his insecurity to speak his truth to his husband and Larry responded in a loving, supportive way. Paradoxically, jealousy and insecurity in your marriage can bring you both much closer *if* you are *both* willing to talk about it.

Whether you're married or single, in a monogamous or open relationship, there's just no avoiding difficult emotions like jealousy and insecurity. You may be jealous of people at work, or insecure when talking with someone whose life you admire. These emotions are not unique to marriage. And yet, in an open marriage, jealousy and insecurity are usually brought to the surface quickly, in a way that single guys and men in monogamous marriages seldom experience.

How do we begin to work with these uncomfortable feelings? First off, let's be clear that *we* are responsible for our feelings. No one else can "make" us feel jealous. We will not take on the role of "victim" and say things like, "He did it to me."

So, no victimhood drama, okay? That said, we want to be considerate of our husband and work with him to trigger his hot buttons as little as possible.

You and your husband defined jealousy and insecurity for yourself in the questions above. I'd now like to share some other men's definitions with you. These are much better than any textbook definitions of jealousy and insecurity—they come from clients I've worked with over the past two decades.

I asked them, "What is jealousy?"

Chad: "Jealousy is when you don't trust your man, whether you have a logical reason or not."

Abel: "It's when you care a lot and you're scared to lose the man you love."

Christian: "When you feel like attention has been drawn away from you by another man."

Andy: "Jealousy is so much more powerful than I thought: it made me act like a crazy person."

Rabih: "Being jealous is wanting to keep what you have and keeping it away from other men."

Benjamin: "It's being possessive: not wanting others to flirt with or touch your man. It's like: 'He's mine; you can't have him.'"

Chibuzo: "It's completely irrational, but I can't help feeling it anyway."

Niels: "When you love someone and they do things to make you feel like they don't care so much about you anymore."

Peter: "When your man's attention is on someone else and you feel angry and helpless to change it."

Garjoca: "A jealous man will do anything to make it look like he's bigger than he is because he feels so small and helpless."

Timothy: "When you really love a guy and he does things to make you feel like you're not his #1 anymore."

Will: "When you notice that your husband's attention has shifted away from you to someone else."

In addition to asking men to define "jealousy," I also asked them, "What is insecurity?"

Charles: "It's all the things I hate about myself and feel judged about."

Olan: "An insecure man will bully his husband to make him feel better about himself."

Michael: "He will try to control his husband because he's afraid that his
husband will see that he's really not so great."

Yannick: "Insecurity is when you are not okay with yourself."

Ben: "An insecure man feels he is not worthy of having such a good man
and fears his husband will find a better man."

Edon: "For me, insecurity is low confidence and low self-esteem."

Curtis: "It's feeling inadequate."

Jim: "Insecure people want to be liked by people and will go out of their
way to please others, because they don't want people mad at them."

Sidney: "It's a lack of trust in yourself and who you are."

John: "Insecure people compare themselves to others to see how they stack
up against the competition."

Craig: "An insecure man will read his husband's e-mails and texts to see if
he is lying to him."

Hasim: "We insecure people are afraid of being rejected and most of our
perceptions are false."

In working with our own jealousies and insecurities, it's important to
remember that *we*—ultimately—are responsible for our happiness. We can't
expect our husband, or anyone else, to "make" us feel secure. Most couples
I've worked with would readily agree with this (at least, in theory), but would
concur that it's awfully hard to live it 100 percent of the time. We want to feel
safe and secure, to know that there are people we can depend on. This is one
of the main reasons why many gay men get married: we want a husband we
can depend on.

But depend on for what? What are we expecting of him? That he makes us
feel loved and appreciated? Well, he can't really do that for us, can he? We
may want to be able to have sex with other men and come back to him as our
rock, our foundation. But—often—if we are really honest, we don't want to
return the favor. We'd like to be the one who gets to have all the fun without
the insecurities that come with our husband having his fun too.

Let's look at an example of this.

Ira and Eric have an open marriage. They had an open relationship for
several years before they got married. Things seemed to be going well for
them, until something changed and they made an appointment to come to see
me for couple's counseling.

Ira: "I love being married to Eric. It works really well in almost all ways, but this open marriage stuff isn't working for me anymore. If I'm honest with myself, I never really wanted it, but it was so important to Eric that I just went along with it. I got used to it and thought it was okay, but lately, it seems like Eric is much more into his 'friends I fuck' than he is in having sex with me."

Eric: "I knew that Ira wasn't as much into it [an open relationship] as I was, but he seemed to be okay with it and said that—sometimes—he enjoyed it. So, this is a big surprise for me."

Ira: "I knew how important it was to Eric and I didn't want to lose him, so I sucked it up and pretended it was all fine. I can't pretend anymore."

Eric (spoken to me): "Okay Michael, so what do we do now?"

This situation is more common than you might think, so let's address it.

Rarely, in an open marriage, are both husbands equally excited about having sex with men outside the relationship. In most cases, one man is more into it than the other. This is another reason why ongoing communication is crucial to sustaining an open relationship over time. Ira isn't the first man who's ever "gone along with" an open relationship because he didn't want to lose his man. You may call Ira passive or codependent, but labels aside, Ira did the best he could at the time with the knowledge he had.

Now, he's more honest and also more unhappy. What happens when one husband finds that an open relationship doesn't work for him anymore? Usually, jealousy and insecurity are at play. In Ira's case, he tolerated Eric's having sex with other men because he didn't think he had a choice: he could either accept it or lose Eric (which may have been true, we can't really know). In working with Ira and Eric, it became clear that the best immediate option for them was take a break from their open relationship—to "close" it—and let things calm down a bit for both of them.

Ira: "I need more attention from you and I am no longer willing to have so little (sexual) time with you."

Eric: "I'm sorry you didn't speak up and, honestly, I'm angry about that. I'm not a mind reader. Are you saying that if we're not monogamous, you don't want to be married to me anymore?"

Ira: "Right now I don't know what I want or what is the right thing to do. I do want to be married to you, but I'm not happy with our sex life."

Many gay marriages go through periods where the relationship is sexually "open" for some time—a month, a year, several years—and then it may "close" for a while. Changing situations require changing the form/structure of the relationship. In the above case, Ira became more jealous and insecure as he perceived Eric having more and better sex with other guys, leaving little for him. "Closing" the relationship for a while—to focus on *repair* of trust and connection—was the most constructive thing to do. Once the relationship stabilized, Eric and Ira could talk more honestly about what they do and don't want.

> Ira: "I want to have sex with you at least once a week—hopefully, more. I want to feel that I am your #1 priority."

In their counseling sessions, I asked Ira to give more specifics on what being "your #1 priority" would look like. Otherwise, a vague goal like that is hard to satisfy. It turned out that Ira wanted to have a "date night" once a week where it was just the two of them, no cell phones, no working from home— just the two of them. Eric was willing to do what Ira asked, but he explained why he really liked their open marriage.

> Eric: "I like variety in my sex life. I always have. It's not you, Ira; you're great. But our sex life has gotten very predictable these past few years, and I miss the variety I get from being with other guys."

For a while, it appeared that the two of them were at a stalemate: Ira wasn't comfortable with Eric continuing to have sex with other men. I asked them both if they could stay in the present and not project into the future, focusing on making their relationship as good as it could be *today*, knowing that things may be different tomorrow.

Ultimately, after a few months of a closed relationship, Ira and Eric agreed to slowly open up their marriage (again). They also made some changes as to how they'd have sex with other men: they would only have sex (with another man) as a couple, so that Ira wouldn't feel insecure or jealous and Eric could have some of the variety that's so important to him.

At the time of this writing, their relationship continues to "relax" and open up further. Ira likes Eric to watch him and the "other" man have sex. This reduces his jealousy and insecurity. It's still hard for him to watch Eric with other men, but that's shifting.

> Ira: "The more secure I feel with Eric, the easier it gets for me to see him with other men. It's a slow process, but it's changing."

Eric also feels good about it.

> Eric: "I like that Ira is more assertive. He's asking for what he wants in bed and surprising me, at times. He's not as predictable as I thought. And I like watching him with other guys; it's a turn-on for me. I do miss being with other guys on my own, but I think that it may take some time before Ira's ready for that."

Not *every* nonmonogamous couple has problems with jealousy and insecurity. But in my experience, most couples in open gay marriages experience these challenges *at some point* in their marriage. Often, it's at the beginning, when having sex with other men is new for both of you, and there's a whole lot of uncertainty and unease.

This was true for Todd and John: they had been monogamous in their two years of dating and didn't think much about opening up their marriage until their first anniversary party, when a friend of theirs asked them, "So, are you guys gonna be monogamous forever?"

After they got over the surprise of that question, Todd and John talked about the possibility of opening up their marriage, but felt that the time wasn't right. Neither of them had ever lived with another man, so *that* alone was enough of a challenge for them to take on. Their friend had, however, planted a seed in their consciousness. As Todd said, "From that moment on, we thought about it, but it wasn't for another year or so that we gave it serious consideration. By that time, we felt pretty stable in our marriage and were ready to begin our explorations."

In some open marriages, everything goes along just fine until one of the husbands begins to "have feelings" for someone he's having sex with. This may not be a big deal if he and his husband can talk about it. But it can become a big deal if he considers it a shameful secret, which—ironically—only amplifies his feelings for the "other" man.

Stan and Pete had been happily married for five years and had been nonmonogamous since they first began dating, about seven years ago. They had started out with a lot of rules about what was okay and not. They laughingly made up the rule: "And no falling in love with anyone we have sex with."

It wasn't so funny when Pete found himself growing extremely fond of his friend-with-benefits, Stephen. Pete tells it best.

> "I never gave most of my fuck buddies a lot of emotional energy. Sure, I liked them as people, but they never threatened my marriage to Stan. And then Stephen came along and I thought, 'Wow, if I weren't married to Stan, I'd sure go for Stephen, he is an amazing guy.'"

Fortunately, or unfortunately, Stephen felt the same way about Pete, but he didn't want to be a homewrecker, so he temporarily stopped spending time with Pete. This made Pete, to his surprise, quite depressed and sad. He tried to keep it a secret from Stan, because he was so ashamed and embarrassed, and didn't know how Stan would react if he told him the truth.

Eventually, of course, Stan noticed and pushed Pete to say what was bothering him, and that's when they called me and asked for help. They found themselves in a situation that they'd never expected and didn't know how to move forward. Luckily, they were both willing to talk about it and were committed to their marriage (and each other).

Initially, during counseling, they agreed to close their marriage for a while to "recalibrate" (Pete's words). As they talked, they mutually decided that Pete needed to take a break from being with Stephen—and even talking to him—because "I was beginning to fall in love with him." This was painful for Stephen too, and he came to one of Pete and Stan's counseling sessions so the three of them could hear each other and "be on the same page," as Stan said.

It took about three months before Pete and Stan were ready to reopen their marriage. It took six months before Pete and Stephen were able to be together (platonically). Fortunately, at that point in time, Stephen was dating a man that he was very fond of and chose to be monogamous with.

Would you call this a happy ending? They did.

I have also seen jealousy and insecurity become a problem when one of the husbands goes through a difficult time (e.g., loses his job, has a health problem) and old insecurities are activated. William and Travis were considered a "power couple" in their community. They were highly visible and often spoken as "an ideal couple": two successful, handsome, healthy, and prosperous gay men in their early forties in a very happy open marriage. William was a corporate lawyer and Travis ran his own public relations firm. They had a beautiful home with the requisite number of adorable dogs and had recently purchased a lakeside summer home just an hour from their city.

Then William's law firm hit a tough spot and laid him off. He was in shock: "How could this happen to me? I've been there so long. I thought they liked me." Travis was reassuring: "It's okay honey, I can cover us financially for a while, and you'll get another job soon." William was worried about their two mortgages and the scuba diving trip to Africa for which they had just paid $12,000 (nonrefundable, of course). It is not insignificant that William was making about $500,000 a year to Travis' $100,000, so both men were quite concerned over the loss of the major money-maker in the marriage.

William's self-confidence quickly took a dive; he couldn't get another job as easily as he'd hoped and began, to great distress, to realize how much of his status was due to his career as a highly paid corporate lawyer. Unemployed, he had too much time on his hands. He began to arrange a lot of Grindr hookups to fill his now-empty days.

Travis, meanwhile, was quite focused on bills. As the sole breadwinner, he felt a lot of pressure to bring in more money, so he worked longer hours and had less sex then before—with William or any of the other guys he usually "played with" (his words), coming home at night exhausted, plus working weekends to pay both of those hefty mortgages.

It's easy to understand how Travis became resentful of William's now-abundant sex life and how William's self-esteem was in the gutter.

> William: "I felt like a piece of shit, a total fraud. I thought I was such hot stuff, untouchable. Now, my self-confidence is totally shot. I feel like I'm nothing without my job. Even all this sex isn't making me feel any better, it just fills up all the empty hours in the day."

Travis was jealous of William and William was incredibly insecure. Not a good combination. This "power couple" had become tremendously imbalanced and their disparate sex lives (too much for William, not enough for Travis) became a bone of contention. In a counseling session, Travis told a depressed and disoriented William,

> Travis: "Baby, I love you, but right now I just want to kick your ass. You're not trying hard enough to get a job. You need more job interviews and fewer hookups."
>
> William: "You're right, but how can I get another job when I feel like a piece of shit? Who's going to hire me in this state?"

William began individual therapy to work on his self-esteem and how he felt "like nothing without my job." He also began doing volunteer work to fill his daytime hours with something besides "meaningless sex" (his words). Travis decided to temporarily lay off one of his employees, lowering his payroll so he felt less pressure to work eighty-hour weeks. And they began to rent out their lakeside house to bring in more money.

Eventually, of course, William did find another job, but at a considerably lower salary. They decided to sell the lakeside house to lower expenses and found other areas where they could economize.

"And where are they now?" you might ask. They are still together and happier than before. I'll let them tell you.

> William: "For the first time in my life, I feel grounded. I feel solid in myself. I was raised to be the perfect child, the great achiever, the golden boy— and when I thought I couldn't do it, I felt worthless. Getting laid off was the best thing for my personal growth, but it was sure hell on our marriage."
>
> Travis: "I agree with William, this was actually a good thing, in retrospect. Before, we were both way too wrapped up in our jobs, our status in the community, spending lots of money, being the perfect gay couple—we believed our own PR, which is hilarious because I'm a PR person. We don't believe it anymore."

William and Travis worked through their jealousy and insecurity to become a much stronger couple. The structure of their marriage changed a great deal as their priorities shifted. They used individual and couple's counseling to work through their anger and disappointment in themselves and in each other. They kept talking about "the hard stuff" even when it was uncomfortable.

Ironically, as their status in the community cooled a bit ("We're no longer considered 'the hot couple'" Travis told me, "and it's okay"), their personal satisfaction—individually and as a couple—grew exponentially. Loving each other through their problems brought them much closer.

Let's talk about rules in open marriages. Most couples have some sort of rules, guidelines, or structure in their marriage: the degree of structure, its rigidity/flexibility, and its adaptability vary greatly among couples. Some couples swear by rules; they codify and amend them on a regular basis. I'd like to give you some examples of how married gay couples can create and adjust their rules. But first, you and your husband might find these questions useful to explore your own needs/desires for rules in your open marriage.

Questions for Discussion

- Do you and your husband have any rules about having sex with other men?
- If so, did you make them up ahead of time, or did you wait until a situation occurred and then create rules for future situations?
- If not, how do you handle unexpected situations?

Eduardo and Felix are a couple I worked with. They both liked to feel "in control," so having a solid structure for their open marriage was important to both of them. Each of them came up with his own set of "rules" and then they hashed them out together in couple's therapy, creating the rules that they wanted to begin their marriage with. Here are a few of their initial rules.

- No kissing other guys
- No seeing another guy more than once a week
- No seeing another guy more than three times total
- No sleeping over with another guy
- No hanging out with them and their friends
- No meeting their family

With these rules, Eduardo and Felix found the right amount of "structure" for their open marriage. It really doesn't matter how much structure/rules you and your husband want: you can always adjust it later on. What matters is that the structure that you create *together* works for *both* of you.

While it may seem overly restrictive to some men, the above rules were a good foundation for Eduardo and Felix. It gave them the confidence to move ahead. And yes, they loosened up their rules over time. But these rules were great for them at the beginning.

Other couples keep it much looser: they don't create a fixed set of rules. Instead, they take it as it comes and adjust as they go along. Tomas and Larry, if you recall, were pretty flexible in how they handled their open marriage; as their situations changed, they adjusted the structure of their relationship.

Probably the most adaptable couple I know is Ivan and Samuel. Both men were extremely secure in themselves, successful in their careers and personal lives, and had been in several long-term relationships before they met and—eventually—married. Each man had experimented with monogamous and open relationships and had learned what worked for him and what didn't. I think they put it much better than I could.

> Ivan: "I was no young innocent when we met. I had been in three really great relationships that had gone through periods of being monogamous and open. I knew the pros and cons of each. I knew my triggers for insecurity and jealousy and how to work with them. I was so happy to be with Samuel because it seemed like he had as much experience with this stuff as I did."
>
> Samuel: "Neither Ivan nor I was naïve or young when we met. We'd both been around the block and were pretty worldly. This was great and I hoped we could have a marriage of equals. We started talking about monogamy from our first date: what we liked about it, didn't like, etcetera. We decided after our third date that we would experiment with an open relationship and keep the dialogue going so we could adjust it when need be."

It's probably no surprise to you that Ivan and Samuel's open marriage is a happy one. They talk about their jealousies and insecurities, easily identifying them and asking each other for help. Their relationship is adaptable and flexible: they can calmly talk about what's working—or not working—and come to solutions that work for both of them.

It wasn't completely smooth sailing, it never is, for *anyone*, but for these two married men, the transitions from open to closed (and back again) were pretty smooth, and because each man really knew himself and his strengths and weaknesses, the conversations about the state of their marriage were almost always respectful and constructive. In fact, Ivan and Samuel had "wine and check-in night" once a week, where they'd have a glass of wine and sit down and talk about three things.

- What's working well in our relationship?
- What isn't working so well?
- What would we like to do about it?

(I admit: they got these questions from me.)

Addressing your own insecurities can go a long way toward a happy open marriage. However, what happens when your jealousy and insecurities threaten your marriage? Here is an e-mail I received from a jealous husband.

Dear Michael:

I have a wonderful husband, "Ethan." We've been together for about three years now and we're very happy. There's just one problem: I am a handsome, successful twenty-nine-year-old man who is incredibly jealous. This isn't the first time I've had this jealousy problem with a man. I thought that getting married would make my jealousy go away, but it hasn't. I'm afraid I'll sabotage our marriage if I don't change. Help!

Driving Him Crazy in D.C.

Mr. Driving doesn't say whether his relationship is open or monogamous, but in this case, the main problem is his jealousy. Assuming Mr. Driving is in a monogamous relationship, jealousy is bad enough. If Mr. Driving is in an open marriage, his jealousy could destroy his marriage.

If you find yourself in a similar place, ask yourself, is there any basis for my jealousy? There's a big difference between being neurotic and being naïve. If you have reason not to trust your husband, that's one thing. But if you have had this problem with other relationships, it is likely your problem, not your husband's.

Unexamined jealousy *does* push people away; imagine what it's like to be continually mistrusted and questioned. It would drive anyone away, given enough time, frustration, and invalidation. In fact, some men even rationalize,

"Well, he thinks I'm cheating on him no matter what I tell him, so why not just go and do it then. He'll never believe I'm faithful, so why not?"

Jealousy can be a kind of self-sabotage: some men can't accept a great husband. Because they don't think they deserve him, they subconsciously push him away.

Jealousy can also manifest in issues of control. What some people call "love" is actually "control." While it's popular to label someone you don't like a "control queen," the truth is that we're *all* control queens. What matters is the *degree* to which we need to control other people. Some of us need to feel in control because, in past situations, we had little or no control. So we overreact and want total control in the present. This can make our husbands (and other important people in our lives) feel unsteady, shaken, or blind with rage or anger—the emotions can run the gamut.

People may tell you to "back off" on your controlling behavior; it's easy to say but not so easy to do. If jealousy is an ongoing problem for you, it's important that you get to the source of your need to control your husband. If you have lived through a very out-of-control time, particularly as a child, it may seem normal to want to control everything and everyone around you.

For some men, chronic jealousy comes from a strong fear of being alone, desperately needing to be with someone. You can't handle the idea that your husband could ever leave you, so you cling to him desperately and create the very thing you fear.

Whether you're married or not, it's your responsibility as an adult to find a way to live with yourself, regardless of what happens with your husband (or any other man). Jealousy is not a friend; it whispers neurotic thoughts in your mind and encourages you to do things you'll regret.

Eddie, a client of mine, called me one morning at 6:00 a.m. because, while on a business trip, he'd sent jealous, accusatory texts, at 2:00 a.m., to his husband. Now—four hours later—his jealous behavior made him cringe with regret and embarrassment. He told me, "I can't keep doing this, I just keep imagining that he's out there having sex with someone else, but my logical self knows that he's home sleeping—alone—in our bed."

I have worked with clients who've smothered their partners, making them miserable. Another client of mine—Nolan—wouldn't give his husband any room to breathe, move, or have a life of his own. When his husband wanted to have lunch with a friend, Nolan took it personally and felt rejected. He couldn't rein in his paranoid thoughts; he would imagine his husband flirting with every man in sight, and then, that evening, he'd grill his husband like an investigator on *CSI*.

Yikes! What to do?

I helped Nolan learn to control this kind of self-destructive behavior and get a grip on his paranoid/jealous feelings. Today Nolan and his husband are happy (yes, they're still together). Jealousy still rears its head now and then, but now Nolan has a repertoire of skills to keep that nasty ole demon under control.

If jealousy and insecurity are problems for you, you too can develop skills to bring them more under your conscious control. No one enjoys being jealous, insecure, controlling, or smothering, and it may seem like we can't help it. But we can—and our marriage will benefit tremendously. Please use the information in this chapter as a starting point to get to the root of your jealousy. If you need help, work on it with a good psychotherapist—stop driving your husband crazy and letting your jealousy push him away.

CHAPTER SEVEN

Creating and Adjusting to
an Open Marriage

Every marriage goes through its share of adjustments; but for open marriages, being able to make changes and adjustments is even more critical. An open marriage is, as I've stated, a high-maintenance experience. There is no way that you and your husband can set it up and say, "There, that's done. Now we can relax and just let it be." Sure, you may be able to do it this way for a while, but if you and your husband have sex with men outside your marriage, there is just too much going on to sit back and expect everything to be smooth and easy.

I use the concept of "create and adjust" with all of my clients, especially those in open relationships. Every relationship is a creation: a product of two (or more) people's hopes and desires. You and your husband may start out with a very specific vision of what you want your marriage to be. Over time, however, this vision will interact with reality and need some adjustment. This is normal and healthy: nothing good stays the same over time. Good things—and bad things—encourage us to change. Let's look at our case study couple, Tomas and Larry.

As you may recall, they came to me for premarital counseling. They'd talked about what they wanted their marriage to be—created their shared vision—and made lists of what was important to them. When their lists did not overlap as much as they'd expected, they were surprised; they had assumed (after dating for over a year) that they knew what each other wanted. Let's revisit their lists.

Tomas
1. Security
2. Ease of adopting or having children
3. Legal/financial rights
4. Someone to grow old with
5. Get to know my partner sexually and vice versa and be very comfortable with each other
6. Monogamy and no risk of STDs or HIV ever again
7. My parents will finally get off my back now that I'm married

Larry
1. Want to be with you forever
2. Want our relationship to be the "rock" in my life
3. Possibility of children
4. Someone who will be my #1 and always have my back
5. Someone to buy a house with
6. Someone to explore an open relationship with (when the time is right)
7. Financial benefits (social security, taxes, etc.) and someone to plan/save for an early retirement with

From my years of counseling couples, I've learned that the more fundamentally different the two men are, the more adjustments they'll need to make over time. Let's see how Tomas and Larry handled their ongoing process of "creating and adjusting" in their open marriage by focusing on three areas where they had quite different hopes and expectations: money, family, and sex.

Money

Larry: "Money is really important to me. My family was financially insecure when I grew up and I had to wear pretty raggedy clothes and shoes a lot of the time. I became an insurance agent because I knew I could be self-employed and depend on myself. I work hard and earn good money and that's really important to me."

Tomas: "Our family wasn't rich, but we always had what we needed. My dad worked really hard at his job and my mom stayed at home with us kids. When times were tight, we had my grandparents, aunts, and uncles to help us, and vice versa. Everyone hung together and the extended family was pretty tight. I don't worry much about money; everything always works out fine, eventually."

Their Money-Related "Create and Adjust": Larry was the worrier and planner; Tomas was the one who had faith that everything would work out fine. Initially, they liked how seemingly "opposite" they were in these areas. "We complement each other nicely," Larry told me when I first met them. Over time, however, what may initially appear as cute or amusing, for example, "it's so cute how he worries about money all the time" can become, "It drives me crazy how he's so obsessed with money."

Have you ever noticed how the same things you found charming or funny about your husband when you first met can eventually become the things you most want to change about him?

This is normal, don't sweat it. It's simply time to create and adjust.

Begin with talking about what each of you wants. If it lines up easily, that's great. But if not, begin to see where your mutual desires overlap. Larry and Tomas both wanted to be able to feel financially secure, so this is where they began. Larry explained what made him feel more secure (e.g., making a budget for the two of them), and Tomas agreed, as long as they built in a reserve of "fun money" that could only be used for what Larry termed "frivolous" and Tomas called "just enjoying life."

Over time, they kept creating and adjusting their financial strategies as their situation changed. When they met, Larry made a lot more money than Tomas, but a few years later, Larry had stalled out salary-wise at his job and Tomas was recruited by a headhunter for a high-paying management job. This necessitated yet another "adjustment"—not an easy one for Larry, who liked to feel in control of the finances of the marriage. This changed yet again when, three years later, they adopted their first child. Which leads us to . . .

Family/Children

Family, and whether to have one, is a big issue for any marriage. For couples like Larry and Tomas, bringing children into the marriage can be fraught with strong emotional reactions that arise from each man's individual history, particularly, unresolved family-of-origin stuff. Let's hear Larry and Tomas tell it.

Larry: "I am the youngest of five children and I got really sick of competing—for attention, food, everything really—with my siblings.

My parents were fried at the end of the day from working long hours at their lousy minimum-wage jobs and weren't very affectionate to us or each other. I am open to having kids with Tomas, but it really isn't a high priority. If we do have kids, I want to make sure we have the time and money to do it right."

Tomas: "In my family, you didn't worry about providing for your kids, you just made it work, somehow. And it did. I loved being part of a big, extended family, with lots of cousins. My parents only had three kids. I was the only boy—I have two sisters—and I always wanted a brother. To me, big families mean more love; I want to have at least two kids with Larry, hopefully, more."

Their Family/Children-Related "Create and Adjust": Like the money discussion, these two guys have different family backgrounds, hence, different adult experiences with the ideals of family, parenthood, and children. They never talked much about kids until Larry proposed, and, then, it became clear to them how different their vision of their ideal family was. Larry wasn't sure that having kids would be a good idea, since his experience as the youngest of five kids left a lot to be desired. Tomas, on the other hand, always wanted a brother. See the clash here?

Initially, both men agreed to wait a year and then talk about children at that point. Neither wanted to take this on in their first year of marriage. However, as the year went by, Larry grew more reluctant to become a father while Tomas grew more excited about the idea of their adopting a child. And, as that year went by, both men were a bit uneasy to observe each other's "drift."

After a year, the inevitable conversation occurred, and it did not go well. It resulted in a very stressful couple's therapy session with me where each accused the other of being "selfish" and "rigid" and insisting, "he's not listening to me." At that point, it was important to, once again, focus on where their desires overlapped: Larry wanted to make sure that any child they adopted would "have enough time, money and attention from us—which are all things I never got." Tomas's desires for adopting a child—a boy, preferably—came from his desire for a brother and how lonely he felt as the only boy in his family. He was willing to admit that he and Larry both wanted the same things, basically: a family where everyone had enough time, attention, and love, and no one felt lonely or overlooked. From this starting point, they agreed to begin to research becoming foster parents, taking their first united step toward parenthood.

Larry found that being a foster parent was a good "training" for him: as the youngest in his family, he had little experience taking care of children—he was the one who needed care, and didn't get it. By giving their foster children his love and attention, he told me, "I feel I'm reversing what happened to me, in a good way." Tomas took easily to a loving, nurturing role with their foster kids, since he had spent years babysitting for his nieces and nephews and wasn't easily upset by children's demands and temper tantrums.

Two years later, they adopted their first son, Emilio. Two years after that, they adopted their second son (and last child), Alexander. They are still "creating and adjusting" as parents.

Sexual Ideal

While Tomas and Larry struggled with jealousy and insecurity relating to sex outside their marriage, it's not surprising when you learn more about their personal histories.

Larry: "I grew up in a household where any talk about sex was suppressed. My parents were working class and only high school graduates. When I realized I was gay, it was a shock to me and I didn't tell them until I was in my early twenties. They did not take it well. I was really interested in sex from a very young age. I found my dad's *Playboys* and focused on the few pictures with naked guys. I fooled around with the quarterback of the high school football team (my next door neighbor) when I was in eighth grade and he was in eleventh. That was my first orgasm and I wanted more. My parents' marriage was pretty lifeless and I resolved as a teenager never to be in a boring, dead relationship like that."

Tomas: "My dad had affairs and everybody pretended he didn't. This wasn't so unusual in our extended family. The men tended to be macho and the women accepted their husband's affairs as 'how things are.' As a kid, I saw my mom and her sisters cry over these affairs, and I resolved that I would never be cheated on like that by a man. I think this is why an open marriage is still a challenge for me. In a way, it still feels like cheating."

Their Sexual Ideal "Create and Adjust": Larry was someone who found that more sex with more men made him happy, and didn't detract from his love for and attraction to his husband. Tomas, on the other hand, began their marriage as someone who (initially) wanted monogamy but had a hard time advocating for it. He told me once, "I'm horrified how much I've turned out to be like my mother and aunties: accepting their husbands' cheating behavior and keeping quiet about it." It's not surprising that, at the beginning, Larry enjoyed their open marriage but Tomas grew increasingly unhappy in it and was afraid to express it.

It was important for the health of their marriage that Tomas be able to be honest with Larry and break the pattern of suffering in silence that he had learned in his family. Before they could progress as a couple, Tomas needed to be able to tell Larry what he wanted. As Tomas became more involved with the leather community, he began to see that he didn't need to share everything sexual with Larry. For Tomas, once he realized that he could talk with his husband about *anything*, he broke his pattern of repressing his unhappiness and anger.

Part of their "create and adjust" process was juggling different timelines for change: Larry was willing to wait for Tomas to work through his personal fears before their open marriage could progress sexually. If you recall, Tomas grew to enjoy his "play time" in the leather community, something Larry had no interest in. Tomas told me that this felt like a "juicy kind of secret," although he told Larry—who found it exciting—all about his adventures there.

Once Tomas got used to feeling secure with a sex life outside of his marriage, he grew more comfortable with Larry having one too. Today, as parents of two sons, ages five and seven, the couple tells me, "We're lucky to find the time and energy to have sex once a week with each other, let alone other men." However, soon both of their sons will be in elementary school, and Tomas hopes to be able to reconnect with his "fuck buddies" in the leather community and Larry plans to get together more often for "play dates" with guys on Grindr.

Create and adjust. Create and adjust. Repeat. Repeat. Repeat. This is the cycle of a happy, growing, changing open marriage. Most couples start out with some clarity about their mutual and individual goals, but typically, we don't think much about changes we can expect in the future. While it's good to be in the present moment with your husband, it's also helpful to think about the future.

Questions to Consider

- What can you expect to change in your marriage. How would you like to handle these changes?
- What kinds of situations make you most resistant to change?
- How have you accepted/rejected change in the past? What worked or didn't work?
- What is the best way for you and your husband to talk about this stuff?

I've made a short list of some of the most common changes that gay couples experience.

Expected Changes

- Illness
- Death
- Ebb and flow of feeling love(d)
- Aging
- Retirement
- Health challenges
- Relationship may open and close over time

Unexpected Changes

- Loss of job, home, health
- Divorce
- Falling out of love
- Growing apart
- Falling in love with someone else

Since there's no way to avoid this stuff, how do you and your husband want to handle it? With a healthy, ongoing process of creating and adjusting, of course. Right? Sorry, rhetorical question.

In an open marriage, rigidity is the enemy: you will fail if you try/want to keep things the same. And yet, most of us are afraid of change. We cling to an "illusion" of control, thinking that we have the ability to control how our marriage goes. The only control we really have is to admit that, in the vast majority of situations, we don't have much control! What we *do* have, however, is the ability to choose how we respond to situations. By embracing the cycle of creating and adjusting as a bedrock of your marriage, you and your husband will be able to work with all the changes that will come your way, even the really tough ones.

And, thankfully, the process doesn't have to be a big, hairy deal. Adjustments can be big or small. There is really no rational need to fear creating and adjusting—we do it all the time (unconsciously) in our daily life. We continuously have an idea about something we want, put it out there, give it our best shot, and see what happens. Rarely does it come back exactly as we expected. So, we adjust what we have created. It's as simple as driving to work and finding bad traffic on the road you like to take, so you adjust and take another road.

The same principle works with more important things. You want to buy a certain house that you've fallen in love with; your husband doesn't like it. You want to spend the evening with a hot, out-of-town guy you've been talking with through OK Cupid who's finally in town and free, but your husband wants to spend the evening with you because he's feeling a bit down and needs some alone time with you.

Over the years, I've noticed two typical change scenarios for gay couples: the first is when you want to adjust and he doesn't. The second is when he wants to adjust and you don't. Regardless of who is initiating the change, the dynamic is the same. Let's look at an example.

Skyler and Tim have been happily married for two years. They had an open relationship while they were dating and continued it into their marriage. After about a year and a half of marriage, Skyler said, "I'd like to take a break from this open marriage stuff; it's kind of exhausting, to be honest. Let's be monogamous for a while and see what happens." This was bad news for Tim, who was quite happy being married to Skyler and having rewarding sexual experiences with other guys. Skyler wanted to adjust what they had created; Tim didn't.

When they came into my office, each was pretty adamant that what he wanted was "fair" and that the other was being "unreasonable." Isn't this typical of how we argue as couples? We're right and they're wrong; why don't they see this and just admit it?

If only it were that easy.

Skyler wanted to take a break from nonmonogamy, but Tim didn't. And Skyler didn't want to be monogamous while Tim wasn't. He wanted Tim to do it *his* way. Not surprisingly, Tim bridled against this. A happy, open marriage isn't about who's right or who's wrong—as if there really is such a thing—it's more about how happy can you *and* your husband be as you negotiate your life together.

Skyler found himself tired of all the time and energy it took him to be nonmonogamous with Tim. He said, "It's so tiring finding these guys and then getting to know them and then having sex with them and then dealing with all their personality peccadillos. I want a break." Tim said that he understood, but didn't feel the same way. Where were their common points of interest?

Their common points of interest was that they loved each other and enjoyed sex with each other and with other men, but that Skyler wanted a break and he wanted Tim to take a break with him. After a long, honest discussion, they reached this agreement: (1) Skyler would take a break from sex with other men, (2) Tim and Skyler would schedule more alone time together and have sex with each other more often, and (3) Tim would limit his sexual encounters with other men to once a week for the next month. They would see how the month went and then discuss the situation again at that time.

What happened was that Skyler just needed a break from sex with other men and wanted to reconnect more with Tim. Tim was open to giving this to Skyler as long as he didn't experience it as a "demand" from Skyler. Once their connection had strengthened and Skyler "rebalanced" himself, he was, once again, okay with resuming their open marriage. Skyler decided that he had been seeing too many guys too often and it was exhausting. Instead, he focused on seeing fewer guys and getting to know them better. It was clear to both of them that it really wasn't about Tim seeing other guys, it was about Skyler not being happy with how he was handling his end of the open relationship and wanting comfort and support from Tim. Once he got it, he stopped trying to make Tim want what he wanted.

As a psychotherapist, I am often asked by clients—single and married, "Why is it so hard to embrace change and be willing to create and adjust?" One major obstacle to change is the negative stories about ourselves that we repeat over and over again. These stories bring us pain and keep us stuck in the past.

- "I'll never be a good husband."
- "I always screw things up."

- "My childhood was awful."
- "My last relationship messed me up so much that I'll never get over it."

By repeating these stories, we stay stuck in them.

We want to believe we'll be a good husband, that we can do things right, that our childhood was pretty good in many ways and that we will love this man better than we did the last one.

But why is it so hard to shift our mindset? Because we cling to our precious stories. A friend of mine calls it "My Precious Story." She told me that for many years she wanted to be right and self-righteous more than she wanted to be happy and free. Now, in her seventies, she usually laughs when "My Precious Story" appears. She doesn't believe her own stories anymore.

And she is happier than she ever was when she believed them.

In her book, *Why People Don't Heal and How They Can*,[1] Carolyn Myss writes, "Your biography [aka 'your precious story'] becomes your biology." What we tell ourselves about who we are and what happens to us creates not only our mental health, but also our physical health.

Freud said that our subconscious always says "Yes" to whatever we tell it. When I say, "I'm such a loser. I'll never be happy," my subconscious says "Yes." When I say, "My life is changing and I am leaving my past behind," my subconscious also says "Yes."

What stories do you want your subconscious agreeing with? If you want to change "My Precious Story," try these three techniques.

1. Be willing to be wrong about your precious story; one of my precious stories was "I had a rotten childhood and I'm permanently scarred by it." This is a pretty heavy story to believe and, not surprisingly, it did not create happiness or freedom for me. I began to say, "I am willing to be wrong. I am willing to be wrong." It sounds simple, but it is quite powerful. Saying this may bring up some strong emotions for you. That's to be expected; just keep saying, "I'm willing to be wrong." It starts to create some "space" in your psyche, where your rigid beliefs can start to relax a little.

2. Begin to tell yourself a "new" story. For example, "In many ways, my childhood was pretty good. I'm grateful for those good times." Your new story focuses on the good, the possible and remembering what went

well. If some guy—not your husband, obviously—you're interested in stops returning your texts, instead of telling yourself a story such as, "Guys never find me attractive. I always do something wrong." Tell yourself a new story such as, "I am an attractive, desirable man and I attract great guys to me." Focus on what is good and what you want, not what negative things happened to you in the past.

3. When you are tempted to make up a new negative story, such as, "Why does my husband never do any housework unless I nag him?" it's tempting to keep this kind of story going by telling yourself, "He's so lazy," "He doesn't appreciate me," or "He's never going to change." This will make you feel even worse and doesn't create any possibility of *adjusting* a situation that you have *both* created. Instead, go for something more neutral like, "I don't know. Maybe I could find out." This keeps your self-destructive stories from growing stronger and stronger, making any process of change almost impossible.

"My Precious Story"—whatever yours is—has a lot of power to affect your life and your marriage. You can use this power to keep yourself stuck in those old, negative stories or you can replace them with new stories that open up your consciousness and make way for good, new things, people, and experiences to come to you.

The choice is yours.

One of the main reasons that open marriages succeed is that couples find ways to adjust to the changes that this kind of relationship *will* bring. If you want a safe, predictable marriage, opening it up is not the way to do it!

Sexual passion will likely decrease as emotional connections deepen. This is good for long-term bonding and feeling safe and loved, but not so good for an exciting sex life. However, the price we pay for an open marriage is opening our marriage up to a continual process of adjustment. Bringing other people into your sex life—while married—will force you to reexamine your relationship on a regular basis. It's really constructive, on the one hand, but definitely not for the rigid, timid or emotionally fragile. It's taking on a big challenge with potentially big rewards, but there is a price to be paid.

An open marriage is a potentially demanding, intense path of personal growth for *both* of you. I find it very helpful when working with couples to encourage them to talk with each other about who each man *wants* to be. This is no small thing: your vision for *yourself* is a powerful, guiding force in your life. If your husband doesn't know where it is that you want to go (and grow), then he's missing out on a crucial piece of knowing you and supporting you. And, of course, vice versa.

Questions to Consider

- Describe the man you want to be. Have your husband do the same.
- Is either of you surprised? If so, what surprised you?
- How can you and your husband help each other to become the men you want to be?

Joey and Ricardo had been married for five years and were together before that for fourteen years. They really thought that they knew each other. They had negotiated their open marriage through various stages of "open" and "closed" and felt really solid as a couple. Yet they had never talked about their own ideas of who they wanted to be/become. When I suggested this, they looked at me like I was crazy.

> Joey: "We don't need to do anything like that. That's a little silly for us, at this stage of our marriage, don't you think?"
> Ricardo: "Yeah, we know each other so well, I think that would be pretty pointless."

Well, they did it anyway (at my urging) and—surprise, surprise—there was a great deal that they didn't know about each other. I'll let them explain it.

> Joey: "Ric and I each sat down—at Michael's urging—and wrote out a description of the kind of men we wanted to be. I included men that I admired and qualities that I wished I had, but didn't."
> Ricardo: "I didn't want to do this, but decided to try it anyway. I found myself remembering who I was, as a little boy, and the dreams and visions I had for myself that I'd forgotten. It was like opening up a box of things I once wanted, but gave up on. It was intense."

Here is a sample of what each man wrote:

> Joey: "I want to be the kind of man who is kind and protective of others, especially children and animals. I want to be like my Uncle Ed, who

took care of everybody and was loved by all. I want to be more like my friend Stephen, who is very forgiving and doesn't hold a grudge (like I do). I want to be the kind of man who is respected by those who know him. I want to accept getting older more gracefully. I want to learn to speak Spanish and return to playing guitar again."

Ricardo: "When I was a little boy, I loved to be outside. I loved to run in the fields near our house and feel free and happy, like a bird. I told myself, when I grow up I want to fly away from this small town and move to a big city and meet lots of new people and have an exciting life, going to plays and art galleries—all the kinds of stuff that our town had none of. I had forgotten these dreams. I wanted to become a man who was cultured and sophisticated and had lots of friends he could talk about fascinating things with."

Despite their nineteen years together, neither Joey nor Ricardo knew all this about each other. They were both surprised and pleased and, most importantly, they now could help each other to become the men they wanted to be.

I have seen that sharing this kind of experience with your husband creates a very deep bond; what could be better than knowing that the man you love is there supporting you to become the man you want to be? And that you're doing the same for him? This is creating and adjusting at its best: you learn new things about each other and help each other to "adjust" your life together so that these new goals/hopes can become a reality.

An open marriage puts the focus on your journey together and how you can help each other along the way. It's not about focusing on a destination; it's about the process—because we never get "there" (this mystical "there" where everything is great and never changes). We are always incomplete, wanting more, growing more, learning more.

Your open marriage is a process—it unfolds. It's movement and change. It's new men coming and going into your life and your bed, it's new emotions (both comfortable and uncomfortable) and finding yourselves in situations that you may never have imagined.

It's a bit like buying a car; you can decide you want a dependable car like a Honda Accord or a Toyota Prius, and that's all well and good. It may not be a very exciting car for you; it may not invoke your passion and enthusiasm, but it's not very demanding.

Or you can buy a Maserati (or something more affordable) that is an amazing machine, capable of great feats, and excites you. *But* it will take a *lot* more maintenance, time, and energy to keep it running well. And when it has problems, they may be *big* problems, expensive problems, problems that aren't easy to solve.

An open marriage is like a Maserati; it can be amazing and exciting, but is typically high-maintenance and demanding of your time and energy. Some of us are up for the challenge; others are not.

The Maserati marriage demands security in yourself (do your own inner work) and flexibility in your marriage—it's really a lifetime of creating and adjusting. A great marriage—not just a good one—is one where each man does his *own* inner work and supports his husband to do the same. I've seen this kind of relationship in many of the open marriages that I've assisted; they can be amazing, high-functioning, and extremely fulfilling—*if* you're willing to do the work.

Two strong, happy men together is a beautiful, powerful thing.

CHAPTER EIGHT

Balancing Sexual Expression with Emotional Connection

An open marriage can really feel like a balancing act: you want to be close to your husband *and* have great sex with other guys. You want to have both trust *and* passion in your marriage. You want excitement *and* comfort in your life. How can you balance all this?

Most of us want Superman in bed (passion) but Clark Kent (dependability) at tax time. We want to have the excitement of sex with several—or many—men, but also keep a strong and loving connection with our husband. We don't want our marriage to become sexless, yet we don't want our hook-ups to become too emotionally demanding.

That's quite a balancing act, isn't it?

From my experience of counseling gay couples, I have observed that, over time, this balance between sexual expression and emotional connection will typically shift many times. These shifts are especially strong and frequent in open marriages.

Let's talk about the idea of "emotional monogamy": this is my phrase for being emotionally committed to your husband but not necessarily physically/sexually exclusive. For many of my clients, *this* is a cornerstone of their open marriage. Your husband is your #1 man and vice versa. There is probably no one you are closer to, although (I hope) you have good friends too. The two of you have no doubt that you will be there for each other, no matter what life sends your way. You obviously care for and love other people (friends, family, colleagues), but not as powerfully as you love your man.

Okay, *that's* emotional monogamy.

When I meet a couple that is considering an open marriage, one of the most important questions I ask them is: "Can you separate sex (physical expression) from love (emotional connection)?" Why? Because a couple that can is likely to find the balancing act required of an open marriage to be fairly easy.

Let me give you a good example: Alexander and Eleuterio are a couple in their late thirties. They had lived together for two years and were talking about getting married; specifically, they were considering an open marriage.

> Alexander: "I used to be a real slut. I was on a lot on hookup sites and had lots of sex. But, I never felt any connection to any of these guys, until I met Eleu. Although we met on Grindr, I knew he was special. Up until meeting him, it was easy to separate love and sex. With him, they go together. But I still get horny when he's working for several nights in a row and we barely get to see each other."

> Eleuterio: "I work as a security guard at a club. Guys are always hitting on me, and since being with Alex, I always say no. But do I want to say no to every single guy for the rest of my life? Not really. I love Alex; he's my man, but I want to have fun with other guys too, while I'm still young and cute."

A couple that cannot separate love from sex—or finds it difficult to do so—is likely to find open marriage to be a very bumpy road. Jonathan and Francisco are another couple I've worked with. When I first met them, this is where they were.

> Jonathan: "I want to have an open marriage, because I really like sex. But I have this history of falling in love too easily, especially after I've slept with someone. I don't know how this open marriage thing will work for me."

> Francisco: "I love sex, but I am very insecure. It would be great if I could have sex with other guys, but knowing that Jon is doing it would make me crazy. I know it's selfish, but I want him to be monogamous, so I won't be insecure, while I get to do what I want."

Obviously, these two guys have a *long* way to go if they're going to make an open marriage work for them. Unless they work through their individual issues, their open marriage is likely to be a short one!

In every open marriage, a man determines how to balance the love and sexual energy he gives to his husband with how much emotion he allows himself to feel for his sexual partners. For Tomas and Larry, their love for each other was paramount, but the amount of emotional energy they were willing to invest in their sex partners was quite different.

> Larry: "I only have so much time, energy and love to give. I choose to give it to my husband. He's my first priority. This isn't a problem for me because I enjoy my time with my sex partners—I call them my 'Grindr Guys'—but I don't love them. I like them, I enjoy their company. We respect each other and are friendly to each other, but I don't love them. My love is special, powerful, and deep. I only feel love for people I'm really close to, like Tomas and a few of my relatives and close friends."
>
> Tomas: "I feel like I have lots of love to give to everyone. This is how my family was, there was never a shortage of love, no matter how many of us got together, or didn't. So, with the guys I have sex with, I have plenty of love to give them too. It's not the same kind of love that I give Larry, but it's still love! I love each of these guys in my own way and I feel they love me too."

Each man has found his own balance of emotional connection (love) and physical expression (sex).

In an open marriage, how do you balance the often-conflicting desires of your heart, mind, and genitals? Is your heart (love) energy purely for your husband? Are your genitals for everyone you have sex with? And what about your head (thoughts)? Do you need to "like" the men you have sex with, or is that optional if you find them attractive enough?

These are questions that men in open marriages are confronted with on a regular basis, so let's take some time here to address them.

Questions to Consider

- How do you keep your husband your #1 man?
- How do you stay in love in an open marriage and not end up feeling like "roommates"?
- How can you get your thoughts, emotions, and sex drive to work together?

In any meaningful sexual relationship, we need to balance the desires and demands of our heart, mind, and genitals. When you meet a guy and feel an attraction, how and when do you decide to have sex with him? Is it right off the bat, when your heart and mind barely know the guy? Or is it later on, when your libido has been moderated by the wisdom of your mind and the feelings in your heart?

This married gay couple articulates the dilemma quite well.

Fred: "I need to have some kind of emotional connection with men I have sex with. There needs to be some kind of relationship; I can't just do it with someone I barely know. For me to be aroused, I need to know the man, like him and be attracted to him."

Zack: "I don't want to have an emotional connection with the guys I have sex with. It would just make my life too complicated. I already have strong emotional bonds with Fred, my parents, my siblings, my nieces and nephews, and my good friends. For me, having sex with a guy is fun, playful—an adventure. I don't want it all clogged up with emotions."

Both Fred and Zack are very clear on what works for them. Fred wants his mind, heart, and genitals all "activated" and working together with the men he has sex with, while Zack wants to keep them totally separate, except for his relationship with Fred.

The Three Musketeers: Your Heart, Mind, and Genitals

Do you remember the Three Musketeers? Their slogan was: "All for one and one for all!" This is a motto associated with the heroes of the novel *The Three Musketeers*, written by Alexandre Dumas père, first published in 1844. In the novel, it was the motto of a trio of French musketeers who looked after each other during their many adventures, triumphs, and hardships together (sounds a bit like marriage, doesn't it?).

To me, the heart, mind, and genitals are the "three musketeers" of a successful relationship. Your heart is all about your feelings for someone, your mind is what you think about him and your genitals symbolize your sexual attraction to him. When you have all three engaged in a relationship with a great guy, your relationship has the maximum potential for a deep connection: respect, admiration, and awesome sex! While most of us want the three musketeers in our relationship with our husbands, we may not want all three musketeers "involved" with every man we have sex with. Let's look at the heart first.

Your heart is all about emotions and feelings. If you *want* an emotional connection with someone you're considering being sexual with, I encourage you to take some time and check in with yourself: What are you feeling? What emotions are you aware of? This is your heart speaking. To hear it, you have to look inward. Is your heart happy when you think about this guy? When you hear his voice, do you feel good? When you're near him, does your heart beat faster? Your heart may be telling you that there is an emotional connection there.

You can also use this same process of awareness if you do *not* want an emotional connection with someone. For example, here are three guys I've counseled on why they prefer to keep sexual expression *separate* from any emotional connection.

> Eduardo: "I love my open marriage and having sex with guys other than my husband, but I absolutely *cannot* fall in love with guys I fuck. I can't. It has happened before, and I have to really watch myself. If I start to notice that I am feeling a strong emotional connection with a guy I'm having sex with, I explain to him that I can't go there and that we need to stop seeing each other."

> Timothy: "One of the rules my husband Jeff and I have is that we can't fall in love with anyone but each other. This isn't hard for Jeff, but it is for me, so I've come up with this rule for myself that I never have sex with anyone more than three times. That's about how long it takes me to get to know someone and begin to have deeper feelings for him."

> Gavin: "I confuse love and sex sometimes, so I have to be careful. One thing I've learned is that once I kiss a guy, my emotions start to say, 'Wow, he's great. I wonder if I could love him.' It's irrational, I know, but for me, kissing is super-intimate. So, I don't ever kiss guys I'm having sex with. I only kiss my husband. It's extreme, but it works for me."

Every man gets to decide how much he wants to open his heart to the men he has sex with. In an open marriage, it's an extremely important decision: if it's hard for you to separate love from sex, it may be crucial for the health of your marriage to be very careful about how much you let yourself love your sex partners.

Now let's check in with your head.

By talking about your "head," I mean the rational, linear, logical part of your brain. This is where most of us live the vast majority of the time—thinking, judging, and analyzing.

Sometimes we have lots of "voices" in our head, and they fight each other. For example, let's say you just had sex with a really terrific guy. You may hear one voice in your head that says, "There's potential for a real connection with this guy, he's a lot nicer/smarter/funnier than I expected—could he be someone I'd like to get to know? Someone I'd like to have more than sex with? Could this guy be someone I'd like to hang out with?"

You may also hear another—more cynical—voice that says, "Oh yeah, right, like this hookup is going to turn into a deep, meaningful friendship. Don't be an idiot, you got off, so move on!" You might hear both voices giving you conflicting advice simultaneously. This isn't unusual, but when you can't stop arguing with yourself, it can be crazy-making! This is your head at its worst.

There are lots of articles about getting in touch with your feelings (heart) and getting clear on what you're thinking (mind), but surprisingly few on making peace with your testosterone-driven friend: your penis. Watching man-on-man porn, you'd think that hard penises and great orgasms are all that counts in gay life. Very few porn videos show more than genitals in charge; where is the intelligence, the emotion? Heart and mind have been left behind. Sure, there's kissing in some of them, but do they ever have intelligent conversations? Heart-to-heart talks? Any real emotional connection?

Rarely.

Far too much of gay culture emphasizes the genital aspect of our relationships and leaves the mind and heart far behind. Indeed, the mind and heart are almost seen as "girly" or "feminine" parts of man-to-man relation ships. And yet, without the involvement of the mind and heart, our relationships—from marriage to friendships—are doomed.

Really good sex—and any successful ongoing relationship—requires the simultaneous involvement of your thoughts, emotions, and libido. Simply put: why not let your genitals become good friends with your thoughts and feelings? They really *are* like the Three Musketeers: "All for one and one for all."

Sexually Addictive Behavior

I'd like to take a moment here to talk about sexually addictive behavior. You may think that because you're in an open marriage you can't be touched by this. Not true. You can be happily married and yet, it's your penis that's running—or ruining—your life.

In my experience, married gay men who engage in addictive sexual behavior are rarely in touch with their emotions; their genitals are running wild without any emotional connection to the guys they have sex with. They may have plenty of love for their husband, but feel absolutely nothing for any other man they have sex with. It's all-or-nothing, extreme thinking. Let me share a couple of examples with you.

> Jeff: "Before I married Joshua, I had a lot of anonymous sex. And I liked it. But it was hard to stop. One reason I got married was that I wanted to stop all that anonymous sex and focus on one hot guy: my husband. But in the back of my mind, I keep wanting to hook up with guys I don't know, have sex with them and never see them again. I miss it."
>
> Edward: "I was a fat, ugly kid and it took me a long time to get over it. Now, I look good, but that ugly kid inside me still wants validation from attractive men. Brandon, my husband, gives me lots of validation, but it's not enough. I fantasize about hooking up on Grindr when I'm out of town on business. I haven't talked it about with Brandon yet, because I'm embarrassed that I *still* need validation from other men to feel attractive."

Men like Jeff and Edward may be married and in open relationships, but their emotional hunger cannot be satisfied either by their husbands *or* the guys they have sex with, so they need to keep looking for the next man and the next one after that.

For them, there will *never* be enough sex, because it's not sex that fills the emptiness inside them, it's their unmet needs for a real emotional connection (which, if they'll admit it, scares them tremendously). The fact that we can have lots of sex doesn't mean it brings us any real satisfaction.

We seldom benefit from relationships totally focused on sex. When we're conscious about the role our heart, mind, and genitals play in our sexual relationships, we can maintain a good balance of the three. Some days the balance may be off, but overall, the best relationships are those where your mind is attracted to someone, your heart feels affection and connection, and your genitals get just the right amount of attention.

Feeling Alone in Your Marriage

It is surprising how many men in open marriages feel alone in their marriage. This usually comes from expecting too much of your husband. You may have a very strong emotional connection to your man, but not much of a connection to anyone else in your life (e.g., friends, family, coworkers). This is a setup for unhappiness.

> Nic: "I am pretty much a loner. I've never had many friends; I enjoy my own company. Charlie, my husband, is like that too. We have each other; that's all we need. I have sex with other guys every now and then, so I don't need friends."
>
> Mike: "I'm a shy guy, so for me to open up to someone is agony. It took me a *long* time to trust my husband, and, now that I finally do, I am so pleased that I have one person in the world that I can talk to about things. I have sex with other guys, but I only trust my husband."
>
> Jake: "I have a lot of social anxiety; it's not easy for me to meet new people. I was so glad when I met John [his husband], because finally there was someone I could easily relate to and confide in. I don't really need to be close to anyone else now; I have John."

These three guys sound pretty happy, right? Perhaps I'm too pessimistic, but I've seen a lot of couples who started out like this, all starry-eyed and wrapped up in each other, who had that "You and me against the world" mindset. This may work in the movies, but in real life, it rarely does.

No matter how shy or introverted you are, you need more than one person to be emotionally connected to. It's great that these guys are so connected to their husbands, but that places an awful lot of pressure on their husbands to be their "everything." And honestly, no man—however handsome, loving, or amazing—can be your everything. It's a setup for failure.

So, all you shy/introverted/socially scared married guys, you still need friends. I know it isn't easy, but having a close friend or two besides your husband can make your life so much easier. In reality, no one's husband can be there for them—emotionally—all the time. We *all* need someone to talk with *about* our husbands when our marriage goes through challenging times. One man I know put it very succinctly: "I need someone to talk to about my husband, but the only person I'm close to is my husband. So I'm stuck."

Don't be stuck. No one person can meet all your emotional needs. Spread your needs around! And besides, different people can give you different kinds of emotional support. I'll let my friend Bob tell it.

> "My husband is great at being the quiet, strong rock. But sometimes, I need someone to vent with, and that's my friend Charlie. My friend Greg, on the other hand, is really good at strategizing, like when I want to ask my boss for a raise. Each man has his strengths, and usually, among the three of them, I get what I need."

Exactly.

In addition to having friends outside your marriage, I recommend that you have friends you *don't* have sex with. Some men in open marriages are tempted to sleep with all their friends. Don't. Keep some relationships simple and non-sexual. Why? In general, the more men you have sex with, the more emotion and drama you're inviting into your life.

Sleeping with large numbers of men makes for much more complex interactions between you and these men and between you and your husband's men (remember all the men he's bringing into your marriage too).

As two very sexually active married men told me,

> Gareth: "The more men my husband and I have sex with, the more we find ourselves dealing with these guys' emotional demands and neediness."
> Ted: "When you and your husband have sex with lots of guys, it's a lot of fun, for sure, but we continually find ourselves asking, 'What can I offer, when and to whom?' It can get very intense and demanding."

It's a rich but demanding way to live, not for the emotionally unstable or easily overwhelmed. I've found that most men in successful open marriages have a high tolerance for sensory stimulation—they don't easily get overloaded. At the risk of oversimplification, monogamy is—simpler. Some married men find monogamy to be less rich and fulfilling, but others find it a lot less work and much less complicated.

And speaking of the challenges of an open marriage, I've had more than a few clients ask me, "Where do I find good guys for 'friends with benefits'?" Or, as a friend of mine put it: "I love my husband and my close friends, but where do I find men I like *enough* for sex and some kind of friendship?"

Good question. With that in mind, let's talk about sex parties and hook-up apps, two very popular ways that some married men meet their "friends with benefits." Here's an interesting e-mail that I got from a man in an open marriage that addresses the former.

Dear Michael,

Last week a friend of mine invited me to go with him to a sex party that he heard about on Grindr. My husband didn't want to go with me, so I went on my own. It was in someone's hotel suite and there were a lot of naked men there. I've been to bathhouses before, but this was more intense. Guys were having sex with each other all over the place. There was no privacy anywhere, and that made me uncomfortable. The worst part is that lots of the guys were having bareback sex, even though there were jars of condoms available. What do you think of this kind of sex?

More Like a Virgin in Miami

Here is my response:

Dear Mr. More:

After receiving your e-mail, I am curious what you mean by "this kind of sex." Do you mean anonymous sex, public sex, or sex without condoms? However, before jumping into that, here's my definition of good sex:

Good sex is physically healthy (no one seroconverts or gets STDs as a result) as well as spiritually and psychologically healthy. You can tell you've had good sex because when it's over, you feel good about yourself, your partner(s), and life in general.

Good sex can happen anywhere: bathhouse, sex party, or bedroom. That's the good news. The bad news is that good sex isn't always easy to find. Sure, you can get off, but is that good sex? The best sex usually involves your heart, head, and genitals. If your genitals are the only part of you really involved, then don't be surprised if you feel a release of tension and then a letdown. You may feel lonelier than ever; this is your heart and head saying, "Hey, why didn't you let us in on this?"

When your heart, head, and genitals are all involved, you have a good chance to experience what The Body Electric School calls a full body orgasm and psychologist Wilhelm Reich called orgastic potency. This is sex at its best; it leaves us feeling physically more alive than we were before. It's the opposite of loneliness and isolation; it's connection.

Reich insists that the best sex needs to be between two people whose hearts are open to each other, minds are secure enough to "surrender" to the other, and genitals are highly aroused.

I applaud you, Mr. More, for being open to trying new experiences. I don't have any judgments about sex parties, bathhouses, orgies, threesomes, and so forth. It doesn't matter whether your sexual experiences are at sex parties or the penthouse suite at the Ritz-Carlton; it's the quality of the connection you have with the man/men you're with that makes the sex good or not, not the location or other externals.

Lots of people have judgments about going to places like bathhouses and sex parties to find sex partners. In my e-mail, I get quite a few questions about sex parties: they're quite popular all over the United States (and abroad). Guys ask me what I think about them—are they a good thing or a bad thing? Should they stay away from them or embrace them with open arms (and legs)?

Frankly, I don't have an opinion about sex parties. Nor do I have an opinion on where and when people have sex. I don't think the externals are what make sex fulfilling or not. You can have wonderful, deep, loving sex with a stranger in a bathhouse and meaningless, superficial sex with someone you know very well in a romantic room set with candles, your favorite music and a blanket by the fireplace. It's more about having a good connection with someone else, as opposed to who topped whom, who came first, and who stayed hard the longest.

People have been having sex in as many places as you can imagine ever since time began. Making some situations right and some wrong isn't helpful. Why do people go to sex parties? Don't assume you know their motivation; we never know someone else's motivation for doing something, especially something as complex as having sex. So instead, focus on yourself. Ask yourself, What's *my* motivation for going to a sex party? Is it to have fun, meet other guys, be social, get off, feel attractive, combat loneliness, boost my self-esteem?

For some married men in open relationships, sex parties make life easy. One client told me, "There are all these men there purely to have sex. It's great. It's exactly what I'm looking for. Lots of hot guys who only want sex, not love or romance."

That said, I have the following suggestions if you are considering attending a sex party. Consider this my guide to "Sex Party Etiquette."

- Party tip #1: Sex parties are not about making new friends. Sex parties are about having sex. Don't confuse a sex party with a social gathering, whose purpose is primarily to meet and talk with people. If that's what you want, go to a social event. Be clear on your motivation. If you want Italian food, don't go to a Chinese restaurant.
- Party tip #2: Communication at sex parties isn't like a social event. Smiling or being friendly to someone at a sex party might give him the impression that you're interested in him. Instead of "nice," aim for "neutral" and you should stay out of trouble (or get into trouble, if that's what you want).
- Party tip #3: At a sex party, everyone is fair game and no one is a mind reader. If someone you're not interested touches you, simply take their hand off your body, politely say "no thanks" and walk away. No muss, no fuss, no attitude. And if you approach someone and they take your hand off their body, don't take it personally. Move on and have fun with someone else.
- Party tip #4: No matter what your HIV status is and even if you're on PrEP, use condoms. No matter how tempted you are, stay healthy, avoid STDs, and help your brothers to do the same.
- Party tip #5: Be respectful, playful, and open to new experiences. Ask for what you want, and see if you get it. Have good boundaries; be able to say no to what you don't want and stick to it. Don't have "pity" sex, where you feel sorry for someone and give him what he wants. Take good care of yourself and have the kind of experience that makes you feel good about yourself.

Let's look at another way to meet potential "friends with benefits": dating/hookup apps.

Much has been written about dating apps and most of us are quite familiar with them. (If you're not, put this book down and Google "Grindr" or "OK

Cupid" and familiarize yourself. Then come back to the book.) I am the first to admit that I have used some of these apps; I even met one of my boyfriends on one (no, I'm not telling you which one).

Some apps are more for dating and romance (OK Cupid; Plenty of Fish) and others tend to be hookup-oriented (Grindr; Scruff). If an app requires a face pic, it's usually more relationship-oriented. If body part shots are prominent, it's probably more about hooking up. Depending on the way you and your husband have structured your open marriage, certain apps will be a better fit for you than others.

A word (or two) of caution: if you are relatively new to the gay community and these apps are your first exposure to us, that's not so good. If you buy these apps' logic—without questioning it—you're likely to end up with a very narrow definition of what's required to be popular. Not a perfect face or body? Not white enough? Too old? The message may be that you don't belong, so just go away and don't bother us.

How can you experience the benefits of these apps and connect with men you'd like to get to know? More specifically, how do you *not* get sucked into the unrealistic images of physical beauty that are apparently de rigeur for online success? Use them judiciously. Let's hear from someone who learned this one the hard way.

> Christian: "My husband and I like to share guys and, since we each know what the other likes, we take turns going online and 'hunting.' Am I the only guy who has spent hours online, trying to connect with some hot guy, only to be shocked afterward at how much time I spent on my 'hunt'?"

Christian is not alone; I recommend that, if you and/or your husband look for guys online, that you partake of these apps just as you do high-calorie desserts: enjoy them sparingly. And don't forget your sense of humor! Without it, some of the mean comments you may get on these apps could make any one of us want to run home and hide under the covers.

What if you're having fun on the apps? Then, go for it. But again, get some vegetables with your desserts. Spend time with your husband and your (real-life) friends and monitor the time you spend staring at your phone. And don't invest too much energy in the hopes that the latest pics of you (alone or with your husband) that you carefully took of each other in your bathroom (perfect lighting, your chin at just the right angle to make your nose look smaller and your eyes bigger) will get more hits from hot guys.

Dating/hookup apps are great for making an initial (albeit, superficial) connection with *lots* of men. It's a numbers game: the odds are better the more men that see you (and vice versa). So, if you're into the online scene, take a chance, be respectful, friendly, and funny. And be prepared for *anything* to happen.

I recommend that you and your husband view the world of dating/hookup apps as a game: it's something you both might enjoy, but there is no guaranteed outcome.

And—if you find yourself online a bit too much—you might ask yourself: Am I looking for validation? Maybe I'm not feeling so good about myself, I've gained a bit of weight or noticed a new wrinkle (or two) today. If you get online validation: good for you! Maybe that's all you needed. I've had clients tell me that they like online chatting more than actually hooking up. The chatting makes them feel "connected" and less alone. And who can't relate to that?

Please humor us gay elders who predate the Internet: we grew up in a very different world. We had to meet men in person and see what they looked like, how they talked, if they looked us in the eye, how they laughed. We got a wealth of nonverbal information that let us quickly sum someone up as a "yes" or "no."

Regardless of the app you use, sexual compatibility can only be discovered face to face. Photos and demographic information only take you and your husband so far; you've got to meet these guys in person for the real deal to happen (or not).

The Man Machine

In some open marriages, I have seen the sex life of the two men become like a machine: repetitive, relatively emotionless sexual experiences that just leave them feeling more and more empty, which, ironically, just encourages them to search for even *more* sex.

A big part of this machine-like sexual hypnosis is (gay and straight) media's obsession with how we look. There is a strong media push to encourage our insecurity about our bodies, our faces, our hair, our waistline, our skin, our teeth and—the old standbys—our pecs and butt. The advertising world—

which drives all media—want us to buy their clients' products to assuage our insecurities, but there is an even more unfortunate result of these media messages: we start to think of ourselves, and other men, as less-than-human, in essence, a "man machine." Here are two media images (one from a gay publication, the other from a heterosexual magazine) to illustrate my point.

"We've assembled the hottest guys" claims a gay website with a photo of a beautiful young man in a Frankenstein-like laboratory. The image encourages us to see men as only as good as our assembled parts. Both heterosexual and gay media invite us to scrutinize each other's "parts" and ignore the whole person. We choose our best "parts," photograph them in the best possible lighting, and then advertise them (exhibit A: all those Grindr screenshots of chests, butts, and penises) in the hopes of finding sex/love/whatever.

A national men's magazine gives us this cover line: "America's New Male Body Obsession: From Film to Fashion to Fad Diets." Reading this, I naïvely assumed that the magazine would address the sickness of body obsession. How wrong I was; they *encourage* it! I guess I've been working in mental health for too long; I've forgotten how print and electronic media will do anything to promote the products of their advertisers.

A healthy body image won't sell many products. But the "new male body obsession" is a virtual motherlode of neurosis, designed specifically to get us to buy stuff—as the cover story says: "from film to fashion to fad diets." This magazine so graciously points out the movies that we should see to see just what kind of body we should be obsessing over (Zac Efron, Ryan Gosling, and hunky vampires) and the kind of fashion we need to buy to best advertise that body (tight clothes—expensive and uncomfortable). Even after all of this, I still had a fragment of hope that the magazine would debunk some fad diets. But no—they just tell you all the different fad diets you can choose from, and encourage you to buy the books that promote them.

Let's be clear: this isn't about self-improvement. It's about unhealthy, self-absorbed narcissism. We are instructed to "look in the mirror . . . because, in the end, we all want to look as good as David Beckham does in briefs." Really? Is this a high priority for most men you know? What about qualities like integrity, charm, personality, intelligence, kindness, and courage? It's all about being David Beckham's body twin. Ugh.

A confession here: I go to the gym regularly, love my yoga, and aspire to eat well. But I do it to please myself, stay healthy, and feel good—not to look like some celebrity. I don't think it's the activities, food, or clothes we choose that matter as much as it is our *intentions* behind our choice of exercise, diet, or fashion.

If you were my client and your intention was to have a body like Ryan Gosling's, I would ask: Why is this important to you? What do you expect from looking like that? If physical beauty meant automatic mental happiness, I'd sign up too. But it doesn't. And physical beauty is temporary. Ryan Gosling won't look like that forever, but since he appears to be a young man of depth and intelligence, it probably won't devastate him.

As gay men—whether we're married or not—we are being strongly pushed down the path toward unhealthy body obsession and seeing ourselves as a series of attractive or unattractive "parts." You know the drill: "Oh, he has a beautiful ass but his face isn't much," or "He has a great chest but his legs are too skinny." Forget the whole person; it's all about the parts. Dr. Frankenstein, here we come!

Have we really sunk this low? Are we this easily manipulated? Are we really happy to be a "man machine"? Isn't this what's called sexual objectification? Ironically, this is what the heterosexual world used to accuse gay men of: obsessing on sex and our appearance. From a mental health point of view, feeling good about how you look is great; feeling obsessed to look like a movie star is not.

We are more than good-looking body parts; we are not machines. Thinking of our bodies and those of our gay brothers in a "parts" mentality just encourages addictive sexual behavior. "How's that?" You ask. Because, in this paradigm, we're just looking for the best "parts" we can find to match up with our best "parts" and then we'll see what the "parts" do when they're brought together. Is it really any wonder that this machine/body parts paradigm for sex is going to result in a whole lot of anonymous, repetitive sex?

I hear it from my clients:

James: "I'm obsessed with my chest. I want to have a really buff chest for Pride this year, so I can walk around with my shirt off and get all the hot guys to look at me. This year, it's all about my chest."

Rory: "I work out with a trainer, and he's always having a contest for some body part: who has the best thighs, butt, pecs, arms, quads, lats—I've won a couple of times, but I'd like to win again."

Benjamin: "When I go on Grindr, the only way I get laid is to show pics of my best body parts: my butt and dick. If I try to come across as a sincere, good guy, nobody's interested. It's all about the pics of your best body parts: that's marketing, baby."

Lucas: "I work as a go-go dancer at a gay club. Everyone wants to have sex with me; they all like my chest and my legs. But I wonder: What happens when I'm not young and pretty anymore? Will anyone still want me?"

Daniel: "My husband has a naturally great body; I don't. I have to work like hell on it. I have good legs though, so I go to the gym five times a week to work on my upper body. It's a lot of time and energy, but I want to get laid."

Jack: "I model part time and have no trouble getting dates, but I go to the gym—twice a day on most days—because I keep seeing places that look fat or pudgy. Maybe I should get liposuction, so I wouldn't have to worry so much about my little muffin-top."

Adam: "I like to swim and I hate lifting weights. But my best friend told me that if I want to keep hooking up, it's gonna take more than swimming. I need to have bigger muscles if I want to do well on Scruff. So (sighs), I guess I'll have to go back to the gym again."

You may think that these quotes sound extreme, but they are but a small sample of what I hear on a regular basis from my single and married gay clients.

We are men of depth, character, and wisdom. We are not just a collection of attractive body parts. Let's question the logic of "the man machine" and begin to unhook from media-driven body obsession and insecurity. There's no denying that some men are more attractive to us than others—we all have our individual preferences. And there's nothing wrong with admiring someone's arms or butt or legs, *but* let's keep it all in perspective. As human beings, we have much more to offer than our bodies. Our bodies will change over time. There's no avoiding that, no matter how hard we try and how much money we spend. Remember "The Three Musketeers"? Instead of focusing purely on what our genitals want, let's bring our head and heart into the picture too. This will help mitigate the tendency toward body-part oriented sex and "the man machine."

Aging and Sex

A healthy mid-life "crisis" (whether you have it at thirty, forty, or fifty) can be more of a tune-up than a traumatic event: you don't need to dye your hair, buy an overpriced sports car, or dump your husband for someone younger. Instead, maybe it's time to go to the gym less and do something physical that you enjoy more, like yoga or hiking. Or it could be time for you and your husband to finally get your finances in order or plan for the rest of your life together. It can be a really great time of life, not something to dread.

Aging does bring physical changes, but brothers, let's not panic. As we age, we'll probably experience gradual—not dramatic—shifts in our bodies, minds, and feelings. Aging may make sex more difficult, particularly if we have age-related physical problems that affect the frequency and quality of sex, whether with our husband or someone else.

Some of us deal with aging by consciously trying to accept the changes in our bodies, minds, and sex lives, while others choose denial as a coping strategy. This denial may manifest in the form of repeatedly looking for and hooking up with much younger men. Are you hooked on twinks? Obsessed with younger men? Trying desperately hard not to act your age?

If so, you're not alone. Read this:

Dear Michael:

I am a happily married man in an open relationship and I have this ridiculous crush on a much younger guy from my gym. He is one of the most gorgeous guys in town. I am forty-five, but I have this schoolgirl crush. You know why? Because he walked by and said "Hi" to me. I would never pursue having a sexual experience with someone who looks like this because I know I would end up in the dumped older gay man's loony bin, like what happened before my marriage when I dated a man much better-looking and eleven years younger than myself.

Was this guy from the gym just being friendly? We have not spoken but I go to the gym a lot more often. Why am I so fascinated with this much younger man, and what should I do about it?

Bewitched, bothered, and bewildered in Boston

Here is my response:

Dear BB&B:

It is challenging being a mid-life gay male, especially when the current gay ideal (as shown in most of the ads in gay media) seems to be a twenty-four-year-old, muscular, six-packed white male who shaves his face, chest, and armpits. If you believe that this is the epitome of homo handsomeness, it may be hard to find anyone in their forties, fifties, or older who fits your image of desirability. Thank God for the leather, bear, and other communities whose parameters of male beauty are more open minded.

You didn't tell me how old your husband is, but let's assume that you prefer men who look like Mr. GymBunny. Have you ever asked yourself why? Have you ever wondered why younger guys are your preference (if they are)? For some of my clients in open relationships, there is a factor of unavailability involved; it's yet another version of "I only want what I can't have." For other men, it's more about not feeling so old; with a younger guy, you can *pretend* that you too are young and youthful. It's one way *not* to tell yourself the truth about how old *you* are.

Do you find guys your own age or older unattractive? If so, what's "wrong" with them? What do they lack? Poreless skin and a beautiful body are nice to look at (and fantasize about), but what about personality? Intelligence? A sense of humor? Kindness and patience born from experience?

Why do you see yourself in the "dumped older gay men's loony bin" (a great phrase, by the way)? You don't say where your relationship with the younger man went awry, but how and why did you get dumped? Could it have been because you chose someone who didn't appreciate all your good qualities? Maybe it would take someone of wisdom, taste, and experience to really value all you have to offer. And where are you most likely to find that? I'm not saying that younger men don't have these qualities, but you're more likely to find them in men who have lived, loved, laughed, and are still here to tell us about it.

Why is your self-esteem so low? You seem shocked that Mr. GymBunny even speaks to you. I wonder if you don't see yourself as worthy, desirable, or attractive. If you were my client, we would address this. Any real stability of your self-esteem cannot be based on physical beauty, which will, inevitably, change. If you want to feel good about yourself *now*, you need an *inner* appreciation of yourself *just as you are*—whether your pecs are perfect or not.

You say that you are fascinated with good-looking, younger men. Does this mean that you won't give the time of day to men who aren't? What about us average-looking guys? Do we merit your consideration? Or do you just pass us by, focusing only on younger, perfect physical specimens?

Do you see where this is likely to take you?

I suggest you take a good look at "why I am so fascinated with this much younger man": don't do anything about it right away. You might use the above questions as a starting point to do a little digging in your psyche; look at your past relationships, where they succeeded/failed, what types of men you're attracted to, and what types of men would appreciate you. It's very "safe" to fall for men who are unavailable—they're unlikely to stick around and get to know you.

Some men use an obsession with unavailable men to avoid looking at how emotionally unavailable *they* are—not only to the men they have sex with, but also to their husbands. Too many open marriages are—sadly—described as "housemates who live together and have sex with others, but not each other."

Real intimacy is scary and vulnerable. You might get hurt. Your heart may be open to someone and then be broken (or stomped on). A much younger or unavailable man—while attractive in his elusiveness—is unlikely to see past your façade, your veneer of whatever it is that you want the world to see. For these reasons, he may seem "safe" to you.

Some guys in open marriages keep it pretty superficial with most of the men they have sex with. And why not? That way, you can hide your ugliness—all those parts of yourself that shame and embarrass you—by not letting them get to know you. It's an effective defense mechanism and usually, it works.

However, in a healthy, intimate relationship, there's no way to avoid emotional ugliness. When you really get to know your husband, you're going to see all the stuff he hides from everyone else (and vice versa).

In an open marriage, I've repeatedly seen the temptation to distance from your husband when times are tough and invest more time and energy in your sex buddies. While this may seem like a good idea in the short run, it's a bad idea in the long run. Avoidance of emotional problems can play out in sexually "acting out" with other men.

You can see that this will—inevitably—*not* lead to a happy ending.

Bob and Grant have been married three years. Bob was a successful lighting director for a big theater company and Grant was a CPA for a small tax firm. Bob and Grant were quite happy in their open marriage, until their lives changed quite dramatically: Bob's beloved boss left for a better job and Bob absolutely hated his new boss. He began to dread going to work. Grant tried to be understanding, but Bob just wanted to complain. One day, Grant (not-so-tactfully) pointed out that Bob was acting like a victim. This made Bob really angry.

Bob: "How dare he call me a victim. He has a sweet little job with a great boss. He has no idea what it's like to work for someone who wants to replace you with his lighting director from his previous theater."

Grant: "I don't know why Bob is acting like such a baby about this. He's become a real drag to be around—and forget sex between us, it's just not happening."

Bob started avoiding Grant as much as possible. He started working during hours that he knew Grant would be home. He also started having more sexual encounters than usual, which was easy for him with a new play coming into his theater and a large cast of attractive men.

Grant became despondent, wondering what to do. It was only after a lot of insistence on his part that the couple came in for some counseling.

Grant: "It feels like our relationship is falling apart. I don't know what to do. Bob's become this other person and I don't know how to be his husband anymore."

Bob: "I'm sick of Grant's lack of empathy. He's so prim and proper and judgmental. I have met this really great guy in the new cast and he really seems to understand me. When I complain about my boss, he listens and doesn't judge. And the sex with him is phenomenal. Of course I don't want to come home to Grant. Why would I?"

Both men still loved each other, but their marriage had become a hollow shell. Their interactions, now few and far between, were unsatisfying and cold. Emotional ugliness had reared its head. Grant was seeing a side of his husband that Bob had kept hidden from him up until now, and he didn't know what to do about it.

Bob began to distance himself from his husband when times got tough. He started investing more time and energy in his relationship with new sex buddy, trying to avoid the big gaping hole in his marriage. Grant, equally pissed off, began to hold a grudge against Bob. He too began to invest more time and energy into his sex partners, as he and Bob grew further and further apart.

People who love each other can do really awful things to each other. However, holding a grudge or avoiding problems in your relationship won't help your marriage. While it's difficult in troubled times to keep your marriage healthy, both parties need to find a way to let go, forgive, and move forward. Therapy can help with this (it did for Bob and Grant).

Does this all sound too hard? Never fear, there's the good stuff too: love, affection, and a renewal of sexual attraction can return when a couple's problems and tensions are resolved. Here's Bob and Grant after a few difficult months of hard truths and couple's counseling.

> Bob: "I never had such an awful boss; it made me really insecure and I didn't know how to handle it. I tried to avoid it, but it didn't work and I aimed my anger at Grant, not my boss. Grant and I have never been through a bad time like this. I wondered if we would make it through, as a couple. However, after working through our shit in therapy, our marriage is stronger than it was before the storm hit."
>
> Grant: "I never realized how judgmental I am, and how I needed Bob to be a certain way. When he changed, I didn't like it, so I tried to shame him back into the Old Bob that I loved and missed. When it didn't work, and I saw that both of us were detaching from each other and spending more and more time with our sex buddies, I pushed Bob to go with me to couple's counseling, so we could work through this stuff."

The fact that your relationship is in a bad place now doesn't mean that your love is dead and your marriage is doomed. Feelings of love and affection ebb and flow in the best marriages—don't judge the future of your relationship by whether you feel love for your husband today. These feelings usually return as your relationship improves. When bad shit happens, notice if you have a tendency to avoid it, blame it all on your husband, and/or turn to your sex buddies for comfort instead of talking with your husband. If it's too hard to do on your own, get some professional help.

Romance and Your Open Marriage

After all this talk about sex, man machines, sex parties, and online hook-ups, talking about romance may seem out of place. Not at all! Let's talk about romance—with your husband. This is the "emotional connection" side of your open marriage. If your sex life together is great and rewarding, well done! But if not, perhaps it's time to dig a little deeper in your relationship with your husband.

Whether you like a bit of romance with the men you have sex with (or not), I highly recommend that you put some time and energy into fostering a culture of romance with your husband.

Questions to Consider

- What is romance for you?
- What is it for your husband?
- Do you have enough of it?
- Do you want romance in your sexual relationships outside your marriage?
- If so, how do you see that playing out?

Your husband is your #1 man, your rock, the man who has your back, the guy you want to be with through thick and thin, right? He may not be your most exciting sex partner, but it sure helps when he is the most important person in your life and you treat him that way (and vice versa). Otherwise, why are you married to each other?

Over the years of working with gay couples, I've observed a real temptation—especially in open marriages—to neglect the romantic relationship with your husband and focus your passion on other men. Don't go there! If you have a lot of amour and passion to go around, feel free to share it with the guys you have sex with, but make sure that your husband gets the biggest and best part of it.

And if you're the type of guy who says, "I'm not very romantic": this will be especially helpful for *you*.

Some clients—particularly younger men—have asked me: "What exactly is romance?" I once heard a woman say that she fell in love with a man because he bought her a clothes dryer. He even had it delivered to her house. The woman was struggling financially and had to take her clothes to a laundromat to dry them. Her lover saw a need and filled it. That's romance! Talking about love is easy. Romantic actions—like Mr. Dryer Man's—speak volumes.

Romance isn't fake, either; it's real. It needn't be big and dramatic, it can be small and subtle. You can pick up a $1.99 plant at Home Depot for your husband, just to let him know you're thinking of him. You can unload the dishwasher even though it's *his* turn. You can make the bed or wipe off the sink after you shave. Real romance is consideration and appreciation. But first, it helps to be aware.

Questions to Consider

- What little thing could you do to make your husband happier today?
- Are you more of a talker or a doer in showing your husband how you feel?
- When was the last time you said or did something to show him you care?

For some men in open relationships, it's easier to be romantic with men *other* than our husbands. After all, we don't see them all the time, they're not as familiar, they're more surprising—you know. However, this is a great way to gradually siphon the joy out of your marriage.

Remember how I talked earlier about how an open marriage is not for the easily overwhelmed or confused? You've got to juggle your energy, love, and affection between more than one man. If you're having sex with five men (including your husband), that's five times the guys to "please" than someone in a monogamous relationship. Use your energy wisely.

Some guys have lots of energy.

Manny: "I have tons of energy; I always have. I have no trouble keeping my boyfriends *and* my husband happy. I can just tell when one of them is a bit 'off,' so I give him an extra bit of attention until our relationship is balanced again. Of course, my husband is the main recipient of my energy: he gets about 50 percent of it and I split the other 50 percent between my family, friends, and my fuck-buddies."

Some of us have more moderate amounts of energy.

Dean: "I am a really mellow guy. I rarely get too excited or annoyed about something. The men in my life know this. I'm not the gift-giving type, so my husband has learned (finally) not to take it personally. I do remember important days for him, like his birthday and our anniversary, so I give him 100 percent of my time and attention on these special occasions. We both hate to dress up and go out, so we celebrate things in a very low-key way. My sex partners are also pretty mellow guys; otherwise, we wouldn't enjoy each other's company."

Whatever your energy level and regardless of how many men in your life you're sexual with, find a balance that keeps your marriage going smoothly while your sex life with other men hums along too. This is easy to say; not so easy to do. After all, the title of this chapter is: "Balancing Sexual Expression with Emotional Connection." The word "balancing" is crucial here, because that's a skill that must be continually created and adjusted in an open marriage.

Maybe the word "romance" feels cornball for you. True, the word itself may seem hopelessly old-fashioned, but what we're really talking about is satisfaction, depth, and meaning. And who doesn't want that in their marriage?

Your Old Friend Fear

Fear is a common experience in open marriages: when you and your husband are being sexual with other men, all kinds of fears can come up.

Questions to Consider

- What fears does your open marriage bring up for you?
- What fears do you have about being sexual with men other than your husband?
- What fears do you have about your husband being sexual with men other than you?

Fear is a big obstacle for many of us. We're afraid of getting hurt, falling in love with a husband who doesn't love us back in the same way or with the same intensity. We're afraid of rejection by men we want to have sex with. We're afraid that someone—somehow—may get past our defenses and hurt us.

We're all, on some level, afraid of having our heart broken. But let's be honest: we've all had our hearts broken and we will continue to have them broken and heal again and again. This is the nature of being alive. People break our hearts—not just our wonderful husbands, but friends, bosses, family members—even pets break our hearts when they die and leave us lonely. You can't get through life without having your heart broken repeatedly. Once you accept this, and know that you will always heal, you will lose a big chunk of the fear.

Here's an exercise I teach my clients to work with their fear(s).

1. Begin by noticing when you're afraid. Just observe it; don't judge yourself for it. Rather than beating yourself up and forcing yourself *not* to be afraid—as if that were possible—try instead to *explore* your fear. Take a more neutral, observatory stance: notice your fear as you might a piece of lint on your clothes, for example, "Oh, there's a piece of lint," and "Oh, there's some fear."

2. Once you notice your fear, check in with your body: notice any body sensations like a tight jaw, uneasy stomach, or clenched hands. Just notice, don't judge. Your body may automatically relax just from slowing down enough to become aware of what it's feeling.

3. Notice where in your body you feel your fear the most. Focus your attention there and visualize that you are breathing into this place. Allow the fear to change or stay the same. Remember: you're not forcing anything—let this be a gentle, easy process for you. You've been trying to "beat" your fear into submission for years, and it hasn't worked. That's not the way to do it.

4. As you breathe into your fear, you can ask it a question, such as "What do you want me to know?" Let yourself listen to the answer. Keep breathing. Take this process slowly. If you rush it, you're likely to miss the wisdom. You may have another question for your fear. If so, ask your question and let the fear respond.

An open marriage can bring up a lot of fears for both you and your husband. It really helps to have ways to work with these fears. Don't avoid them; they are there to show you something. If you are willing to listen to what your fear is trying to tell you, there is a lot it can teach you.

As a married man, there is no way to avoid difficult emotions like fear, anger, sadness, and numbness. Being married brings up all our unresolved emotions. Aren't you glad you know that now? It's actually a good thing in the long run, because we can use these uncomfortable feelings to learn more about what makes us tick and—ultimately—to make our marriage better.

As men, most of us were socialized to try to beat our unpleasant feelings into submission (as if we could). Instead, any time you notice fear (or anger or numbness or any other emotion) arise in your marriage—or in any important relationship in your life—try this exercise. For most of my clients (and myself), it helps transform the fear from enemy into tutor and, eventually, friend.

Holding Your Center in an Open Marriage

Dear Michael:

I went to one of your workshops on "Emotional Monogamy" and found it helpful. So I'm writing to you with a follow-up question: I love my open marriage; overall, it's going really well. But sometimes there's just too much going on. Too many men coming and going. Too many personalities to deal with. And that's just the guys I'm sleeping with. My husband has the same thing going on his side.

How can I calm down when the two of us have so much going on and so many men in our lives? It's a good problem, I know, but it's making me feel very uncentered. A friend told me that I should meditate. I am a pretty Type A guy and my friend thought that meditation might calm me down. What do you think?

Stressed out in Seattle

Dear Stressed out:

I think you describe some of the challenges of an open marriage very succinctly: How do you stay centered in the midst of so many men and so much activity? How do you find time for yourself, when you want to make sure you give time and energy to your husband as well as the other men in your life?

Your friend is wise to suggest meditation. I was quite a skeptic myself—plus, I'm not good at sitting still—but meditation has been scientifically proven to have health benefits like lowering stress levels, improving general all-around health, and decreasing feelings of anxiety and panic. Unlike most things we enjoy, it's hard to imagine any negative aspects of meditating—and there are many different ways to do it.

For some men, meditation has a bad rep: we think it's new age-y, religious, spiritual, or something strange and foreign. To me, meditating is basically getting quiet with myself (you don't have to sit to do it) and noticing what's going on. I'm sure you've already done this—unconsciously—hundreds of times during your life. The difference now is that you're going to do it with *awareness*.

I encourage all my clients to find some way to spend a little quiet time with themselves on a regular basis. It helps keep us sane, especially when your open marriage brings new men, experiences, problems, and excitement into your life on a regular basis. You *definitely* want to find *some* way to calm yourself down: Xanax, alcohol, and recreational drugs are what some guys choose when they're stressed out, but meditation is free, easy, and has no side effects (except feeling better).

Some types of meditation focus on repeating a word or phrase to yourself as a way to focus your attention. Other types encourage you to focus on a candle flame, or a point in space, or a place on the wall, to center yourself. Most of us have a hard time just sitting still for a few minutes and need some help chilling out; by having a focus, it's easier to quiet ourselves down.

I once heard Louise Hay, whose book, *You Can Heal Your Life*, is a worldwide best seller, say that meditation is when you sit and listen, and don't talk. You just listen and see what you get.

Most of us need something like meditation (or yoga or prayer) to quiet down and pay attention to what we are thinking and feeling. Living in a society that encourages us to *do* something (or buy something or drink something or eat something) when we feel anxious or worried, it's hard just to *be* ourselves and *do* nothing. It sounds easy, but for most of us, it isn't.

Many people have great ideas about starting to meditate and set goals of twenty, thirty, or even forty-five minutes twice a day. Good luck with that! Having unrealistic expectations like this may doom you to fail; it's just too much for most of us.

Instead of starting with twenty minutes or more, why not start with five minutes or less?

In my humble opinion, it's more important to start meditating and to keep doing it than to do it for any specific length of time. I suggest—rebel that I am—that you start with one minute today and see how that feels. You can always go up to two minutes tomorrow and three the next day. Why set yourself up to fail by expecting long meditations from the start? Set yourself up to succeed: start small.

If you are interested in finding out more about meditation, Google it; there is probably a group in your area that meditates together (this makes it much easier).

Follow your intuition and check out meditation to see what it may offer you. The worst that can happen is you have a few more minutes of peace, serenity, and relaxation than you usually do—such a problem!

PART III

EXPLORING MONOGAMY

CHAPTER NINE

Sex, Monogamy, and the Three-Year Itch

In part 2, we looked at many ways that an open marriage between two men can work, now let's focus on how two married men can explore monogamy. It may sound a bit trite to say "explore monogamy," but honestly, to *really* explore it can be an incredible adventure.

I looked up some definitions of "explore." These are some of my favorites.

- To travel in or through an unfamiliar place in order to learn about or familiarize yourself with it
- To examine or evaluate options and possibilities
- To look into closely; to scrutinize
- To investigate into; to probe

Let's not make assumptions about what monogamy is or must be. Just as with an open marriage, the possibilities are infinite. Granted, most people *assume* that they know what a monogamous marriage looks like, feels like, smells like—but I encourage you *not* to assume anything.

Legal gay marriage is a very new phenomenon; we have the perfect opportunity to invent it (or reinvent it) to our own specifications. Let's travel in and through this unfamiliar place called marriage; let's examine options and possibilities, look closely and scrutinize what marriage has been (up until now anyway), and probe the possibilities of what *your* gay marriage can be.

Questions to Consider

- How do you and your husband keep your married life interesting?
- What do you enjoy most about being married to your husband?
- What has surprised you most about being married?
- What is the hardest part of being married?
- What would you like more of in your marriage? Less of?

Over the years, I've heard all too many gay guys claim that "monogamy is boring" or "monogamy is so hetero." It's interesting that people often put down what they have never actually experienced. There is *nothing* boring about creating a wonderful life with one man. About twenty-five years ago, I went to a workshop for therapists and the wise (twice-married) facilitator said, "Nothing will bring up your unresolved shit like a committed, monogamous relationship. Nothing!" Hearing this was, for me, like being hit over the head with a frying pan: "BONG!" it said. "Listen up Michael, you need to hear this."

I've thought a lot about this over the past twenty-five years, and here's why I think it's true: You may think that you've worked through most of your personal baggage (what we psychotherapists call your "Family of Origin" issues) but the ultimate test may be a monogamous relationship.

You could probably say the same things about an open relationship; but with an open relationship, you don't have to work through all the stuff that comes up from monogamy. Men in open relationships sometimes avoid dealing with difficulties in their marriage by focusing on their sex lives with other men. In a way, these other men offer "temporary respite" from the problems of their marriage.

In a monogamous marriage, there is no such sexual diversion; you *have* to work it out with your husband—or not.

You might, after reading the previous section, think that, as the author of this book, I favor open marriages over monogamous ones. Not true. As a psychotherapist and an openly gay man with a relationship history of my own, I see advantages and disadvantages to both. Neither is better; they're just different. In this book, it is my pleasure (and challenge) to talk with you about both and to invite you to "explore" what works best for you and your husband.

In my work with gay couples, here are some of the major challenges I see with monogamous gay marriage.

The Benefits

- Emotional stability and security
- Predictability in sex can make it better over time
- Physical and emotional intimacy may be easier to sustain with your husband
- Social acceptance is greater for marriages that follow the heterosexual model

---

The Difficulties

- The Three-Year Itch
- Sexual boredom and monotony
- Much of gay life doesn't support monogamy
- It can be hard to keep your own identity and not lose yourself

---

We will be addressing these issues—and more—in this section.

It takes a lot of work for two men to be a happy, monogamous couple. Much of gay life is not very "couple-friendly," particularly if you live in an urban area. For many gay guys, life is about getting laid, looking good, partying, going out, and making out with men, men, men! This emphasis on self-pleasuring doesn't align well with coupledom.

Boredom in gay marriages is another reason monogamy often fails. Here are four married gay guys on this topic.

Travis: "I'm so bored with him. Our marriage started off with a lot of energy and optimism, but now, it seems like we're always fighting about stuff like whose turn it is to empty the dishwasher."

Sven-Aag: "The excitement's gone. We used to do all these great things and now—we seem stuck in a routine. The most exciting part of our life is our new puppy. It's the gay version of straight people having kids to have something great in their lives."

Eric: "He's so predictable; I know exactly what he'll do. After all, we've been together now for seventeen years, I know what he likes in bed, for lunch, his taste in movies, and what pisses him off. The mystery is gone (sigh)."

Collin: "I just feel like we [he and his husband] have slipped into some half-alive relationship where the juice—the energy—is gone. How do we get it back?"

Sound familiar?

These statements are typical of how some of my gay clients describe their long-term relationships. While boredom isn't unique to long-term gay marriages, our experience of boredom may be somewhat unique: same-sex couples often find that having a partner of the same gender is both a blessing and a curse. There's a great sense of familiarity with your partner when you share gender, but there can also be a lack of "mystery" and, as a result, boredom and predictability may rear their ugly heads. We'll address this more specifically in chapter 10, "Keeping Monogamy Lively."

Just as Tomas and Larry were our case study couple for an open marriage, in this section we have Ethan and Jake as our case study couple for a monogamous marriage.

As I began to get to know Ethan and Jake, I learned that—after they were married—each of them had (gradually) given up many of their individual friendships so that most of their friends became "our" friends. This isn't uncommon; many couples "blend" their social networks, but it can have some negative repercussions, as Ethan and Jake are discovering.

Ethan: "I feel like I've lost myself. I used to have friends I hung out with, but since they're mostly single guys, we've drifted apart. The only people I see much now are friends of both of ours. It's like instead of 'Ethan' and 'Jake,' it's become 'EthanandJake.' I love Jake, but I miss having a social life of my own."

Jake: "I went into the relationship not having as many friends as Ethan. So his social circle was much bigger. Over time, his social circle became mine too. My friends didn't feel comfortable with his, so I just kind of let them go. I sure regret that now, because I don't really like his friends that much (I don't think they like me much either) and now I'm stuck with them."

Isn't it funny how each guy thinks they gave up their friends for the other? This isn't unusual: it's natural to "share" friends the longer you're together, but if you let go of the people you like the most, you're bound to regret it later.

In counseling, each man was surprised to hear that his husband felt he got the short end of the stick by combining their social circles. It actually helped them "forgive" each other when they realized that they had each done the same (unskillful) thing.

I often find, working with couples, how surprising it is that both men are so similar and do so many of the same things. When I point this out to couples, as I did with Ethan and Jake, they're usually startled; they'd been focusing on how *different* they were rather than how *alike*. It's extremely helpful to see how similar you and your husband are. Over and over again, I've witnessed a man project onto his husband qualities that he doesn't like in himself. Then he can say, "He does that, but I don't" and it's all too easy to blame our husbands for doing things that we do too.

It wasn't hard for Ethan and Jake to reach out to the friends they'd "lost" and reconnect. Most of their friends were happy to resume the friendship; a few even said, "I never knew why you dumped me. I thought it was because your husband didn't like me." Ironic, isn't it, since neither of them saw it that way?

Once Ethan and Jake had reconnected with their old (lost) friends, each of them felt a whole lot happier.

Ethan: "Part of my boredom was that I was missing my friends and expecting Jake and his friends to fill up that space. They couldn't, of course, but I thought that's how it has to be when you get married. My single friends keep me aware of what's going on in the single world, but I don't want to be single again. My friends actually want to be married!"

Jake: "Ethan's friends are more social and flamboyant then mine. I like them, but there are just too many differences. Once I started hanging out with my old friends again, I felt so much better. My friends make me feel comfortable; we've known each other a long time. I only have a few real friends, but we're close."

Ethan and Jake thought they were doing what you're "supposed" to do when you get married: you need to leave some of your friends behind. It *doesn't* have to be this way. Sure, your single friends may find your married life isn't what they're into, or your friends and your husband's friends may not have a lot in common, but that doesn't mean you need to dump them. We'll talk more about not losing yourself in chapter 11, "The Art of Not Merging."

Ethan and Jake used to go hiking and swimming together and lifted weights at the local YMCA together. After a couple of years, this kind of faded out (which happens, you know). So Ethan and Jake began to be bored with each other. But really, they were bored with themselves. Each of them had let things "slide" once they became comfortable in their relationship. There's nothing wrong with comfort and predictability—it helps us feel safe and secure—but often we sacrifice liveliness, spontaneity, and energy in the process.

Each of these young men had also gained weight and become more sedentary: "more Netflix, less exercise" became their (subconscious) mantra. They became dissatisfied with themselves and each other, and came to see me.

Ethan: "We let ourselves go and then we didn't feel good about our bodies. So, we started avoiding sex. We considered opening up our relationship, but that felt like the easy way out. Like we weren't really trying. Would feeling good about ourselves physically help our sex life?"

Jake: "I feel like Ethan and I have become lazy slobs. We don't go out and do things anymore. We stay home, watch TV or DVDs, and pick at each other. It seems like we're always blaming each other for something. Judging each other. Trying to blame each other for being unhappy."

Ethan and Jake weren't happy with each other, but fortunately, they saw that it was caused by not being happy with themselves as individuals. They decided to look at what each of them disliked about who they had become. This is a difficult (and not very popular) step: often, in a relationship, we blame our husband for our unhappiness. It's much harder to admit that we, not them, are responsible for our boredom and unhappiness.

From working with couples, I've noticed that, after about three years of being together, often there's an increase in sexual discontentment and boredom. It doesn't happen to everyone, of course, but I've seen many gay couples hit that wall. I call this phenomenon the "Three-Year Itch."

Dear Michael:

My husband and I have been together for a little over three years now, and we're doing well in most departments, except that we're getting kind of bored with each other, especially in bed.

When we first met it was all hot and heavy and we both were so passionate. And now? We're like old straight married people—we only have good sex once or twice a month. Yeah, we cuddle and stuff, and we really love each other, but we're in a real rut.

Bored Already in Baltimore

Dear Mr. BAB:

Did you ever see that Marilyn Monroe movie *The Seven Year Itch*? It was about the idea that (straight) men get bored with their wives after seven years and may look for a new woman to revive their faltering libido.

For us gay guys, I think that a more appropriate title to describe our relationships would be the "Three-Year Itch." After being together for that long, many gay couples hit a wall called "boredom." It often manifests in sexual boredom, but it can show up in other ways too.

- letting yourself go (gaining weight, not exercising, eating poorly)
- letting your social life (with your partner and on your own) become almost nonexistent
- becoming bored with yourself, your life, your job
- taking your partner for granted

This can be a time when gay couples start to consider "open" relationships or begin to develop fantasy lives that involve other men.

Why? You know too much about your husband to harbor any illusions. You've seen each other at your worst and probably had three years of ups and downs, stony silences, and angry arguments. While this is the cement of real intimacy, it is death to illusions of romantic love. Notice that I said "illusions" of romantic love.

There's this idea in coupledom that falling in love is easy—just let yourself go. The mystery of your new man is enticing and it's a lot of fun to get to know him and to let him get to know you. Everything's new and sex is often a great adventure.

Then, six months or a year or two or three later, all your illusions are gone, and what are you left with? A real relationship with a real man, and this is bound to be both the best and worst of everything you can imagine.

Love is a lot of work. Falling in love is just that: falling. Staying in love is about staying with your man through thick and thin, anger, jealousy, mistrust, and disappointment as well as all the good stuff like affection, closeness, security, comfort, reliability, and steel-belted radial tires. (Sounds like a good car, doesn't it?)

What can we do about the boredom? Here's my definition of boredom (and it might surprise you): boredom is fear in disguise.

Underneath most of our discontentment with ourselves (and others) is fear. What are we afraid of? That our lives aren't enough, that we are not enough, nor is our husband. Fear—masquerading as boredom—is that little voice at the back of your mind that says, "You know what? You made a mistake—and look who you're stuck with now." This voice says, "Dump him and get someone more exciting/intelligent/funny/whatever and you'll be a lot happier."

Fear is the voice of the Three-Year Itch. "You did it wrong," it says, "look how everyone else is much happier and more in love than you are. Get out of this marriage and move on to someone better."

It's an interesting idea: this continual search for someone better. (Some people call it "the search for my soul mate"; sound familiar?) How will we know when we find him? Will we ever get there? No, because this ideal relationship is an illusion.

Every new man eventually becomes familiar. Newness masks fear.

It's like when you buy something new because you're scared or lonely or bored. It cheers you up, right? For about five minutes. Then the fear comes back. Relationships are the same. A new man may make you happy—for three weeks, months, or years—but every man will eventually fall off his pedestal when his burps, farts, and heavy baggage inevitably make their appearance. You can keep running (very tiring), become a monk (boring wardrobe), or face the music and dance—with your man.

We get bored with our husbands because we're bored with ourselves.

Ethan and Jake—during the course of counseling—began to deconstruct their ideas of "boredom" and "discontentment." After a lot of finger-pointing (typical), they took responsibility for their own emotional state (a crucial part of happiness) and took action.

> Ethan: "I was blaming Jake for my laziness and resenting him. I used to belong to a gay hiking club, but dropped out because Jake lost interest. Actually, I just got lazy and used that as an excuse to quit. I started going on group hikes again—without Jake—and met a group of gay guys who were also into mountain biking, something I always wanted to check out. So next I'm going to try that and see if I like it."
>
> Jake: "Once I realized that I couldn't blame Ethan for being so fat, I decided to take action. I didn't want to go back to the YMCA; I was tired of the gym. Instead, I started taking swimming lessons. I always wanted to learn to swim properly—and do all the strokes—but I kept putting it off. I enjoyed it and all my excess blubber started to come off as I became physically active again."

Ethan and Jake's sex life improved tremendously when they felt good about their bodies again. And it was great for their relationship when they realized that they didn't have to do all their physical exercise *together*, as they did when they first met. This took away their excuses not to exercise. Jake was so into his swimming lessons that he eventually joined the gay swim team. Ethan *did* pursue mountain biking and liked it even more than hiking. Each man met new friends who supported and encouraged him to stay physically active and healthy. They couldn't blame each other anymore!

It's so easy—even in a good marriage—to become complacent and stop growing and changing. There is a comfort and ease in a happy marriage, which is a good thing, but sometimes that "good thing" turns into a lack of enthusiasm or interest in growing and changing. Every loving couple is a living creation of two people; every relationship needs time and energy and work and attention and perseverance to survive and thrive.

A loving, growing, thriving relationship is truly a great work to accomplish; perhaps there is nothing more worthwhile. But it's work—work with an amazing potential for happiness. The Three-Year Itch is just one manifestation of the kinds of obstacles that stand in your way of really loving your man, for better and for worse, in sickness and in health, for richer and for poorer—you know! By growing, changing, and thriving as an individual, you contribute this same life, vitality, and spontaneity to your relationship.

Often, in couple's counseling, it's becomes clear that while sex may be the most obvious place where boredom appears, in truth, boredom is *never* just about sex; it's about our life, all the aspects of our life, not just our marriage. A good friend surprised me recently when he commented on an experience we'd just shared: "Oh well, it's something to do." We had gone to a wine-tasting event and while perfectly fine, I guess it wasn't exciting enough for him. This is how many of us look at sex: it's something to do, but nothing great.

It doesn't have to be this way.

Questions to Consider

- How do you keep your sex life interesting?
- What do you enjoy most about sex with your husband?
- What would you like more of? Less of?

We don't need to let our sex life become uninteresting: boredom is a choice. You may feel like it swoops down on you like some evil force, but it doesn't. When you choose to settle for mediocrity, you probably start telling yourself that you're bored. Then it becomes a repetitive thought and soon it's a pattern of habitual thinking that's hard to break.

And don't get married—or stay married—to avoid being bored. It doesn't work. It's not your husband or your sex life that's boring, it's *you*. No matter how wonderful a man you marry, he can't change how you feel about yourself and your life. Boredom kills relationships and people. The cure: pay attention! Wake up! The Buddha is famous for saying not that he was enlightened (whatever that means). Instead, he said, "I am awake!"

You can be too. More and more. Don't let boredom (or the idea of boredom) mess with your marriage. Instead, pay attention to your husband. Become *more* interested in him. Don't assume you know everything about him. Ask more questions. Be more curious. Start noticing when you tune out what he's saying. Instead, consciously choose to become *more* interested. Your boredom with him comes from your boredom with your life, not him. It's a choice you're making.

You can choose differently. It may be hard at the beginning, but it gets easier the more you do it. Many of us think we know everything about our husbands. And then we wonder why we're bored in our marriages. We don't and we can't know everything about anyone else, even if we've lived with him for fifty years.

Be willing to be surprised. Pay attention to your husband. *Be willing to be wrong about him.* Be willing not to know what he will say or do in a certain situation. Boredom is a result of assuming you know what will happen. You don't.

It's not easy to do this, I know. I am often very unwilling to be wrong. But these days, I'm aware of it. Let me share a little story with you:

I had a history of pain in my right knee. I took a bad fall in a ballet class in college, and my knee hadn't been the same since. A few years ago, I went to an acupuncturist that my yoga teacher recommended. The acupuncturist was an elderly Chinese woman who expertly placed the needles and left the room to let them do their work.

After an hour had passed—and the pain had lessened—she removed the needles and started to leave the room. But as she left, I heard her mumble, "knee pain, must not be willing to be wrong." I barely heard her, but nonetheless, I felt like an alarm clock just went off, it was such a loud wake-up call. I quickly sat up on the table and asked, "What did you say?" And she said it again, adding: "Knees are about rigidity: you have to be right, you are not flexible, not willing to be wrong." And, with that, she left the room.

I was stunned; I knew, in my gut, that she was right. I wasn't willing to be wrong. Over the previous months, I had been dating a few guys and it wasn't going well. I was very judgmental about them—each in their own special way—and I wasn't willing to be wrong. My knee was trying to tell me something; it was a wake-up call.

Thanks to this wise woman, I realized that my beliefs about men and the specific men I had been dating were holding me back and making the relationships unsatisfying. I was very rigid and stubborn: "Goddammit, I want my way!" was what my ego was saying. This, of course, is the battle cry of a five-year-old child, not an adult man. It was a good lesson for me. I started saying to myself, "*I am willing to be wrong.*" Over and over again. Not only did my relationships with men improve, but so did my knee!

If *you* are willing to be "wrong" about your husband—whatever that "wrong" is at the moment—and let your self-righteousness go, it will be interesting to see the changes that happen in your life *and* in your marriage. It's like that old adage, "You can be right or you can be happy." I was choosing to be right, and paying the price.

The Eight Kinds of Love

Every time someone is considering saying, "I love you" for the first time to a special man, he may wonder: What exactly is "love"? I recently went to a men's workshop where many different aspects of love were addressed and we, the participants, were encouraged to examine how these different aspects of love appear (or don't) in our lives.

Excited by this, I sat down and wrote about the eight kinds of love that I think are the most interesting and how they enrich or impoverish our lives. Most of these names are from the original Greek words, so they may not be familiar to you.

Philautia: This is self-love, how we feel about ourselves. In the Greek definition, it has two sides: narcissism and self-respect. I think that the concept of self-love is often misunderstood. It doesn't mean thinking that you're so much smarter, better, more beautiful than everyone else (this is narcissism, which will inevitably lead you into trouble). Instead, it means that you see yourself as smart, beautiful, and talented—and so is everyone else! See the difference?

Storge: This word is pronounced "stor-gay" (ironic, isn't it?). This kind of love refers to a parental, mentoring love. It has a protective vibe. I felt this recently when I saw a young gay couple eating at a restaurant, holding hands while a clearly judgmental person at a nearby table glared disapprovingly at their expressions of love. I feel very protective of the young couple: this is the essence of storge.

Pragma: This word describes a deep, long-lasting, committed love, the kind you see in the best kinds of long-term relationships. It's not easy to achieve, but there is a depth here that helps us get through the disagreements and disappointments that any long-lasting loving relationship is bound to experience.

Platonic: You may think you know what this means, but I was told that it means loving the beauty inside people, not their external presentation. This has an interesting implication for friendship; do you love men because of their inner beauty (kindness, sensitivity) or must someone be physically beautiful to be loved by you?

Eros: This is sexual, passionate love, often manifested in the physical. This may be the kind of love you are most familiar with. If so, you might explore the others a bit more. On the other hand, if you have little eros in your life, you probably feel pretty low energy. Eros—in healthy moderation—recharges our batteries.

Ludus: This is a word that was new to me. I was told it is a playful, flirting, teasing love. Perhaps ludus leads to eros (or vice versa). Ludus can also relate to playing games and sports, giving another aspect to the playful quality. Ludus has a lightness to it, a youthful energy. If you find yourself not very light or playful, a little ludus might be just the thing for you.

Agape: In the spiritual world, this is quite a popular term. It is about unconditional love: how we are told God loves us. Whether you believe in God or not, agape is something we can strive for in our relationships. To love with agape means we forgive easily and understand that everyone we love will screw things up at some point. Will we still love them? Can we easily forgive them their humanness?

Epithumia: I wasn't familiar with this term. I was told it is a kind of obsessive desire where you find yourself saying things such as "You are my life; I can't live without you" to someone you allegedly "love." Let's be clear: obsession is not love. Obsession is a very unhealthy form of insecure self-centeredness, where other people exist only to make you happy.

Questions to Consider

- After reading through the list of the different types of love, look at each kind of love—on your own or with your husband—and ask yourself:
- Do I have this in my life?
- Do I want more of it or less of it?
- How could I make that happen?

I encourage you to experiment with this list of these different kinds of love: have fun with it. Discuss it with your husband. See if together you can increase the kinds of love you want and release the kinds you don't.

One of the more challenging aspects of my work as a psychotherapist is working with couples when one of the men has had an affair. I typically hear the "wounded" husband say something such as

Matthew: "How could this happen? How could he do this to me? We got married last year and he promised to be faithful. And I thought he was."

Nadir: "I'm so angry. I feel so foolish. I bet all our friends are laughing at me, because I was the last to know."

RJ: "I don't know if I can ever forgive him. It's not so much that he had an affair—*that* I could forgive—it's that he lied to me. How can I ever trust him again?"

When I work with a couple struggling with the aftermath of an affair (i.e., one person was unfaithful to the other), it's common for the man who cheated to say "I don't know how it happened; I just kind of fell into it." But upon examination, it becomes clear that there is usually a predictable chain of events that led to the affair. I'd like to talk a bit about how affairs "happen" and what you can do to prevent them from happening in *your* marriage.

In my experience as a psychotherapist, here are some of the steps I've observed that make up the anatomy of an affair.

1. You feel that your needs are not being met. Your desires for emotional, physical, and/or sexual intimacy are no longer met by your husband. You begin to—subconsciously—search for someone else to meet those needs.

2. You begin sharing intimacies with a new man, let's call him your "special friend" (hereafter, "SF"). You tell him things about yourself that formerly only your husband knew because your SF *really* understands you.

3. Your focus of intimacy shifts. You share less and less with your husband, keeping your growing relationship with your SF a secret; your husband wouldn't understand, after all, would he?

4. You justify what you're doing. You tell yourself that, if your marriage was really so great, it wouldn't feel like so much work. As a result, the intimacy you have with your husband takes a nose dive.

5. Now comes the moment you've both been waiting for. Something bad (or good) happens and who do you want to share it with? Yes, your SF.

And that fateful—long-awaited—day, you wrap your arms around each other (only wanting to be close, right?) and you find yourself kissing him, realizing that, omigod, you *love* him!

6. Face the music. You explain to your betrayed and shattered husband (whom you still care about, of course) that you never meant to hurt him, and you're so sorry.

How to prevent this scenario? The moment you find yourself sharing secrets with your SF that ought to be shared with your husband, let a warning bell go off inside your head:

Danger! Danger! Big problems ahead!

This is a pivotal point. Instead of heading into an affair, muster your courage, go home, and tell your man that you feel yourself drifting away from him. This is a time for real honesty with your husband: "I'm tempted to be intimate with someone else, but I don't want to."

Ask your husband for help: "How can we get back to what we used to have?" Reaffirm your love for him and—as kindly as possible—tell them what's missing in your relationship.

This is difficult, grown-up stuff. In the short run, it may seem easier to keep secrets from your man and avoid emotionally wrenching conversations. But in the long run, that's how good relationships are destroyed.

Here's an e-mail I recently received.

Dear Michael:

I never thought it would happen to me, but here I am, married to a cheater. I didn't know he was sleeping with other guys, but I started to notice too many things that were weird and he then started being extra nice to me in a way that made me wonder what the hell was going on.

Anyway, I found out, confronted him, and he admitted it. The problem is, what do I do now? Do I forgive him? How can I trust him again? He swears he won't do it again, but can I believe him?

I'm tempted to leave him but he's begging me not to. He said he'll even go to counseling (which is a big step for him). What should I do?

Putting Up with a Cheater in Portland

Dear Mr. Putting Up With:

You ask good questions. Cheating can end a relationship or—surprisingly—make it a lot better. Let me explain.

You wonder, how can you trust him again? Rebuilding trust in your husband after an affair takes time; you can't rush it. He will have to realize this and not pressure you to "get over it." You don't say how long you've been together, but if it's taken you years to build that trust, it may take a while to restore your trust if a whole lot of deception has gone down.

Counseling can help. It's a good sign that he's willing to do it; it shows that he doesn't want to give up on your marriage and that he's willing to change. What I've noticed in counseling couples dealing with infidelity is that if *both* parties involved want to work it out, they almost always do.

If you and your husband are willing to look at what conditions brought about his cheating, you could both learn a lot about yourselves and each other. In fact, many couples I work with—when cheating is the issue that brings them in to see me—end up *closer* than they were before. Why? Because they are forced (by the cheating) to take a good look at their marriage and see the mountains of small resentments that they've been avoiding.

Taking about cheating is pretty damned uncomfortable. This is why couple's counseling can be helpful: it's not easy talking about this stuff, and most of us aren't willing to squirm that much unless we get some professional assistance.

In the short run, it can really suck to hear why your husband cheated on you. But in the long run, you sure can learn a lot about him and yourself. Maybe you had no idea that he felt neglected or unappreciated. Maybe you took him for granted and just assumed he'd always be there.

Every cheater imagines that he's not getting his needs met and that he "deserves" to feel loved and desired in the way he wants. Your husband may have needs that he's never told you about. Maybe he wants more of you emotionally. Maybe he felt that your sex life was dull or dead. I'm not saying this to rationalize his behavior. I am saying that if you are *both* willing to understand why he did what he did, your relationship can become even stronger as a result.

And what about the old adage, "Once a cheater; always a cheater"? It is my experience as a psychotherapist that any habitual or compulsive behavior can be changed if the person wants to change and is willing to do the work to do so.

Cheating is an alarm clock. It tells you both that something's off, something's wrong, something's missing. Often, we have these nagging little voices that tell us, "pay attention; something's wrong," but we don't want to listen to them so we ignore them.

Until the alarm clock gets bigger and louder and we can't ignore it anymore.

No one can tell you to stay or go. No one knows your marriage and what the two of you have when no one else is around. So don't take anyone else's advice unless it aligns with your own. Only you know if this man is worth working it out for or if you're better off dumping his ass and moving on.

Cheating is an intense wake-up call. It gives you information that you probably don't want to hear, but need to. It can be an opportunity to work out all the shit you've both been avoiding—or not.

It's all up to you. You hold all the cards.

Play them wisely.

Do you ever read those little free magazines that tell you all about gay porn stars and their latest movies?

I do.

I read just about everything in front of me; you never know what you might learn. I found an interesting article in one of them. The basic premise of the article was don't get fat or your man will leave you. "Really?" I said to myself as I read this little piece of alleged wisdom. "Is that true? If your body changes, will your husband leave you?"

Needless to say, this is not an example of good mental health. So I was inspired to write this in response to that article, to ask the question: Do you love a body or a person?

As we age, what is most likely to change? Our bodies. Only with massive plastic surgery and intense daily workouts are we likely to avoid any physical changes. And, even then, we'll still get older. Look at Cher, God bless her, she does it all and even she looks older—well, a little older.

Beautiful bodies are wonderful to look at, feel, make love to. No doubt about it. I too am drawn to those gorgeous young twenty-somethings at my gym; they are visual perfection. How could you not be attracted to them? The only problem is, would they be good love objects (Freud's words) for you? In other words, could you love them well and could they return it?

Over the years I have been privileged to be a psychotherapist to porn stars, go-go boys, escorts, and even a male madam who asked me to do psychological evaluations of candidates for his stable of escorts. (I declined.) Many of these young men were bright, creative people who were experimenting with their sexuality and supporting themselves by doing so. Most of them ultimately left their sex-oriented work and moved into other fields.

It is clear to me that even porn stars and go-go boys realize that their amazing bodies are temporary assets. None of them thought they would be able to sustain their beautiful, fat-free bodies for long; most of them accepted aging and the physical changes that go with it.

So why can't we?

Do we expect our husband to look as amazing in a year, or two or three, as he does now? Do we start to hint "You better not get fat; you know I like those muscles." or "Isn't it time you went back to that trainer?" Some men claim to fall out of love with their husband when his body changes. In those cases, it's clear who they love: the body, not the man who inhabits it.

Have you ever talked with older gay couples who have happily stayed together for years and years? You may look at their bodies and not find them to be your physical ideal. But guess what? If you live long enough, this will be you. And your husband. Former beautiful boys become elders who are beautiful in their own way (if you're willing to see it). These folks may have been brought together by physical attraction, but that's not what kept them together. They learned to love their husband as a whole person: body, mind, and soul.

A dear friend of mine has been married five times. She said that the first four were "all about the bodies. I loved these hot younger guys, but in the end, all you have left is friendship—that's why George [husband #5] lasted."

By focusing on our husband's aging/changing body, we are pulling a fast one; by doing so, we avoid looking at our own body, our own life, our own unhappiness. We get to blame our dissatisfaction on them.

Derek: "How can I be attracted to you if you don't take care of yourself?"
Xavier: "I'm not into you anymore. You used to turn me on, but lately, eh . . ."
Kyle: "I used to be so hot for you, but honey, you're not aging well."

Let's be clear: I'm not talking about an unhealthy body, I'm taking about a body that *naturally* (and normally) ages: hair goes gray, thins, or disappears; waistlines get larger, biceps aren't quite as big, and that perky butt isn't quite so perky.

Who do you love? The body or the man inside it? What you choose will determine the kind and quality of your marriage.

Choose carefully.

Everyone wants to have great sex, but the "ingredients" seem elusive. It is my observation that great sex requires elements of both aggression and tenderness. As men, we all have a healthy need to "conquer," "win," and "be the best." How in touch with this are you?

When there is *too* much aggression in your sex life, however, you can easily feel that sex is all about being in control, all the time. There's little emotional connection: basically, you're just using your husband to get off.

Too much tenderness, on the other hand, can lead to a mushy, messy enmeshment where it's hard to tell where you end and your husband begins. It's great for intimate friendships and parental relationships that demand a lot of love and empathy, but too much tenderness is—surprisingly—not very helpful for great sex.

You can use the questions below as bases for a discussion with your husband. Be not afraid! It can only result in your sex life getting better (and more balanced). So take a deep breath, both of you, and ask yourselves and each other:

Questions to Consider

- How would you define great sex?
- What makes it great for you?
- Where would you place yourself on the sexual spectrum from tender to aggressive?
- Can you express your healthy aggression? Do you enjoy it?
- Can you express your tenderness? Do you enjoy it?

Talking about this stuff with your husband will open a lot of doors. They may not be doors you're comfortable opening and walking through, but in the long term, being able to talk about your sex life is crucial to keeping it alive and fulfilling.

How can you find the right balance of aggression and tenderness in your sex life with your husband? Awareness and curiosity help a lot. There is no one way to do this; each couple has to find their own way on this path. It's not so hard, however, to tell if your balance is off. If your sex life with your husband feels empty and emotionless, you need some tenderness. If your sex feels energy-less and boring, you both might benefit from some healthy aggression.

What might that look like? Tenderness is often expressed as warmth, compassion, empathy, and a genuine caring about another person. It manifests in sexual behaviors like maintaining eye contact, breathing together, gentle touching and caresses, and sweet kisses. Checking in with how your husband is feeling is another way of expressing tenderness: "Do you like that?" and "Does this feel good?" are questions you can ask him to let him know that it's not all about you.

Healthy aggression may be a new idea for you. Aggression has gotten a bad reputation, but healthy aggression is *conscious* aggression. It is not about acting out like a spoiled child or a self-obsessed narcissist. Healthy aggression is a way of expressing your sexual energy; at its best, it's playful and passionate. There is a mutual consent component; both you and your husband need to be okay with how aggression is expressed. Each of you needs to be able to say, "No, that's too much" or "I really don't like that" so that any aggressive behavior can be modified or stopped, depending on what you've both agreed upon.

Healthy aggression isn't like a porn video, or, it can be. Your way of expressing it may be different from your best friend's. You may like to take your husband's clothes off roughly and push him over the sofa for passionate sex. Here are some other examples.

Peter: "My husband and I have a set of clothes that we like to rip off each other. We keep them in a special drawer and when we're in the right mood, it's a real high to tear these clothes off each other and have wild, bad-boy sex. We've been together for seven years now and our sex life is still very hot, to the envy of our friends."

Jack: "When we have sex, my husband and I are very clear on how we like to use healthy aggression: sometimes it's rough talk, sometimes physically forceful, strong movements. At first, it made us laugh when we tried this stuff—it felt so fake—and we almost gave up. But eventually, we found that we can enjoy it and let it lift our libidos without taking it too seriously."

Pedro: "My husband and I like to alternate who gets to be the aggressive one. Sometimes he's the one who initiates sex and calls the shots; at other times, the roles are completely reversed. I like to throw him on the bed sometimes and ravage him. I like it when he does it to me too. It keeps things fresh."

Will: "We know it's trite, but my husband I like role playing during sex and, sometimes, to keep it lively, we'll reverse the roles in the middle of having sex; for example, one of us was the 'naughty schoolboy' being punished by his 'teacher.' But the schoolboy got bored with this, so he spontaneously reversed the situation, took control and became aggressive with his 'teacher.'"

Bruce: "My husband and I have a lot of fun with healthy aggression. One day he took on the role of the 'sexy plumber' (from a porn video we both like) and when he finished unclogging the drain, he (happily) ravaged me."

In long-term relationships, a bit of healthy aggression can keep your sex life alive and spontaneous. Like Jack (see above) mentioned, it can seem "fake" or "phony" at first, if it's new to you. However, don't give up so easily; keep experimenting and see if there is a way that it can work for you and your husband. As two men together, it's really helpful to have a *healthy, mutually agreeable* way to express your aggression during sex.

Tenderness and gentleness are great for feeling safe, secure, and loved, but they're not so hot for excitement and eroticism. In my experience as a gay couple's counselor, too much familiarity isn't conducive to great sex. If you and your husband are "joined at the hip," your sex life may be suffering. Great sex requires some unpredictability; this is where healthy aggression can come in.

If your sex life has plenty of tenderness but not enough "juice," talk with your husband about adding some healthy aggression. If your sex life has plenty of action but isn't very fulfilling, "try a little tenderness," as the song goes. Find the right balance and get ready for some great sex.

CHAPTER TEN

Keeping Monogamy Lively

Balancing Emotional Stability with Spontaneity

Okay! It's time to look beyond your sex life and examine other important aspects of a happy monogamous marriage.

One of the problems I have seen in many monogamous couples is that they feel like the "life," the "juice" has gone out of their marriage. There is plenty of emotional stability, but not much spontaneity. For other couples, there is too much change and drama, but not enough stability and predictability. How can you and your husband find the perfect balance for you?

You can't, because there is no perfect balance. And even if there were, that balance would change over time.

In this chapter, we'll look at and discuss marriage-related topics such as spontaneity, anger and hurt, self-esteem, getting older, parental challenges, retirement, money, body image, feeling safe, mirror work, health and illness, comfort and security, age differences, disappointment, improving our self-care, resilience, and lots more. All of these factors either contribute—or do not—to keeping your marriage lively.

The bottom line: keeping your marriage lively is dependent on keeping *yourself* happy and contented.

We often expect that getting married is going to change our lives dramatically, that so many of our problems—loneliness, depression, anger—are just going to magically disappear. They don't. In the short run, they may actually get worse, but keep reading . . .

When you're married, particularly when you and your husband are monogamous, it places a great deal of focus on just the two of you. Other people are important (and I sure hope you both have friends), but basically, it's you and him. You quickly see the best and worst in each other. This kind of vulnerability brings up our unresolved issues in a way that being single seldom does. This is where emotional stability is really helpful: we want to feel safe in our marriage. We want to know that our husband isn't going to walk out when things get tough.

On the other hand, if we have too much stability, we may begin to be bored in our relationship and wonder why it isn't everything we'd hoped for. This is usually a path of slow death for a marriage. Little by little, the vitality seems to drain out of your relationship, and often, neither of you will know why. Here's an e-mail from a guy who can't figure out why he isn't happier in his marriage and his life. I call it "We have it all, but it's not enough."

Dear Michael:

I feel like such a fool. I have a great job, good health, a loving husband, and a bunch of loyal friends—but I still feel empty and miserable inside and find myself crying for no reason. What's wrong with me? Why can't I just be happy and grateful for all the good stuff in my life? My husband thinks I'm crazy and is afraid I'm going to have an affair, but I don't think that would make any difference either. Having it all—which I do—just isn't enough somehow. Help!

Signed,

Messed up and ungrateful in Minneapolis

Dear Mr. Messed Up:

First of all, you have insight and self-awareness, so please give yourself credit for that. Years ago, I heard gay billionaire/philanthropist David Geffen say, "Everyone should be rich and famous at a young age so they'd realize that this alone will *not* make them happy." You don't say if you're rich or famous, but the idea is useful regardless.

Many men achieve their childhood expectations—marriage to a great guy, a fulfilling career, and loving network of friends—only to find themselves feeling empty and disappointed. "Is that all there is?" the refrain from that old Peggy Lee song, may temporarily be your song too.

Where do you go from here? Let me posit some questions for your consideration:

First off, how useful is it to look to externals for happiness? The world outside us always changes: people leave or disappoint us, jobs end, health shifts, etc. It may be more helpful to look for happiness internally. Looking inside yourself is not easy or comfortable, but it is *very* productive.

Questions to Consider

- When you look inside yourself, do you like what you see?
- Does everyone else see you as a great success and you don't?
- How do you want to see yourself?

It matters far more what *you* think about yourself than what your boss, husband, parents, or friends think about you. Their kind actions and words of love/praise are useless if they don't ring true to *you*.

You, Mr. Messed Up, may be ready to go deeper. In my experience, we don't have breakthrough "aha" moments until we're really ready for them. Ironically, a good marriage can allow you to feel secure enough to see the sadness and disappointment that's always been there, in the background, waiting until you were together enough to face it and deal with it.

Maybe you're ready to move beyond previous drama—or trauma—in your life. When times of struggle and upset are over and you're feeling pretty strong in yourself and in your marriage, *this* is the time to look beneath the surface of your life and ask yourself, what's going on down there?

Crying jags can give you useful information; they are likely telling you that something is off and that it's time to look into yourself (not at other people, places, or things) and see what's going on with you—thoughts, emotions, body sensations, etc.

Another set of questions that may be helpful involves looking at what's next in your life; if you've achieved most of your childhood dreams, you're now seeing just what they've brought you. Perhaps the life you thought you wanted isn't the life you want any more.

I once heard actress/film producer Salma Hayek (*Frida*) talk about her long, frustrating search for happiness. She spoke of her success as an actress in Mexico and how surprised she was to find herself feeling empty and unfulfilled. She asked herself, "This is not my dream—why am I here? How did I get here?" Perhaps you are in a similar place. This could be the result of an unexamined life. But it needn't remain unexamined and you needn't remain "empty and miserable inside" and keep "crying for no reason."

When you pay attention to your internal life and ask yourself some good, juicy, life-altering, bone-crunching questions, your potential for happiness and gratitude will grow tremendously regardless of your job, health, marriage, and friends.

Questions to Consider

- When do you typically feel empty or miserable inside?
- Where do you think those thoughts and feelings are coming from?
- What can you do to help yourself feel better?

There is a definite silver lining to this cloud: having all the things you thought you'd wanted now gives you the opportunity to see all the parts of your life that you've been avoiding and need attention.

Let's look at Ethan and Jake, our case study couple for a monogamous marriage. As you recall, Ethan and Jake had been together as a couple for about three years when they came to me for help with their marriage. In the previous chapter, we saw how, after a lot of finger-pointing, each man took responsibility for his unhappiness in the marriage. They saw how they had both unnecessarily sacrificed friendships for the marriage, thinking it was the "right" thing to do.

They also blamed each other for not exercising together and not taking good care of their bodies. When they realized that they didn't have to do all their physical exercise *together*, this took away their excuses not to exercise. As a result, Jake joined the gay swim team and Ethan learned mountain biking. Each man met new friends who supported and encouraged him to stay physically active and healthy. They each took responsibility for their physical health and no longer blamed each other for being "lazy." Not surprisingly, they began to feel good about their bodies again and their sex life was revitalized.

Ethan and Jake had become complacent and stopped growing and changing in their physical and sexual lives, but found a way out of their stasis. In this chapter, let's look at how they learned to balance their needs for emotional stability with their desire for spontaneity.

Ethan: "I like how comfortable I am with Jake, but things at home have become too predictable for me. I want to go out and be with my friends more. Sure, I love him, but I want more variety in my life, and I'm not getting it from him. I think he feels hurt by this, though."

Jake: "Ethan and I got back on track as far as our sex life, but once that was good again, I noticed that I wasn't happy with other parts of our marriage. I feel that Ethan and I have emotionally drifted apart. We're spending so much time doing our own separate activities that it feels like our emotional closeness is slipping away. It feels like things are falling apart for us."

This is a classic case of one man wanting more emotional closeness and the other wanting more emotional space. What to do?

No matter how good your life or marriage is, there will inevitably come a time when it feels like things are (temporarily) falling apart. You can wait until those moments and panic, or you and your husband can do a little preparedness planning—you know, like you do for tornadoes and earthquakes.

It's impossible to be an adult and not have things periodically fall apart. As a wise old friend of mine used to say, "Remember Michael, no one's life is shit-free." She was so right: you lose your job, your partner dies (both have happened to me), or someone close to you loses a child. When things fall apart, how can we comfort and sooth ourselves?

Some people go into denial, pretending that everything is fine. I do not recommend this. While it's common to feel overwhelmed and want to "put on a happy face" when things fall apart, it's far healthier to let yourself feel numb, sad, angry, or confused. Plus, putting on a happy face takes a lot of effort and—eventually—it's not sustainable.

Ethan: "Things were already a bit uneasy with us and then Jake's mom went into the hospital for tests; she had all kinds of physical problems. This just made him even more clingy, which drove me crazy. I understood he needed me, but the needier he got, the more I wanted some space of my own. It wasn't a good combination."

Jake: "I am close to my mom, so when she went into the hospital, I lost it. I knew that Ethan felt I was clingy, but I couldn't help it. I needed him for emotional support and I felt like he gave it to me sometimes but pushed me away at other times."

In order to not push Ethan away, Jake tried to hide his emotions and "man up." This only served to make him more emotionally fragile and to confuse the hell out of Ethan.

> Ethan: "Now he says he doesn't need my emotional support. He tells me to go hang around my friends, that he'll be fine. But I don't believe it."
>
> Jake: "If I let myself feel what I'm really feeling, it will be too much for Ethan, so I'm just holding it all in. I've done it before, I can do it again."

All or nothing; black or white. This kind of thinking only makes us feel worse. It doesn't work to let everything out (total spontaneity) or hold it all in (total repression). I suggested to Jake that he imagine that his emotions are like toothpaste in a toothpaste tube. You don't want to squeeze the whole tube out at once and feel that flood of emotions. So you squeeze out a little bit at a time.

> Ethan: "Thank God Jake is learning to find the middle ground emotionally. This all or nothing stuff was making me so confused. First, he needed me too much, then, he didn't need me at all. Moderation—that I can work with."
>
> Jake: "I like the toothpaste tube analogy that Michael gave us. I was raised not to show emotion, to keep it in until you feel like you'll burst—which is just what I did over and over when I was younger. Letting my emotions out a bit at a time also is something that Ethan seems able to handle."

This wasn't all Jake's "problem," of course, although Ethan made him out to be the needy one. Ethan was needy too; he didn't want to feel overwhelmed by his husband's emotions, but rather than talk with him about it, he wanted to "run away" and hang out with his friends when the going got tough. Ethan and I talked about that. He had a history of feeling "smothered" by other people's emotions.

> Ethan: "In my family, my mom was super-emotional and my dad said little. I was pretty stoic, like Dad, and of course, picked a husband who was more like my mom, which Michael pointed out, to my great dismay. I have to learn not to run."

Jake: "I have a history of stuffing my emotions, because no one in my family talked about their emotions. We just didn't. Every once in a while one of us would blow up because we couldn't stuff anymore. The blow-up passed, no one mentioned it, and then things returned to normal again. This was our pattern. So, of course, when Michael pointed out that I picked a husband like my father, it totally made sense."

During therapy, Jake learned to gradually "squeeze" his toothpaste tube of emotions in a way that didn't overwhelm his husband. Ethan, in turn, learned not to run away from Jake's now more-moderate displays of emotion. Each man had picked a husband like one of his parents and was playing out the pattern he knew from childhood. This isn't unusual; most of us do some version of this.

Ethan: "Usually, with my emotions, I think that if I let myself feel this [emotion], I'll lose it and feel crazy, because that's what my mom did, so I expected Jake to do the same thing. Working with Michael, I learned that if I don't let myself *begin* to feel what's going on inside me, I'm much more likely to lose my peace and find reasons to get annoyed with Jake."

Jake: "I needed to find a way to calm myself down when bad things happen, like my mom's hospitalization. I had relied too much on Ethan for my emotional stability. Now, I want to rely more on myself and figure out ways to do it without asking too much of Ethan, especially since a lot of emotion still makes him wanna run."

Ethan runs from strong emotion and Jake doesn't know how to modulate his. Often, we pick partners not only who remind us of our parents, but with whom we can work out these unresolved family-of-origin issues. One husband feels too much; the other feels too little. One man is okay with a lot of emotion; the other cannot tolerate it. These situations typically bring out the best and worst in a marriage; we can either learn from our husband and become a bit more like him (the ideal situation) or we can find fault with our husband and say he's doing it all wrong and should be more like us (the typical situation).

This brings up an even deeper question: How can we calm and comfort ourselves when it feels like things are falling apart?

Psychological attachment theory says that if we are not "reflected" in a positive way by our caregivers during the first eighteen months of life, it will always be hard for us to comfort ourselves. We need to "internalize" the ability to self-sooth, and we get it by being soothed as a baby by secure, loving people who know how to do that.

Many of us didn't get that good stuff. So, are we doomed? Thankfully, we are not. We can learn self-soothing skills, but it takes some work. Here are some ways to sooth and calm yourself when the shit hits the fan.

Do Things That Calm You Down Emotionally

Ethan: "As a kid, the only place I felt really safe and calm was outdoors, so I have always liked being outside. When I need to calm down, I like to mountain bike or hike and be in nature."

Jake: "It calms me down to play video games. It always has. It lets me leave the problems of the world behind and go into a fantasyland for a few hours. I know Ethan thinks it's silly and that I should have outgrown it by now, but it works for me."

We all have things that calm us down. What are some of yours? For me, it's reading, listening to music, working in the garden, walking, playing with pets, talking with a (calm) friend. Discover what calms you down; make a list and—in times of chaos—do things on the list, with your husband or on your own, at least one a day.

Be Physically Comfortable

Ethan: "I always feel good when I'm outside. I love sitting in a jacuzzi or a sauna at night, under the stars. I also like going to the gym and exercising, but those are my inside activities for when the weather's bad."

Jake: "I really like staying in bed and reading on my iPad and of course, video games. Swimming also helps me feel comfortable in my body. I love how calm and peaceful it is to be underwater and how the water feels against my body."

It's a good idea to know what things make you feel comfortable. Why not make a list of what works for you and ask your husband to do the same. Then, compare lists. What things make *both* of you feel comfortable? Why not do them more often?

Watch Your Self-Talk

Ethan: "When things fall apart for me, my self-talk is usually, 'Just ignore it; it'll go away.' This is what I was raised with. But now I see that ignoring a problem in my marriage doesn't work very well. So these days, I'm telling myself things like, 'I can handle this. It's just emotion' and 'Talking with Jake helps the problem go away.' This seems to work better for both of us."

Jake: "In my family, our unspoken mantra was: 'Don't feel it; feelings are dangerous.' So I tried not to feel anything, which, of course, doesn't work. Now I'm trying self-talk like 'Feelings are a normal part of life; they won't kill me' and 'It's okay to express feelings; I don't have to push them away.'"

Isn't it ironic how similar Ethan and Jake are? Both of them tried to avoid what they were feeling, having grown up in environments where feeling emotions was a bad or scary thing.

For many of us, when things fall apart, we usually make ourselves feel worse with self-talk such as "This will never get better" or "I'm hopeless." Try saying these phrases out loud: See how they only make you feel worse? That's not self-soothing.

When things get really bad, it helps a lot to monitor your self-talk. You can either make yourself feel worse or better by what you tell yourself. For example, I encouraged my client with a recent diagnosis of prostate cancer to consider telling himself, "Yes, I have prostate cancer, but I'll do everything I can to help myself and I'll let my husband and friends love me and care for me." See how much better it feels to say stuff like this than, "Omigod, I know I'm gonna die" (which is what he used to tell himself)?

For a client I know who was struggling with crystal meth, his self-talk was pretty depressing. He was saying things such as "I can't believe I'm hooked on meth. What the hell is wrong with me?" This is—obviously—not very helpful. After he and I worked together, he came up with this phrase instead: "I may have a drug problem now, but I can work through this and come out of it. I was clean and sober before; I can do it again." He told me that the more he repeated *this* phrase, the more optimistic he felt. Eventually, he got into an outpatient drug treatment program and is now happily clean and sober.

Ask for Help

Ethan: "I've never been good for asking anyone for help. This is a tough one for me, but I'm willing to give it a try. I have a lot of friends, but we don't talk much about feelings. I am starting to try this out with my female friends, because it's easier for me to start with them. I hope to work up to my guy friends, but that may take a while."

Jake: "I realize that I have depended way too much on Ethan for my emotional comfort and never could figure out why he seemed to shrink away from me when I needed him. Through counseling, I've learned to 'spread my emotions around,' not just give them all to Ethan. I talk more with friends and family now, and as a result, I'm not so needy with Ethan."

Jake expected Ethan to handle almost all of his emotional needs, which didn't work well for either of them. However, most married men have realized that, once we've been with our husband for some time, he *does* know how to help us when we feel worried or anxious (and vice versa). A key factor here is not expecting our husband to do it *all* for us.

We'll check in with Ethan and Jake later in this chapter. For now, let's hear from a few other married gay men on how they ask their husbands for a (reasonable) amount of support when times are tough.

Xavier: "When I get all worried about something, like applying to PhD programs and wondering how I'll pay for them, I ask my husband to rub my shoulders and tell me he loves me. It always helps me feel less stressed out."

Clayton: "My Dad died recently and I asked Kyle [his husband] to just hold me and let me cry. I asked him not to try to problem-solve or fix anything, just to hold me so I could feel safe and loved. It made us both feel better and closer."

Sammy: "I recently lost my job and—the next week—my best friend told me he was arrested for domestic violence. This threw me way off-balance. Davis [his husband] asked me what I needed and I told him,

'Reassure me that I'll get another job and that Tadd [his best friend] will get help for his anger problems.' It helped me to hear that and not believe all my own negative thoughts."

I don't encourage you to lie to yourself (or to ask your husband to lie to you just to make you feel better); I *do* encourage you to find the most loving truths that you can and to repeat them to yourself or have your husband say them to you. And if it seems like everything is going downhill, try a phrase such as "Out of this experience will come something good, I know it." Now *that* is a phrase that can bring you comfort no matter what personal hell you're going through.

When things fall apart, you *can* comfort and sooth yourself. However, some of us expect our husbands (or friends or family) to do it all for us. Unfortunately, it doesn't work that way. While it's great that you can count on your husband when things fall apart, ultimately, it's up to *you* to learn how to make yourself feel better. I've seen more than a few marriages falter when one partner *expects* the other to make him feel better—in other words, do it *for* him.

> Hafez: "I was single for a long time, very lonely, looking really hard for a good man and thank God, I found him. I don't know anyone as great as Stan, my man. I lean on him hard, I know, but it seems like he's okay with it."
>
> Brad: "I was married to a woman for years, and was 'The Rock' in that relationship. When I came out and got a divorce, I realized that I was tired of always being the strong one. With Niels [his husband], I feel like I can finally relax and let someone take care of *me* now."
>
> Sloan: "I have a very intense job (VP of Marketing for a Fortune 500 Corporation) and I just get so sick of making decisions all day. When I come home, I want someone else to make all the decisions and make me feel good. Tim [his husband] does that for me."

There's nothing wrong with leaning on your husband, but if you depend on him to "make me feel good" or "take care of me," what happens when the time comes that he can't? Yes, eventually the time will come when your man, no matter how wonderful, will not be able to meet your needs. What will you do then? How can you become more resilient so that you are less needy with your husband and more able to take care of yourself?

Becoming More Resilient

The same bad thing can happen to two guys: one gets really down and depressed for a few days/weeks; the other bounces back to "normal" within a few hours. What's the difference?

When I worked for Child Protective Services, we talked about "resilient children" and how they managed not only to survive abusive/neglectful parents, but to actually thrive in tough situations. Let's look at how *you* too can thrive when bad things happen.

Most successful people had a lot of obstacles thrown in their way, but somehow, they kept going. How can we? Here's a little quiz.

> When you're stuck in a bad situation, which answer sounds most like you?
>
> 1. "This sucks, but I'll get through it and be stronger when it's over."
> 2. "Why is this happening to me?"
> 3. "I know that this is going to screw me up forever."

Obviously, #1 is the answer for the most resilient of us, but how do we get there? It's all too easy to drift into #2 (I know that I do), and if we're really going through a rough time, we might even opt for #3. If you want to become more of an answer #1 kind of guy, here are some suggestions.

Be Grateful for What Works: Stop every so often and tell yourself three things you're grateful for. Gratitude builds resiliency. You might also tell your husband three things you appreciate about him—strengthen your marriage as you build your own resiliency.

Keep Learning New Stuff: Resilient men don't sit back and watch bad TV for hours (not usually, anyway). They keep growing and getting smarter and more skillful, so that when bad things happen, they know what to do.

Build a Strong Support Network: No one can do it alone. What kind of support do you have in your life? People who reinforce your weaknesses and problems or people who believe in your talents and abilities and encourage you? Do your husband, friends, and family tell you, "Oh, you poor little victim" or "You can get through this. How can I help?" Hint: Choose the latter.

Combine Optimism with Critical Thinking: A guy I know can build or fix anything. Since I'm far from being able to do that, I asked him how he does it. "Well, I think I can figure just about anything out, so I just keep going until I do." When you combine skill with self-confidence, you can accomplish almost anything.

Have an Internal Locus of Control: Resilient people believe that the actions they take will affect the outcome of an event. They know that they have the power to make choices that will affect their situation, their ability to cope, and their future.

Be a Good Communicator: Assertiveness comes with resilience; we ask respectfully for what we want and negotiate until we get it, or most of it anyway. A resilient person is calmly assertive (and drama-free).

Identify as a Survivor, Not a Victim: When dealing with any potential crisis, avoid thinking like a victim of circumstance and instead look for ways to resolve the problem. While the situation may be unavoidable, you can still stay focused on the most positive outcome possible.

Ask for Help: While being resourceful is an important part of resilience, it's also essential to know when to ask for help. During a crisis, of course your husband is your #1 support person, but also consider getting assistance from psychologists and counselors specially trained to deal with crisis situations.

Cultivate Good Problem-Solving Skills: In difficult situations, we sometimes develop tunnel vision and don't notice important details or take advantage of opportunities. Resilient individuals, on the other hand, are able to rationally look at a problem and work toward the best possible solution.

Embrace Change: Flexibility is an essential part of resilience. By learning how to be more adaptable, you'll be better equipped to respond when faced with a crisis. Resilient people can utilize tough times as an opportunity to try new things and move in new directions.

Nurture Yourself: Eating junky food, ignoring exercise, and not getting enough sleep are all common reactions to a crisis. Instead, by taking extra-good care of yourself, you can boost your overall health and resilience and be better able to handle whatever life sends your way. Nurture yourself and encourage your husband to do the same. It will strengthen both your individual resiliency and your marriage.

Regardless of your situation, your marriage, or how you were treated as a child, you *can* become more resilient. When you're faced with a crisis or stressful situation, you can't always choose what happens, but you can choose your response and become more resilient. Since bad things happen to all of us, learning to bounce back quickly from trouble is a really good quality to cultivate.

Why not start now?

Questions to Consider

- In what ways am I resilient?
- In what ways am I rigid and inflexible?
- How can I become more resilient?
- How can my husband and I help each other to be more resilient?

Improve Your Self-Care: Go to the Mirror

Mirror work is something I first tried about thirty years ago. I went to a workshop where author/teacher Louise Hay encouraged us to talk to ourselves in a mirror. I thought it was pretty weird and resisted it at first. But today I frequently use it in my counseling practice and in my personal life.

For many of us, looking at ourselves in the mirror isn't easy. We often start—automatically—to criticize ourselves: "Oh, I look old today," "My hair looks bad," or "Boy, I sure am fat, aren't I?"

This is the kind of stuff that encourages us *not* to look in a mirror; who wants to criticize themselves over and over again? (Only masochists, and I hope that doesn't describe you.)

Why would you look in the mirror and talk to yourself? Because it's one of the best ways I know to help yourself through a bad time and to "be your own therapist." There is something about looking in your own eyes that is very powerful. Perhaps it's because when we gaze (not stare) at ourselves in the mirror, we cannot avoid dealing with whatever it is that's bothering us.

I've had clients who start crying when they begin to do what I call "mirror work." Many of us are afraid to take a good look at ourselves; we try to avoid it. We're afraid we're going to see some really awful, ugly man meeting our gaze. As a result, we can get very out of touch with what we feel and want.

Then we wonder why we're so unhappy.

Mirror work isn't a miracle panacea; but it *can* be very helpful if we're feeling stuck or unhappy and want to get out of it and feel better.

Mirror work helps us not only to *see* ourselves, but to *listen* to ourselves. Many of us avoid listening to ourselves, thinking that we'll be happier if we don't. It doesn't work. Ignoring how we feel is very unwise. Sure, we don't need to pay attention to every little thing, but ignoring stuff that continues to bother us just ensures that we stay stuck in it.

When should I do "mirror work"? you may ask. Well, it can be really helpful in the following situations.

When things are bad, make eye contact with yourself in the mirror and say

- *"How can I help you feel better today?"*
- *"What can I do today to enjoy my life more?"*
- *"What can I do about (name your problem)?"*

When times are good, you can go to the mirror and say

- *"Thank you for this great husband/home/career."*
- *"I am really happy about _____. Thank you."*
- *"I am so grateful for my marriage/health/friends."*

When you're having a hard time talking to someone, talk to them in the mirror, as practice:

- *"I would like us to have sex more often"* (said to your husband, of course).
- *"I deserve a raise because _____"* (said to your boss).
- *"Mom, I need you to stop calling/texting me so much"* (no explanation needed).

Mirror work doesn't take long. If you have a minute, that's enough. If you have more time and find yourself crying or angry, give yourself as much time as you need to get to the bottom of your emotions. If you're crying, ask the man in the mirror: "Why are you so sad?" and then listen for the answer. You'll get one, and it may not be what you expect.

Mirror work "works" because it forces us to really look at and listen to ourselves. It's often hard because what we see and hear is painful. The potential benefits of this kind of work are great: we have a chance to slow down and pay attention to ourselves at a level that we rarely do in this rush-rush, crazy deadline world.

That's why I do it myself and use it with many of my clients. You can do it on your own and encourage your husband to do it too. It's usually best to do it on your own, because you connect with yourself on a deep level. I've had couples do it together, with mixed results. It's usually *much* better for you and your husband to do it on your own and *then* rendezvous afterward to talk about how it went.

(I'd like to thank Louise Hay for starting me on this path in 1987. She is a *very* wise woman. I've learned a lot from her in the past thirty years *and* she is the happiest ninety-year-old person I know.)

Youthfulness, Mental Health, and Your Marriage

One way to keep your marriage lively is to feel youthful. I don't mean imitating young people, I mean being as youthful, vital, alive, and healthy as you can be, regardless of your age.

I recently turned sixty-three and I am damned proud of it. I have my share of wrinkles and gray hair, but I *feel* youthful and healthy. I'd like to share some of what works for me—and my married clients—in hopes it will be useful to you too.

Meditate: It teaches you to listen to your body and tell yourself the truth about what's going on with you, and helps you get in touch with your desires, motivations, and fears. Meditation has been proven to help relieve stress, decrease chronic pain, and improve sleep—and has recently been found to slow down cognitive decline. And it's a great activity to share with your husband, even if it's only five minutes a day. What's not to like?

> Sean: "Michael kept urging me and my husband [Don] to try meditation. I resisted, until a friend told me that he tried it and it helped lower his blood pressure. So I grudgingly tried it; it really did calm me down. I told Don about it and so now, every morning, we sit quietly together for a few minutes and let our minds go as empty as possible. It helps us stay calm and is one of the best things we do together."

Pay attention to your body, but don't obsess: take care of your health so you don't worry unnecessarily. Don't weigh yourself too often. Let your clothes be your guide—if they don't fit comfortably, then decide how you'd like to handle that. Exercise is wonderful, but it only works in the long run if you find something you enjoy. Try new things and experiment with combining them. Too much routine can be deadly; keep yourself interested.

Terrance: "I've been unhappy with my body my whole life. After marrying Curtis, I finally started to be less obsessive about my weight. Curtis loves me as I am, why can't I? So I'm experimenting with things I like to do. The thing I like at the moment is walking—taking long walks. I have graduated to steep hills and just got a new pair of super-supportive walking shoes. Curtis joins me on the walks a lot of the time; it's a nice, healthy thing we do together."

Notice what you eat: try this Zen "paying attention" exercise.

- Step 1: Only eat when you are really paying attention to what you're eating (for most of us, we can only eat about three bites before we start to zone out and go on autopilot).
- Step 2: When you stop paying attention to what you're eating, stop eating.
- Step 3: Refocus and come back to the present moment: What are you eating? Do you really taste it? If so, go back to Step 1 and begin eating again.

This exercise sounds simple, but it is very powerful. It works particularly well with whatever your comfort (i.e., habitually addictive) food is. For me, after the first few bites, I'm usually over my "craving" and can leave the rest alone. This exercise alone helped me kick an ice cream "addiction."

Yuri: "I have quite a sweet tooth. When Michael told me about this, I thought it sounded ridiculous. But I tried it and damned if it doesn't work. I can usually only eat a few bites of dessert before I start to shovel it in. So then I stop eating until I can pay attention to what I'm eating. I can't do this all the time, but when I do it, it really helps. I've actually lost a couple of pounds just by paying attention! I'm trying to get Bill [his husband] to try it. So far, no go. But I'll keep putting it out there and we'll see how it goes."

Be a little "goofy": let go of the seriousness of life. About 5 percent of things are seriously important; the other 95 percent aren't. Can you laugh at the silly things you do? Try it and watch your blood pressure drop and that crease in your forehead disappear.

> Ken: "I take things so seriously. When Michael and I talked about this, I thought he was being rather foolish, encouraging me to be 'goofy'. But I thought about it some more and decided, what do I have to lose? So, I signed up for a hip-hop dance class. I was always curious about it, but never had the guts to do it. I actually like it. It really has loosened me up and my husband [Carl] says I'm a lot more fun when I come home from the class."

When in doubt, try moderation: a little dessert, one glass of wine, one morning to lie in bed, one afternoon to do nothing but read magazines—moderation is a wonderful thing. Living in the extremes is exhausting.

> Ivan: "I have a very addictive personality; when Michael suggested this, I thought it would be impossible. So, I took baby steps—indulging in a bit less of things I normally obsess over—and it wasn't so bad. I don't think I'll ever be a really 'moderate' person, but I'm becoming less intense and habitual in my eating, drinking, and bar-hopping. My husband is very happy about this, no surprise there."

Give of yourself: This is the fastest way out of self-pity (which is terribly aging). Get out there in the world and help someone else. You don't need to be Mother Teresa to make a difference. Got an hour a month? Some worthy organization would love to have you. Do something that makes your heart happy; a happy heart is a youthful heart.

> Finn: "I am not the giving type; I've had to fight for everything I've got, and I'm not big on sharing. However, I thought I'd give it a try and was surprised how good I felt about myself. I guess I don't have to be as

selfish as I used to be. My husband says that when I come home from my volunteer work, I'm at my very best. So I guess I'll keep going."

There is a lot of pressure on us as gay men to look youthful, but much more important is that we *feel* youthful. You and your husband might want to consider some of the above suggestions, as well as these.

Questions to Consider

- What does it mean to be youthful?
- How youthful do I feel?
- What do I do that keeps me feeling alive, vital, and energetic?
- What do I do that makes me feel old and over the hill?
- How can my husband and I help each other to feel alive and youthful, regardless of our biological age?

As we get older, it's hard to tell what activities are a good fit for us as married gay men. How do we know when we're too old for something? Who will tell us and should we even be listening to them?

This letter puts it in a rather surprising way.

Dear Michael:

Last night my friends and I went to a "Foam Party" at a local gay club. We were having a great time, looking at cute guys in their speedos, and then we saw a bunch of old guys in their fifties dancing in the foam in their baggy old swimsuits. It really turned us off. Don't you think at that age you need to stay home with your knitting? Just kidding, but not really.

Mr. Foam Party (age twenty-five)

Dear Mr. Foam Party:

I like your question, despite your impertinent comment about knitting. As gay men who are getting older (if we're lucky), how do we know what's age-appropriate for us? It's easy to say, "Oh, just do what feels right to you," but what about being "appropriate"? And what is "appropriate" anyway? Maybe it's about being nonoffensive. But then, isn't it impossible not to offend someone just by being yourself? If life is all about not offending people, none of us would have much fun at all, would we?

When I was twenty-five, I dreaded being fifty. It seemed so far away. I remember calling one bar—patronized by older gay men—a "wrinkle room." All my friends called it that too. We thought we were just having fun and being cute. Cut to the present: As you age into your forties, fifties, and beyond, what and where is your place in the gay community? Can you and your husband go to events for gay elders *and* foam parties, or is that just too weird? Can you enjoy both knitting *and* going to gay bars and clubs patronized by younger gay men? Or should you "know better," "stay in your place," and avoid situations where much younger gay men may be hanging out?

We're talking about Ghettoization by Age. I wish that when I was twenty-five I had known some cool older gay guys who enjoyed life and didn't base their happiness on a perfect body or face. But in all honesty, I was like you, Mr. Foam Party, I only wanted to be around people my age. Why do we ghettoize by age? Fear is behind all of this. We cling to people like us—in age, race, income, education, religion—because it's comfortable and familiar.

By ghettoizing by age, we miss out on so much. We miss out on variety. We miss out on learning from those older and younger than we are. Don't we all need each other? Can't we all learn from each other? Can you see older gay men at a foam party and see yourself (still enjoying life and trying new things) in twenty-five years? Or is it painful to see a fifty-year-old gay man having fun because you can't visualize yourself at that age as a happy, fulfilled elder?

Questions to Consider

- What do I think I'm too old for?
- How did I decide that?
- Do I have access to the carefree, playful (ageless) side of myself?
- How can my husband and I be more playful with each other?

You may think that these questions don't really apply to you and your husband. "After all," you may be saying, "we don't worry about what's appropriate or not, we just do what feels right." But isn't it worthwhile to consider *how* you decide what feels right? Age-appropriate attitudes and behaviors may not seem so interesting to you when you're in your twenties and thirties, but they get increasingly more relevant in your forties, fifties, and beyond.

Mr. Foam Party doesn't mention if he's married—probably not—but for those of us who are, if there is a significant age difference between you and your husband, you've probably already had to deal with this stuff. For example, if he's forty-six and you're twenty-seven, I'll bet that aging and age-appropriate behavior have already been topics for you both, as they have for these four men.

Sven: "I'm twenty-two years older than my husband—he's forty-two and I'm sixty-four—and age has been a big challenge for us, from when we first started dating. He felt that I was acting too "old" and rigid and I felt that he was acting too "young" and immature. It was a continual source of disagreement for us. Each of us tried to pull the other into our own age category, and it didn't work."

Kevin: "My husband is forty-four and I'm twenty-nine, and sometimes I do feel the age difference. He's already talking about saving for retirement and I just want to go out and have fun. We've had some difficult discussions about how to meet in the middle—it's an uneasy topic for us."

Joaquin: "My husband is sixty-eight and I'm fifty-two. He wants to retire soon and I don't. Also, he's starting to have all these physical problems and our sex life has taken a big hit. How do we work all these age-related problems through? We were both so healthy and active when we first met. Now he's not, but I still am. Help!"

Khayal: "I have a husband who wants to act, dress, and party like my friends and me, but we're in our early twenties and he's in his late thirties. He imitates us and it drives me crazy. I keep telling him, 'I *like* it that you're older, calmer, and more mature. Please don't try to act so young; it's *very* unattractive to me.' He doesn't listen though."

As Mr. Foam Party's e-mail illustrates, it's common in our community to make fun of people who are not aging in a way we consider "attractive." This is one reason that plastic surgery and injectibles like Botox and Restylene are increasingly popular with gay men. Once the domain of straight, wealthy women, these expensive and invasive procedures promise a lifetime of looking twenty-five, thirty-five, or whatever.

This is self-hatred repackaged as "Don't I deserve it?"

This kind of backward logic (i.e., the outside is what matters most and the inside is secondary) makes a mess of our lives—and then we wonder why it's so hard to maintain the health of our marriages. Meaningful relationships are not about sharing the same plastic surgeon; they're about depth of personality, feelings, integrity, humor—all the stuff you can't sculpt with a surgical blade or syringeful of Botox.

Regardless of your age, it's healthy for you and your husband to eat well, take care of yourselves, exercise, and be good to your bodies. It's unhealthy to obsess on your *image*—or his—at the expense of your inner feelings and emotions.

I must admit, I'm tempted to ask Mr. Foam Party, "If a foam party isn't the place you'd expect to find a bunch of fifty-year-old gay men, can you find a way to celebrate with them anyway? Do you see how one person thinking and living a little outside the box can make it possible for *all* of us to move outside that same damned, tight little box?"

But after all, I'm sixty-three years old, so I won't be impertinent and ask this young man such a challenging question. Instead, I might say to him, very politely, of course, "We're all in this together; can we enjoy growing, maturing, and aging together too?"

Beneath Anger, There Is Sadness

Have you ever noticed that, when you argue with your husband, there is always hurt beneath your anger? In the beginning stages of couple's counseling, a lot of angry words usually fly across the room. The couple isn't ready yet to address their hurt and sadness; they'd rather vent their anger and frustration with each other. While this is often a necessary step, it's not very helpful for long. Sure, you can vent, but venting without exploring the *reason* you're venting is usually a waste of time.

I can tell that a couple is really ready to do some good work on their relationship when they start to show some vulnerability. This isn't an easy place to get to. It's scary to be vulnerable; your husband can really hurt you when you show him your weak spots. However, if you're going to stay together as a couple, you both need to go beneath your anger and get to what's below.

In 1996, when I was a middle school counselor in San Francisco, I (foolishly) volunteered to facilitate an "anger management group" for the most out-of-control boys in the school. Most of the boys in this group were in trouble with the law; they stole cars, belonged to gangs, carried guns—you know, they were just the kind of people I usually hang out with.

One of the main things I learned from facilitating this group was that underneath anger, there is always sadness and hurt. *Always.* No exceptions.

When I was in middle school, in 1966, it wasn't safe to be gay in my small Ohio town. I felt trapped and helpless. I begged my dad to move our family to a bigger town, where I might fit in (and I thought, desperately, that there might be more people "like me"). He refused, telling me, "You'll just have to wait till you go away to college."

I was sad, hurt, and subsequently, very angry. What did I do with my anger? It wasn't safe to show it openly, so I started scratching my arms—until they bled. I wasn't exactly a "cutter," I was a "scratcher"; same difference. And it did feel better; I had an external way to express my internal pain.

When I turned sixteen and got my driver's license, I drove very fast and recklessly. I would borrow my mom's car and go 120 mph on country roads. Sometimes I was going too fast to stop at stop signs.

The anger didn't stop when I got to college; I was afraid to come out there too. It was 1971 and as an undergraduate at the University of Cincinnati, I began to sleep with other boys (clandestinely). I also bought a used Pontiac GTO (with a 396, V-8 engine) and I drove so wild and so fast that no one was willing to ride with me.

Fast-forward about twenty-five years: I was facilitating a meeting of the anger management group—for those middle school boys—and they wanted to talk about cars. Sure, I said, go ahead. So they went around the circle and these tough, macho little guys talked about the cars they knew, loved, and dreamed about. It was pretty typical stuff until one of the guys, the same young man who had been arrested the week before for stealing a car, said, "Yeah, I remember my uncle's Cadillac. It was pretty fine. Then one day, I saw someone shoot him dead in it."

The group went silent. This boy didn't cry. He just looked down at the floor. No one knew what to say.

Finally, the sadness and hurt came out. Slowly, one by one, all of the boys started to talk about people they knew who had been shot, killed, or hurt.

A few months later, I was driving home from the supermarket and found myself becoming more and more angry at each stop sign. I started to curse other drivers, for no reason. I yelled inside my car (I'm glad the windows were up). After driving a few more blocks, I pulled the car over and looked at myself in the rear-view mirror. I asked myself, "What is going on with you?" as my therapist had encouraged me to do.

To my surprise, I began to cry. And cry. And cry. Sobbing in my car, I started to say, out loud: "I hate my job. My boyfriend doesn't really love me. I don't love him either. I don't like living in San Francisco. And I feel so lonely I could die."

My sadness and hurt had finally broken through my anger. The boys had taught me well.

I encourage you and your husband to break through your anger too; anger is always a cover-up for what lies beneath, and what lies beneath is the real treasure. It's this kind of vulnerability that will bring you two closer, but there's usually fear in the way. And that fear has a basis in reality: when you let your man see your weakest spots, it is possible that he could use them against you. That's a risk we all take. However, if you don't take the risk and let him "in" (and vice versa), you can expect endless repetitions of the same arguments, over and over.

Adam: "I don't know why Humberto and I have the same arguments over and over again and never seem to make any progress. We're both pretty hot-tempered, so we need to get our emotions out, but once they're out, we get stuck on how to move beyond them."

Uri: "I had individual therapy and instead of being so angry with Wes [his husband] I started to let him know how much he hurt me by things he did. Well, it didn't work! He just kept being so defensive and throwing it back at me. My vulnerability just made me an easier target for him. I need him to be vulnerable too!"

Uri puts it very well: it doesn't work if only *one* of you is willing to be vulnerable. *Both* of you need to be willing. Otherwise, the still-angry one will just let the vulnerable one have it. He tried to take away his husband's anger by addressing and working through his own. It was a good start, but he couldn't do it alone.

Adam and Humberto, on the other hand, are both so stuck in their angry patterns that when they express how pissed off they are, they don't know where to go from there.

We can't take away our husband's anger, but we sure can address our own. When you feel angry, I encourage you to dig a little deeper and find the hurt beneath it. Tend to your hurt and sadness, and I'll bet your anger and rage go away too. This is how we can take care of ourselves, and by extension, take care of each other.

Let's look at another underlying cause of anger in marriages: disappointment.

Questions to Consider
- What do you do when you're disappointed?
- How do you handle it?
- How does your husband?

Recently, I experienced a surprising disappointment. I had contacted the mayor's office of the city where I live, asking for assistance with a city-related problem, and did not receive the help I'd asked for. My phone calls and e-mails were not returned and I was not treated well. Trying to make things right, I wrote to the mayor's office, explaining my experience, asking for an apology for being treated poorly and an acknowledgment of mistakes made. What I got was a complete denial of any mistakes made at all. Wow, was I disappointed. I had asked for help and did not receive it.

There is no avoiding disappointment: things don't go the way you want. Someone—your husband, perhaps?—doesn't do what you think is right. You want something and you don't get it. So what can you do about it? Here are some ways that we typically react. Some are more helpful than others, but let's list them all:

Sadness: This is a natural response. I was sad when the guy from the mayor's office didn't apologize. I was sad when two people in that office treated me poorly and wouldn't own up to it. I wanted to be treated with respect and kindness. When it didn't happen, I sure felt sad.

Revenge: "You hurt me; I'm going to hurt you." While this sounds appealing, it really gets you nowhere. In fact, if you keep perpetuating (and escalating) the revenge, it often gets jacked up so high that it makes you miserable—and then it's really hard to stop it. I've seen many couples play out various (subtle and not-so-subtle) revenge strategies with each other—always with poor outcomes. It just doesn't work.

Confusion: "Why did this happen to me?" We try to understand, but we can't. We can't know how other people—like our husband, friends, and family—feel and why they do the things they do. Sometimes, our mind just keeps spinning and spinning, trying to understand; have you ever found it hard to sleep because your mind was spinning like this? Your mind can't figure it out, but it doesn't want to admit it.

Self-Blame: "What did I do to bring this about?" This is a useful question *if* (that's a big "if") we use it constructively and not just to beat ourselves up. For example, it's constructive to ask: "How did I contribute to this unhappy situation with my husband?" And let's be honest; we all contribute to a disappointing outcome, but we don't like to admit it. The next time you feel disappointed, ask yourself, "How could I have handled this situation better?" or "What would I do differently next time something like this happens?" This can be really useful; we *can* learn from our disappointments. (I know I'm trying to learn from mine.)

Other-Blame: This is typically an initial (and normal) response: we blame our husband, our boss, or someone else. It's *all their* fault. We avoid taking any responsibility and play the victim. "I don't deserve this—why are you treating me this way?" It's okay to indulge in this for a little while, but ultimately, playing the victim isn't helpful. It is, unfortunately, a very popular way of coping with disappointment in a marriage.

Acceptance: This is the hardest response of all. Acceptance doesn't mean condoning poor behavior; it *does* mean that there's really nothing more that you can (constructively) do about it and that, by holding onto it, you're likely to prolong your suffering. A client recently told me, "I realized that there's nothing I can do to make my husband admit he was wrong. I could keep torturing myself by saying, 'He should admit it,' or I could accept that I was helpless to change his mind. It sounds simple, but it's not easy."

There's no avoiding disappointment in marriage, friendships, work, and all aspects of our lives, but we *always* have a choice regarding how we respond.

You may go through some of the above responses and wonder: "What do I do now?" I recommend that you allow yourself to feel *all* your emotions and not judge them. Eventually, strong emotions will fade and—hopefully—you'll reach some form of acceptance (and peace).

Do I Have Enough?

As a psychotherapist, over the years I've heard many married couples say that they don't have enough of the good things in life. I'd like to share with you a few of the things that I think really matter in making your marriage feel "full" of good things:

Fun: Enjoyment, amusement, and pleasure—that's a good definition of fun. Fun doesn't have to be expensive or dramatic. You don't need a trip to Europe; you could instead enjoy an afternoon in a park, a hike, or a great comedy movie. Your definition of fun is your own; all that matters is that you and your husband include it in your married life on a regular basis.

Friends: If you have two or three good friends you can call at midnight when a truck hits your car and you're in the ER (this happened to me), then you probably have enough friends. Many people we call friends are really acquaintances; you know a bit about them, but they really aren't people you can count on. A friend may not like your situation, but they're gonna get out of bed and drive to the ER to sit with you for six hours until the doctor will see you.

Alone time: Without alone time, it's easy to lose your center and start to "spin out" when your husband disagrees with you or things don't go your way. You don't have to meditate or pray to be alone; just take time throughout your day to enjoy the sunshine, your cat, or a cup of coffee.

Money: What is enough money? Enough to easily pay all your bills and have some left over for fun. Enough to save for emergencies and toward retirement. Money isn't a goal; it's a vehicle. It's a path to get where you want. You may think that you and your husband need a home of your own, but you might really want to feel safe and happy in your marriage, and you think a home will provide that. Or you may think you need a raise at work, but what you really want is to feel appreciated and valued.

Structure/spontaneity: Some of us are way too structured—we plan things to death and it can make our husband feel trapped or smothered. Without a plan, our anxiety jumps. On the other hand, some of us are so loose that we rarely get anything done (this is also hard on husbands). When I work with overly rigid couples, we focus on how to gradually experience *not* planning. It usually invokes anxiety (at first), but that shifts over time. On the other hand, if you and your husband never get much accomplished, I'd help you both to begin to create more structure in your life and to reward yourselves when you accomplish your goal(s).

Questions to Consider

- What do I have enough of?
- What do I *not* have enough of?
- What is one step I can take to get more of what I want?
- How can my husband and I appreciate all that we already have?

These questions are really just the beginning. I invite you and your husband to sit down and—together or separately—make an "enough/not enough" list. It's good to know that some areas of your life are just fine, and it's helpful to notice where there is a lack, so you can begin to change that, together.

Fat? Old? Ugly?

I cannot tell you how often I have heard gay men lament that they are one of the above. At this point in the book, you may wonder: "Why did Michael include this topic in this section?" I'll tell you why: when we begin to believe that we are fat, old, or ugly—or start to believe that our husband is moving in that direction—we are headed for trouble.

Big trouble.

Let me explain: Of course we will all get older, and we'll probably gain some weight as we age, but who says that this has to be a problem, or that it makes us ugly?

Gay culture, that's who.

I recently saw an ad in a gay periodical: the words "FAT? OLD? UGLY?" comprised the large font headline (nice, huh? so helpful and encouraging). It was an ad for plastic surgery—playing on our worst fears and offering a very expensive (and temporary) solution. If only plastic surgery would solve all of our self-esteem problems, I'd probably sign up myself.

Sometimes I am asked to do psychological evaluations of people considering plastic surgery. The (ethical) plastic surgeons I work with refer clients to me when the surgeons think that the client's expectations are unrealistic. The surgeons are afraid that their clients will be disappointed regardless of how well the plastic surgery turns out.

And often, they're right.

Because more often than not, "fat, old, and ugly" is a state of mind, not a state of body. I have often seen clients who feel *worse* after their plastic surgery than they did before. Why? Because their expectations were unrealistic. Fewer wrinkles, a flatter stomach, and a tighter butt may be nice, but they don't change the way we feel about ourselves. It takes more than that. A change in the outside doesn't mean a change on the inside.

And it's how we feel about ourselves—and our husbands—that greatly affects the emotional stability of our marriage. I work with clients on this kind of self-esteem stuff all the time. Many of us have a lot of family-of-origin negativity to undo. Many of us were told all kinds of strange, negative stuff when we were younger, and 99.99 percent of it wasn't—and isn't—true.

Most negative stuff that people told us was really about them: jealous, unhappy, scared parents/siblings/teachers/lovers may have told you all kinds of unkind things about yourself. To me, this is brainwashing: our innate ability and desire to approve of ourselves got corrupted.

Have you ever seen a baby who said, "I just hate my nose," or "My hips are too big"? Babies love everything about themselves and *you* were once like that. You started out just adoring yourself—your *natural* state—and then, over time, other people brainwashed you and messed with your head. But here's some good news: you can *undo* all those years of brainwashing.

Questions to Consider

- Who told me I was fat/old/ugly? How old was I? Why did they say that to me?
- Is there a core part of me that is immune to what other people think about me?
- How can I get in touch with that place more and more?
- What situations bring up these negative feelings for me?

Remember mirror work? Well, it can be really useful when you're working with a distorted or unrealistic body image. So, look in the mirror at yourself. Don't do this with your husband; do it on your own. You may initially cringe or critique what you see. That's okay; do your critique and analysis, if you must, and then you're ready to do some good, deep work. Look in the mirror; it's time to begin to deprogram yourself. Tell yourself things such as

- *"I am the perfect weight."*
- *"I am handsome at every age."*
- *"I am willing to love my appearance."*

You may not believe this stuff at first: you're planting a seed, and a seed takes time to grow into a great big gorgeous tree. If these phrases really stick in your throat, use the word "willing" in your affirmations: "I may not believe I am handsome today, but I am *willing* to believe it."

If you want to do this with your husband, you can try your "deprogramming" phrases out on each other. Warning: do this *only* if you can do it lovingly and supportively. If you're currently criticizing each other, work on yourself first; *then* you can bring this into couple's work with your (now-supportive) man.

There is an illusion that, if you think your husband's getting fat or unattractive, it's his responsibility to fix it. *Wrong!* It's not his problem. It's yours. So start by working on yourself. No matter how much you love him and want him to be happy and healthy, you can only change yourself. Accepting this will make your marriage a whole lot happier.

But it's a tough one for some of us. We think that if only *he* would change his appearance/weight/clothes/habits/diet—you name it—that we would be content. It doesn't work. Why? Because you'll just find *another* thing to fault him for and then pressure, nag, or manipulate him to change *that*. This kind of "We-have-to-fix-everything-that's-wrong-with-you" behavior will make you both miserable. For many couples, this "you need to change" cycle never ends. Plus, how would you like to be on the receiving end of that nagging?

I thought so.

So stop it. Stop it by focusing on yourself and your unhappiness with yourself. That's all you have any control over. I don't care how much you care about your husband; you can't make him quit smoking, eat healthier, or exercise more, no matter how clever a manipulator you are. And don't you think he would be resentful if you try? Wouldn't you be? Few of us are so naïve that we can't feel when we're being manipulated to do something we don't want to do but that our husband wants us to do.

Don't go there.

No matter who you marry—Zac Efron, I'm thinking of you right now—he's going to age and his body is going to change. So focus on finding your own peace of mind and lay off trying to change your husband. Even plastic surgery is only temporary; but peace of mind lasts.

Fathers and Mothers

When I work with married couples, they're often quite surprised to find how much their fathers and mothers are (unconscious) models for their own adult relationships. To paraphrase Freud, we model our adult relationships on those that our fathers and mothers had with each other. For many of us, this is not good news. However, it may explain why our past relationships may have emulated our parents' relationship (for better and for worse).

This may sound simplistic, but I think there's a lot of truth to it. In my own case, I sure played it out according to Freud's predictions: before I came out, I always picked women who were much like my dad. Whenever these women met my dad, they just loved each other. After I came out, I picked men who were like Dad, and Dad and my boyfriends got along much better than Dad and I ever did.

And yes, I played out my mom's role with all these girlfriends and boy-friends: I was attentive to them, looked after them, and catered to their needs (much more than they did to mine). It took me a lot of therapy to see that I was imitating Mom and picking partners like Dad in my own relationships.

I don't do this anymore, thanks to my own therapy, and now I assist others who want to break their own patterns and *not* have relationships like Mom and Dad's.

For a specific example of this, let's touch base with Ethan and Jake, our case study couple, and see how they're handling their family-of-origin stuff.

Ethan: "One of the things I've learned from our couple's therapy is that I keep acting like my dad and expect Jake to act like my mom. It's a very deep-seated pattern and I'm finding it hard to break."

Jake: "I never realized how much I play out my family stuff with Ethan. I have expected him to be the stoic, silent type, just like my dad. And I ended up just like my mom, stuffing my emotions and trying to make my man happy."

Ethan and Jake realized, with the help of therapy, that they were projecting old family-of-origin stuff onto each other, and it was playing havoc with their marriage. How did they begin to turn it around?

Ethan: "I'm working on changing myself because I sure as hell can't change Jake. I see how being so rock-like makes my world small and rigid. I'm asking my friends, especially my women friends, to help me talk more about feelings. At first, it felt so awkward. But I'm getting better at it. I actually like being able to be more spontaneous and expressive. It still brings up anxiety for me, but less and less as I get better at it."

Jake: "I am starting to be more social and less focused on video games. I've used video games since I was a little kid to escape from my unhappy, repressed family. I don't want to hide behind video games anymore. Being on the swim team has been really great, because I'm with this group of gay guys and we're all focused on an intense physical activity, so the social stuff comes more easily than if I was at a party or a bar."

We all have family-of-origin issues (aka "Mommy and Daddy baggage"), so rather than try to avoid them, which never works, why not face them and work through them? A marriage is a great vehicle in which to do so; you and your husband can talk about your family and how it still affects you. I ask clients, "What about your family is still haunting you?" There's always something, but we're never stuck and we need never play the victim. Try using the questions below to start a conversation with your husband. Freud would be proud!

Questions to Consider

- How much is your marriage like your parents' marriage?
- How is it different?
- How much is your husband like one of your parents?
- How much are *you* like one of your parents?

Retire, But Don't Quit

Earlier in this chapter, we briefly touched on age differences in gay marriages, but I'd like to bring your attention to an age-related phenomenon that many gay couples avoid talking about until we're forced to: retirement. You may be forty years from retiring, but someday, if you stick around long enough, you too will be looking at this interesting but poorly understood phase of married gay life. So let's talk about it and see how you can use it to strengthen your marriage.

Have you and your husband ever talked about retirement? Many of us don't until we're in our fifties or sixties. That's not the most skillful way to do it. And I'm not talking only about the financial stuff, although that's a big piece. I'm talking about the *psychological* aspects of retirement and how it can help (or hurt) your relationship with your husband.

Questions to Consider
- What does retirement mean to you? Describe your ideal retirement.
- Does your husband have a plan for his retirement?
- How similar are your retirement plans? How are they different?

I turned sixty-three last year and am being increasingly asked by friends: "When are you going to retire?" It's a fair question, since AARP started sending me membership cards thirteen years ago. In my case, I don't want to retire because I really like the work I do; having a private practice, doing workshops, and writing books and newspaper columns is (mostly) fun for me, so why would I quit?

However, in reality, someday I might want to work less. Or, if my health changes, I may need to work less. In that case, what would I do with myself? How would I be as a "retired" person? I'm not sure, but I'm thinking about it.

While I haven't had any clients who were big-time lottery winners (yet), I have had a number of clients who've had the opportunity to retire early. For example:

- Corey: At the young age of thirty-five, sold his business for several million dollars. Initially, he was really happy, but after taking several long, luxurious vacations, he misses having a purpose and a structure for his life.

- Ramon: Recently diagnosed with a serious disease, he's in his early forties. He thinks he should retire, but is afraid that if he does, his will to live might falter.
- Ismael: At forty-seven, he inherited over two million dollars and wondered if he should stay with his job because even though it's stressful, he finds it very fulfilling.
- Francisco: Burnt out from his job, he has the money to retire, but is afraid to because "I'm only fifty-three. Without my job, what would I do with my time?"
- Johnny retired at sixty-five and now, at sixty-eight, has been offered consulting work that he might enjoy. Should he jump back into the working world, or stay with "retirement"?

After many years of working with clients approaching retirement, I've concluded that, while it's okay to retire, it's a bad idea to "quit" on life. As gay men, without our work, what do we do to create meaning and structure in our lives? We all—regardless of age—need to have certain elements in our lives to be fulfilled. These include the following.

Mental stimulation: We need to be around interesting people who talk about provocative subjects. The Taoists say, "travel is the best teacher," offering us lots of new people, places, and things to be intrigued with and stimulated by. Do you and your husband provide mental stimulation for each other? Or do you find the two of you becoming intellectually "dull" as you age?

Body: Our bodies need to be stretched and exercised. Regardless of our health (or lack thereof), our bodies need movement, and not movement that we hate. Finding something that is enjoyable is the only way that most of us will stay active. What do you and your husband enjoy in the realms of exercise and movement? Are there things you can do together?

Spirit: This is often overlooked. I'm not talking about religion; I'm talking about a spiritual connection, for example, "This isn't just about me, there's a big world out there and what is my place in it?" and "What am I here to give and what am I here to get?" Do you and your man share any kind of prayer, yoga, meditation, or quiet time? Sitting together quietly for a few minutes in the morning can be a great way to begin your day and strengthen your emotional connection.

Social connections: Loneliness is a killer. Literally. I hear many men tell me that they feel lonely in their marriage. I ask them, are you keeping your friendships alive? Your husband cannot be your everything, no matter how amazing, kind, and loving he is. Social connections are crucial to a good marriage, particularly as we get older. Many couples reach an age where their peers begin to die and they find themselves increasingly older than the majority of their community. If this becomes true for you, will you and your husband reach out to younger people, or will you be critical and judgmental and find yourselves increasingly isolated?

Fun: What's still fun for you and your man? It may have changed since you were younger. Have you given up on fun and become bitter, cynical elders or are you both open to trying new things? As a younger person, I thought gardening and walking were boring. Now, at sixty-three, I really enjoy both of these activities. I still like to dance to interesting music, but nightclubs aren't a good fit for me anymore. As we age in our marriage, what is fun for us and how do we find it?

Most of us won't be able to retire before our sixties, so these questions may not reflect a pressing need for you. But why not plan ahead? Surely, you've changed in the past ten, twenty, or thirty years, and those changes will continue into the next ten, twenty, or thirty years. Talk with your husband about when you'd like to retire (if at all) and how you'd like it to be.

Who knows? It may happen sooner than you think and if you and your husband work toward it together, retirement could it be the most fulfilling years of your marriage.

How Gay Relationships Change as We Age

A monogamous marriage, like an open marriage, is an ongoing balancing act. Every couple has their own preferences as to how predictable or not they want their marriage to be. Some men want a lot of stimuli: change, surprise, and adventure. They welcome spontaneity. Other men are more attracted to stability and the ease and comfort that it brings. How can you and your husband find your own balance?

What we want from marriage—and a husband—changes over time. And as we age, what we can *give* and hope to *receive* from our husband will change as well. I'd like to share with you some of my observations of how gay relationships change and evolve as we age.

In your twenties: Excitement and experimentation prevail; everyone's a potential husband. This is the era when you're supposed to date/hook up a lot, have lots of (safe) sex and a variety of sexual and romantic "experiences." Why not go to lots of parties and try different kinds of lovemaking with a wide range of people? Why not experiment with topping and bottoming, leather and lace, restraints and intense sex? Now is the time. Until the end of your twenties, most of us are still avidly experimenting—and this is a great time to do it.

Jonathan: "I thought I wanted to get married, but I just couldn't find the right guy. I kept thinking 'this guy is the one' but then, each guy turned out not to be. Finally, I realized that I wasn't ready to settle down yet. I need to get more clear on who I am and what I want before committing to anyone."

Eddy: "I am not someone who's into the gay party/bar scene, so I don't fit the stereotype of a twenty-four-year-old gay guy. I like a quieter, more introspective life. I love to read and go to plays and poetry readings. I find myself attracted to older, more stable, guys, but no way am I ready to settle down with one man. I'm still finding out who I am and what I like. I'm still creating myself!"

In your thirties: Your love life is probably growing more selective; maybe you're embarking on marriage or another form of long-term relationship. The struggles of vulnerability beckon—how to lay down your (emotional) armor and really let another man see you, flaws and all. You may start to notice physical changes like hair thinning/loss and a gently increasing waistline. Sexually, you may have a good sense of what you like (and don't) and are getting good at expressing it with your partner.

Travis: "I have dated a lot of guys—I'm a bartender, after all—and a few of them have been 'serious.' I am getting closer and closer to being ready to settle down. The guy I'm dating now isn't my usual 'type,' but I find myself trusting him and opening up to him in a way I never have before. It's nice, but kinda scary too."

Evan: "I noticed that in my romantic relationships, I would let guys get close to me but when it hit a certain point, I'd push them away. I've sabotaged a lot of good relationships that way. I guess I'm afraid to be vulnerable. I'm taking a good look at that now in therapy.' "

In your forties: If you're in a marriage or long-term relationship, you may be struggling with boredom or repetition. If you're single, you may be wondering why. This is a time when some of us begin therapy or some other form of personal growth work to figure out what we're doing wrong in the relationship department. You may be noticing more physical changes and finding them hard to accept. Some of us take up with much younger lovers, in one last gasp of trying to feel/be "young." On the positive side: sex with your husband is typically more of an "art" than an endurance contest.

> Elijah: "I don't know why I can't have a good relationship. I'm forty-two and I've never had a relationship last more than six months. Most of my friends are getting married and I don't have a clue what I'm doing wrong."
>
> Istez: "I've been married for about a year now, and the newness has worn off, which is both good and bad. The good is that I'm more comfortable with Hank [his husband], but the bad is that I'm afraid I'm already bored with the structure and predictability of marriage and fantasizing about having sex with hot guys I see at the gym."

In your fifties: This is hard age for many of us; can we accept that we're now in the second half of our lives? Or are we in denial with liposuction, plastic surgery, Botox, Viagra, and expensive personal trainers? We may have desperately fought symptoms of physical aging when we were in our forties, but as we enter our fifties, can we (finally) make peace with our body, the parts we love and the parts that embarrass us? Sexually, our body may not always do what we want it to do. How can we work with that? Do we still feel desirable when we're no longer young and cute?

> Matthew: "I am finding it really difficult to enjoy my fifties. I am losing my hair and my looks and my formerly great body and it's really hard to accept. I have found a boyfriend who's about twenty years younger than I am, and I know I'm doing it to feel younger through him, but I can't help it. He's not really husband material, but sex with him is terrific."

Paco: "I have made peace with my body—I have a little beer belly now—and my sex drive has really dropped off, which is okay with me. Unfortunately, my husband still has a strong libido, so he's pretty frustrated. I don't want to take all those erection-enhancer pills, but he's pushing me to."

In your sixties: We may be retired—or approaching it—and have more time for ourselves and our husband, but what is our life like now? Are we enjoying a more peaceful life? Can we slow down and enjoy it, or does it make us feel old and out of it? Sexually, can we enjoy being sensual and erotic, or must we always orgasm to feel okay about ourselves? Our penises don't always stay hard when we want them to; how do we handle this? Masturbation may become more interesting as intercourse becomes more logistically challenging. Affection may be more important than sex; wisdom informs physical enthusiasm.

Jim: "I really miss my old sex life. I just can't keep an erection dependably and my husband can. Yes, I admit I'm jealous. Some of my friends say that I need to accept these changes, but I really don't want to! I want my old body back and I really miss being a top (in anal sex). I hate to admit it, but getting older sucks."

Theo: "Mark and I have been together for seven years now, married for one. We're wondering how to retire since neither of us has saved up enough money to quit working. We're thinking of selling our house and moving somewhere cheaper, but we don't want to leave all our friends behind. I wish we'd saved more for retirement."

Munir: "Don [his husband] retired a few years ago, but I still like working. I don't know what I'd do if I didn't have my work and the satisfaction I get from it. Most of my friends are from work too. What would I do without my job? I think I'd go crazy from boredom."

In your seventies (and upward): If you're happy, healthy, and financially comfortable, life can be wonderful. But if you or your husband have health challenges, can you both continue to live on your own? For how long? What will happen when one of you dies and the other is left alone? Are there any gay-friendly retirement communities near you? And what about sex? Is it a thing of the past? I hope not. As one of my eighty-something clients puts it:

'Sex—with my husband—takes a little longer now, but it's wonderful. The need to perform is gone and we can just enjoy whatever happens (or doesn't)."

Daniel: "At seventy-eight, I realize that my time is limited. My husband (age seventy-two) and I are still pretty healthy, so we travel as much as we can afford to—small trips, road trips, cruises. We have planned reasonably well financially, but we watch our pennies."

Jean-Pascal: "I have kids and grandkids from when I was married to my ex-wife, so they play a big part in my life with Jeff [his husband]. We visit them often and enjoy the life and energy they bring into our lives. Jeff and my ex-wife get along really well, so we often have dinner with her and her husband. Life is good, as long as our health holds up."

I hope you've enjoyed these ten-year "snapshots." Please forgive any generalizations; my intention is to put out some ideas that you and your husband can discuss to think about your past, present, and future together.

Questions to Consider

- Using the above ten-year "snapshots," what have you and your husband been through in your time together?
- What are you both experiencing now (good/bad/unclassifiable)?
- What does your future look like if you both keep doing what you're doing?
- Is this the future you both want? If not, what can you change today to make your mutually desirable future more possible?

Over the years, I've noticed there are some prevailing myths in the gay community about how a monogamous marriage "should" be. I'd like to address three of the ones I hear most often.

Myth #1: Having/Adopting
Children Will Bring You Closer

In recent years, gay families are popping up all over the place—and it's great! But if you and your husband are considering becoming parents, please examine your motivation. While having a baby/adopting a child can be a terrific bonding experience, it's a million times more stressful on your marriage than your worst remodeling project will ever be. Imagine the unbelievable commitments of time and energy a child will require; how will this affect your private time with your man? Our case study couple—Ethan and Jake—are considering starting a family. I'll let them tell it.

> Ethan: "I always just assumed that I'd be a dad, like my dad. I didn't come out until I was in my twenties; I dated girls all through high school and college. I always thought I'd have a wife and kids someday. But I didn't want a family with a mom who was as unhappy as my mom was. After Jake and I got married and we began to talk about having kids, I realized that I'd never really thought this one through. I just had these old assumptions."

> Jake: "I never really thought much about being a parent. I wasn't really for or against it, it was pretty neutral. Ethan seems to want to be a dad. But do I? I'm not sure. At this point, we've agreed to think about it and talk about it again in a month or so. If we're going to have a family, now is probably the time to consider it, while we're still young and have plenty of energy for running after the little brats."

In my experience, it's not terribly unusual for a gay couple to get married without having an in-depth conversation about kids. Unlike straight couples, who seem to "assume" that they'll have kids, gay couples don't tend to make such easy assumptions. Maybe it's because, since there's no wife or mom in the picture, we have to figure out *how* to bring a child into our lives.

Adoption is usually a long and tedious process and finding a way to have a biological child is equally arduous and emotionally draining. For us, being dads doesn't come easily. And I think that this is a good thing. Gay fatherhood is something we have to think about, plan for, and work very hard to achieve.

Ethan and Jake are just starting to seriously consider fatherhood and are, fortunately, giving themselves time to weigh the pros and cons. If you and your husband are considering parenthood, I encourage you to make your decisions mindfully. While creating a family together can be amazingly fulfilling, it's also incredibly difficult. Please take plenty of time to consider parenting and fatherhood before you make your twosome into a threesome.

Myth #2: Never Go to Bed Angry

This is my favorite myth to bust. Has anyone ever really pulled this one off? I doubt it. Going to sleep angry isn't great, but—for the vast majority of us—it's occasionally part of our marriage. Even if you go to bed mad and sleep in separate rooms once in a while, it's okay. Yes, it's okay! Don't make it into a big deal; it's a part of life that many married gay men don't talk about because we're embarrassed.

If you and your husband are arguing around bedtime, try taking a "time out" from your argument and agree to discuss the subject in the morning. Right before bed is a lousy time for problem resolution; you'll usually see things more clearly in the morning. You may lose a good night's sleep, but in the long run, it's worth it because your disagreements will be resolved with a lot less Sturm und Drang.

Myth #3: Never Take Your Husband for Granted

Didn't every episode of *Oprah* mention this in some form? It's become so engrained in popular culture that it's almost become a cardinal sin. I say it's time to rethink this one. Doesn't taking your husband for granted mean that you can count on, depend on, and trust him? You need to feel secure enough to lean on your man without worrying that he'll flake on you. This doesn't mean that it's okay to treat him badly; it does mean that you can count on each other and watch out for each other. This is also known as "security" and "dependability."

Should I Stay or Should I Go?

I'd like to close this chapter addressing the topic, how do I know when to leave my marriage? It's certainly not a pleasant topic, but it's an important one. As a psychotherapist for many gay couples, I'm often asked: "Should I stay with my husband or should I go?" This is obviously not a question I can answer for you; my job is to help you look at the big picture—your expectations, the current state of your marriage, your old patterns—to help you make your decision.

Many men feel bored in their relationships and wonder if someone else would be a much better partner. Some guys in monogamous marriages decide to try to "have it both ways" and have an affair. An affair can feel very exciting; your lover seems to have all the qualities that your (boring, predictable) husband doesn't. You feel understood in a way your partner never could.

This, dear readers, is characteristic of an affair. It is full of excitement, newness, and illusions. While we enjoy the excitement and newness, it is the illusions that spell trouble for us.

We imagine that this new, wonderful man will lead us into a whole new life, but it's the rare affair that blossoms into a happy long-term relationship. Affairs usually end badly; the illusions eventually bite the dust and we see that the guy we're cheating with has plenty of problems and annoying habits of his own. Once we wise up, we may wonder why we're giving up someone we really know for someone we barely know at all.

I'm not advocating that you stay in a boring, stagnant relationship. Sometimes a different person meets your unmet needs in a way your husband never could (or would) and you are ready for a *major* change in your life. But in all honesty, this is *not* the case for most of us. For most of us, it's *we* who need to change.

This is such a drag, isn't it? Wouldn't it be great if our husband would do all the changing and we could just lie back in our La-Z-Boy recliner and enjoy how wonderful he is now that he's gotten rid of all those annoying habits? Ah, yes—if only it worked that way.

It doesn't. If we want to have better relationships, we need to work on ourselves first. Couple's counseling can be great, but only if *both* people are willing to change. Change is uncomfortable, scary hard work. Many people aren't willing to go there, so they keep repeating the same scenarios over and over, regardless of who they choose as a partner. If this is you, wake up! It's you who is the problem, not your husband.

If you have a common pattern in relationships, it's all about you, not them. Changing partners probably won't make a damn bit of difference. Oh sure, at the beginning things might look rosy with your new lover, but give it time and the same old you will start to emerge.

Big surprise.

If you're considering ending your marriage, talk about it with your husband, *not* your best friend or your brother, your *husband*. It may be daunting, I know, but the two of you are the only ones who can decide the course of your relationship. If he is willing to change, you have the potential for your relationship to deepen and become really amazing. If your marriage is having problems and you are *both* taking action to do something constructive about it, that's a good sign; couples who take action to save (or improve) a troubled relationship usually succeed.

If you've never had couple's counseling, know that a good couples' counselor is neither on your side nor your husband's, we're on the side of the *relationship*. We are not referees, judges, or juries. Our intention is to help you and your husband overcome your obstacles to being happy together, learning to communicate better, and negotiating conflicts.

People who love each other can do really awful things to each other. However, holding a grudge won't help your relationship. While it's difficult in troubled times to keep your marriage healthy, both parties need to find a way to let go, forgive, and move forward. Therapy can help with this. If your husband *isn't* willing to change, focus on changing yourself (perhaps in individual psychotherapy) and see if your husband will eventually "follow along."

Does this all sound too hard? Never fear, there's the good stuff too: love, affection, and a renewal of sexual attraction can return when a couple's problems and tensions are resolved.

Sometimes a trial separation is a good reality check for a couple in trouble: it gives both parties a chance to see whether they miss each other, what they had together; it can serve as a good motivator for discussions about "How can we be happy together again?"

You may be clear that what's best for you is to end the marriage. If so, do it with as much kindness, grace, and honesty as possible. Love isn't like a light bulb; you can't just turn it on and off with a switch. If you've loved this man, you still probably do. Leaving is rarely the easy, breezy panacea we hope it will be. It's usually fraught with sadness, anger, and uncertainty, for example, "Did I give it my best shot?" "Did we try everything we could to stay together?" "Did I give up too easily?"

If you do end your marriage, I strongly recommend that you be on your own for a while. Do not jump right into another relationship, even if it appears immediately on your doorstep. After a marriage ends, it usually takes a few months for your internal voices to calm down and for you to see clearly where you're at and what you really want next. Jumping right into another relationship usually has a poor outcome. Yeah, you may be lonely for a while, but you need to figure out who you are now and what you want in terms of your next relationship.

I define a good relationship as one where you and your partner help each other to become the men that you truly want to be. Whether you stay or go, let that be your guide.

CHAPTER ELEVEN

The Art of Not Merging

How to Not Lose Yourself in Your Marriage

Often, when I counsel newly married couples, I hear a familiar lament: "I feel like I've lost myself since I got married" or "After moving in with my husband, I feel like I've merged with him so much that I don't know who I am anymore."

You fall in love. You move in. You get married. You get lost. Sometimes, it feels that way and you wonder what happened to the man you used to be. You wonder how you lost all those good qualities that you used to have, all your independence, all those friends. You lament all the activities you used to enjoy that you've given up. It's oh-so-tempting to blame your husband for all of this. Of course, perhaps he's lost himself as well.

In this chapter, we'll talk about how *not* to lose yourself in a marriage, or what I sometimes call "The Art of Not Merging."

Are you someone who is typically overly responsible for other people? Do you usually put yourself last and everyone else first? Do you have tendencies (small ones, of course) toward being unselfish, virtuous, and martyr-like? Do you often deny your own needs and focus on what someone else—like your husband—wants? Then, my friend, you may be what I call "hyper-responsible."

If this is true for you, don't be surprised when you start to feel resentment. Eventually, no matter how much you love someone and want him to be happy, if you're losing yourself in the process, you're bound to feel resentful. This plays havoc with a marriage; you're caught in the middle—you want to make your husband happy, but to do so, you have to deny your needs, making yourself *unhappy.*

Being hyper-responsible isn't good for your husband either. Although he may enjoy being the object around which you orbit, it encourages his self-centeredness and narcissism, which is no good for either of you. If you find that you frequently sacrifice your own well-being for that of your husband or other people you care about, then you're probably hyper-responsible.

You may have been taught to be that way. I know I was. As the oldest of four children, I felt responsible for the younger three. I also was put into the role of my mother's confidante, further cementing myself into the box of "caretaker/helper/responsible one." It has taken me a long time to get out of that box. In many of my past relationships, I was the one who lost himself. I was so happy to have a good man by my side that I would do whatever I needed to keep him happy.

I have clients like this too.

Matthew: "I was raised by a single mom and I had to be the man of the house. I got used to being 'the responsible one' and basically the one in charge when Mom was at work. When I met Joel, I tried to boss him around and he told me, 'No way.' It was a shock: I thought everyone wanted me to take care of them and tell them what to do."

Luay: "I had a father who was meek and mild and a mother who wore the pants in the family. She traveled for business and had affairs with men in other cities. My father just sucked it all up; never said anything. When I grew up, I ended up becoming a modern-day version of my father. I'd do whatever it took to keep my boyfriend-du-jour happy: pretend I agreed with him, deny my own needs, and let him run the show."

Andy: "Sometimes I'm afraid that my husband will leave me. Every time we have an argument, I think, 'That's it; he's gonna leave.' I'm still realizing that an argument isn't the end of the world. I'm embarrassed to say it—because I'm so confident in the rest of my life—but I feel like I've lost myself in my marriage."

Let's return to Ethan and Jake, our case study couple. As I worked with them in therapy, they discovered that they had over-merged their lives; in their desire to share with each other, they had kept almost nothing uniquely their own. Ethan and Jake had lost much of their own identities and uniqueness. In their words, they had become "EthanandJake." Luckily, they were willing to take responsibility for it and not blame each other. This is a step that many relationships are not able to take; it requires maturity and a willingness to be responsible for your own happiness. As a result, they were each willing to take action—to work on themselves and experiment with things that made them happy.

Over time, they discovered that there are things they could share and things they couldn't. These separate interests helped them keep their own identity intact as they also "merged" into "EthanandJake." It's not a bad thing to merge with your husband—at times, that is. But if you have lost yourself in your marriage and your identity as an independent person seems to have slipped away, then it's time to talk about the Art of Not Merging.

It's really great to be part of a couple, it can feel really wonderful to be "Blake's husband" or "Luis's husband," as long as it isn't your *only* identity. Don't make your husband your everything. This leads to resentment and feeling trapped and can lead to an affair.

One former client of mine felt so enmeshed and lost in his (monogamous) marriage that he started having sex with someone he met on a business trip. When his emotionally devastated husband asked him why, he said, "I need something that's just mine—everything is 'ours': our friends, our home, our workplace [both work from their home]—I needed something that was mine alone, and that was my relationship with Silas [the 'other' man]."

I like the idea of "healthy distance" in a relationship. It means that each man needs friends of his own and activities he does on his own. It isn't emotionally healthy to share everything with your husband. A desperate groping for emotional closeness makes you clingy and needy.

Feeling abandoned? Often, this is a sign that you're *really* lost yourself: your whole sense of safety and identity depends on feeling loved by other people, and when those people temporarily (or not) turn their love away from you, you panic.

> Marek: "Any time that Darryl [his husband] made the slightest move away from me, I would panic. I grew up in a family where no one was very close to each other and my parents were really unemotional. As a result, I never had any idea where I stood with people I loved. I brought that into my marriage. I'm working on being less anxious as I gradually get comfortable with Darryl doing things without me."

Adrian: "I was raised by my grandmother, who loved me very strongly, but her love was always conditional: 'I'll love you *if* you do this or *if* you do that.' As a result, I felt that her love could be yanked away from me at any time if I didn't meet her standards. As I grew to love Bill [his husband] and marry him, I realized that I expected Bill's love to be conditional too, and I'd better do what he asks if I expected him to love me."

Juan-Carlos: "My dad left us—my mother, sister, and me—when I was little. The only time I got to spend with him was when I did something good, like got good grades or won some award; then he'd take me out to lunch or to a baseball game. If I didn't perform, I didn't have a dad. Not surprisingly, when I was dating Jeremy, I expected that he'd do the same: only love me when I did something good. I was continually expecting him to abandon me, just like Dad did."

Feeling abandoned is one version of losing yourself. We believe that the only way to make our husband (or anyone) love us is to deny who we really are and perform for them—making them approve of us in order to "win" their love. Luckily, you don't need to be stuck there; with the help of your husband, friends, and others who love you, you can begin to "unhook" from the need to please.

If you were my client, I'd help you to *gradually* begin to figure out what *you* like to do. For some of us, we're been performing for others for so long that we've almost forgotten what we like or don't like. Our personal preferences got pushed aside to make way for the desires of those we wanted to love us. We needed them so badly that we denied our own needs to serve theirs. We'd do or say almost anything to make sure they wouldn't withdraw their love. When we *finally* begin to speak up and say what we want, we usually feel *very* anxious.

It's time to un-brainwash ourselves; we started out in life knowing we were lovable exactly as we are, but then, along the way we were taught to believe that we were worthy of love *only* if we behaved in a certain way. And of course, it was *impossible* to behave in this way all the time. What a setup for insecurity! It's no wonder that many of us have lost ourselves in our years of people-pleasing and feel abandoned if anyone we love *appears* to pull away from us.

I know this one. It has taken me a long time to be able to say to those that I love: "You know, when you did (name the behavior), I felt abandoned. I know it's my stuff and I'm working on it." Most of my friends were really surprised when I said this. "Really," they said, "*that* made you feel abandoned? I'm sorry, that wasn't my intention at all." It helps me to be able to bring it up in a *calm, respectful* (nonaccusatory) manner. And it strengthens the relationship, too—they know I'm working on my abandonment stuff by saying it out loud and owning it, and they're helping me in my process.

It's easy to suggest, "Why not try a bit more autonomy?" But if you've been a people-pleaser for a long time, it usually makes for a lot of anxious times when you start to change. Gradual change is the way out. Begin slowly. For example, the next time you feel like your husband is abandoning you, you could turn to him and say, "You're abandoning me" (your old pattern) or you could try something like I did (in the previous paragraph) by being responsible, owning your emotional reaction and communicating your concerns to your husband calmly and respectfully (your new pattern).

Let's check in again with our Ethan and Jake.

Ethan: "When Jake and I first met, I thought he was very independent and self-contained. He played video games on his own a lot and had his gamer friends that he hung out with. I never thought he was trying to please me. I liked how independent he was back then."

Jake: "I always felt like such a loner: I never fit in anywhere. I became obsessed with video games because it gave me a world where I felt like I could be successful. My [video game–based] fantasy life got me through some very lonely times. When Ethan came along, I wasn't sure what to do. He seemed great, but I was afraid to really trust anyone else."

Isn't it interesting how two men see each other when they first meet and how that changes over time? Ethan was looking for a guy who was independent and Jake appeared to fit the bill. Of course, when you first meet someone, there is a lot that you don't know about him—you can only scratch the surface.

Ethan: "The more I got to know Jake, the more he intrigued (and puzzled) me. I just couldn't figure him out. Most guys were easy to know—not him. I liked that. It made me want to get to know him more. I like a challenge and most guys were just so easy to predict that I got bored with them."

Jake: "I never thought I'd have a boyfriend as popular and handsome as Ethan. I didn't think he was really my type and I was his. So, I didn't think he'd stick around. My friends told me, 'He's gonna dump you. Don't let him break your heart.' I was so wary of getting hurt that I didn't let him in much at the beginning."

It's not surprising that people who are very independent (like Ethan) are often attracted to people who aren't (like Jake), and vice versa. While I won't completely concur that opposites attract, we usually don't want a husband just like us. Why? Because we aren't likely to learn much from him. For example: if two Ethans married each other, there is a likelihood that neither of them would risk vulnerability, so there would be little real intimacy and not much motivation to change. If two Jakes married each other, it would likely be a marriage of high drama and intense feelings of hurt and abandonment.

See why the Ethans and Jakes of the world can be so good for each other? Each provides the other with the perfect learning opportunity to work through his own weaknesses and become the man he truly wants to be.

Ethan: "Jake and I have worked through a lot. I've learned not to be so distant and he's learned to be a lot less clingy. But as Michael pointed out in our couple's counseling sessions, we can't each dramatically change our personalities. Change comes slowly, and our differences are going to surface again and again—and they do."

Jake: "Couple's counseling has helped me to see that my neediness triggers Ethan's running away. And the more he runs away, the more abandoned I feel. I know where this comes from, but it's still hard not to feel it. I want to be more independent and not 'merge' so much into Ethan, but it's hard not to lose myself in him because I love him so intensely."

Undoing long-established patterns like Ethan's emotional distancing and Jake's feelings of abandonment is a long-term process; it doesn't happen quickly. Most of our personality traits are subconscious: we don't usually know *why* we do or say what we do. We say things like "that's just me" or "that's how I am." This book and other tools for creating a happy gay marriage (like workshops and couple's counseling) can help you and your husband to understand *why* the two of you clash personality-wise and how you can begin to deconstruct any repetitive patterns in your marriage that cause these clashes.

When most clients tell me, "we keep having the same arguments, over and over," this is what they're talking about. Sound familiar?

Do you remember how, in previous chapters, Ethan and Jake were talking about starting a family? Well, they've given it some thought—a lot of thought, actually—and are moving ahead. Of course, this brings up its own emotional challenges.

> Ethan: "We're taking the training to be foster parents. This is a way to 'try' parenting. I have no idea how this will go. I would like it to work, but it's bound to really change our relationship. I feel I have a lot of love to give to a child, but I don't know if Jake and I are ready to do this yet. Maybe we should wait until we're older and our marriage is more stable. Oh well, we'll find out soon enough."
>
> Jake: "We talked about the foster parent thing for quite a while, and then, when our friends Harrison and Tom did it and were so happy being foster dads, I wanted to give it a try too. It's scary, though—sometimes I don't feel mature or stable enough to be a dad. Maybe everyone feels that way. Maybe having a child to love, in addition to Ethan, will make me less needy with Ethan. I hope so."

Both men have their doubts about becoming parents; this is a good thing. Healthy doubt is a useful thing, especially when it comes to something as important at adopting a child. Each of them has looked at his own individual motivation and is also considering how bringing a child into their marriage might affect the relationship between the two of them.

> Ethan: "Now that we're going to be foster parents, I wonder if Jake will feel abandoned by me when I start to focus on the kids they place with us. He says he wants this, but he's really used to getting all of my attention. I hope this works, but I'm kinda uneasy about how this will affect our relationship."
>
> Jake: "I am glad we're doing the foster parent thing so we can see how we'll be as parents. I know Ethan thinks I'll feel abandoned, but I only feel that way when he emotionally withdraws from me. I hope that I'll see a loving fatherly side of him when we get our first foster placement. I hope I'll see that in myself too."

Parenthood is a daunting challenge for any gay couple, but Ethan and Jake are talking about it and giving it a lot more thought than many couples typically do. Since they've done a lot of work on themselves in individual and couple's counseling, each of them has developed useful tools for talking with each other about difficult subjects. Ethan is learning how to be less distant and Jake is learning not to lose himself in their relationship.

Let's look at another tool you can use to keep your marriage from becoming neither too distant nor too enmeshed. I call it "healthy distance." I think that a bit of distance enhances not only preserving your own identity, but also emotional intimacy. You don't want to know everything about your husband—as if you could; it kills any sense of surprise/mystery/spontaneity. Resist the temptation to tell him everything you do/say/eat/think. I'm not encouraging you to keep secrets, but don't overwhelm him with minutiae.

If you are so insecure that you need to know where your husband is at every moment, what he's doing and with whom—then *you* have a problem. This kind of insecurity and—dare I say it?—paranoia can drive you (and him) crazy. This can come from a need to feel in control, a fear of abandonment, or a history of being betrayed. Regardless of the source, it can eat away at the trust and integrity of your marriage.

Think of your marriage as two overlapping circles; your life and your husband's life are the overlapping circles. There is the area where they overlap and areas where they don't. There's a lot of "us," but make sure that there's plenty of "you" too. Don't do everything together; keep some interests and activities of your own. That way, you'll have things to share with each other and surprise each other with.

Are you ready for some more ways *not* to merge? Travel together and separately. Yes, separately! Occasional trips with friends or—especially—alone can help you keep your sense of self. And it often shows you both how much you miss each other—and can make for loving (and passionate) reunions. If you're a bit of a loner, this will make sense to you. If you're a real people person, it might be new and unfamiliar. Try it in little steps and see.

Do you believe the idea that husbands should be best friends as well as romantic partners? Many people do. Doesn't it sound logical? The theory: You and your husband know each other better than anyone else, so why wouldn't you be best friends too?

Let's take a good look at this theory: first of all, other people may know you better than your husband does, but in different ways. Your family, siblings, and old friends may know you in ways that your husband does not and cannot. Over the course of your marriage, know that it's normal to sometimes feel closer to your best friend/brother/other beloved person than you do to your husband. Keep your expectations real—real love goes deep; it lasts. How much you and your man *like* each other, however, comes and goes. Sometimes you'll be annoyed with your husband and prefer to spend time with others and vice versa. This is *normal*: just keep reconnecting with your man while sharing your life with other people who love you—and everyone benefits.

If you've lost your sense of self, perhaps you've focused too much on the love of your husband and ignored the love of the rest of the world. That "you and me against the world" thing is destined to leave us dependent on our husband for our happiness and disconnected from the rest of the world. Let's revisit the eight kinds of love and see how they can help you to balance your life with love from *many* sources.

If you're feeling too dependent on your husband, perhaps you need some more Philautia. This is self-love: how you love, cherish, and respect yourself. If you can use more of this, you're not alone.

Jean-Pierre: "I was raised never to praise myself; I'm used to belittling myself when I fail. My husband [James] is the opposite; that's one reason I love him so. I am slowly learning to see the good in me and to be kind to myself. But it sure feels strange."

You could also search out for some more Storge kind of love: this kind of love is parental, mentoring love. It has a protective vibe.

Pedro: "I was the oldest of seven kids, and so I always felt like a parent to the younger ones. I knew that feeling really well, but I never had someone give me that parental kind of love, until I met my friend Bruce in our gay square dance group. He's a bit older and treats me like a kind, wonderful uncle. It's such a good feeling. I feel safe and cared for by him. Finally, I'm receiving what I've been giving out for so long."

You may want some more Pragma: a deep, long-lasting, committed love, the kind you see in the best kinds of long-term relationships.

Patrick: "I have had many boyfriends in my life, but I never really experienced a deep love until I met—and married—Byron. He is so easy to love and I feel so safe with him that I can be vulnerable and let him see all my 'ugly' places and he just loves me anyway. It is such a relief to be loved this way."

Platonic love is about loving the beauty inside people, not their external presentation. Do you love your friends because of their inner beauty kindness, sensitivity) or must someone be physically beautiful to be your friend?

Dane: "I have always picked my friends because of how fashionable and beautiful they were. Being in the nightclub business with my husband, this makes sense. However, I am starting to want more depth in my friendships and have more kindness and forgiveness in my life. The glamour and the elegance I surround myself with are nice and good for my business, but I want something more."

Eros love is passion, energy, and desire. That energy can be directed at anything: your work, your home, your hobbies, and your friends.

Kossivi: "I am happy with my husband, but after being married for about three years, I just felt kind of dull as a person. I was tempted to have sex with other guys and not tell him about it (I almost did), but I talked with a friend about this and he suggested that maybe I wasn't doing anything fun in my life (I work a lot). I used to like to sing, so I started going to karaoke and found that it really energizes me and makes me feel more alive."

Perhaps you could use more Ludus love: a playful, flirting, teasing love. This often manifests as a kind of brotherly teasing among friends.

Spencer: "I play on a gay softball team, and it gives me a really good connection to the other guys. I'm kind of a quiet person, as is my husband, and so I'm not very good at being playful. But with the guys on the team, I am getting better at gentle, friendly teasing and goofing around. It's really great for me. I hope to eventually share it with my husband, too."

Agape is unconditional love; it's how we are told God loves us. To love with agape means we forgive easily and understand that everyone we love will screw things up at some point.

Aidan: "I have always had a strong connection with God, but growing up as a Catholic, I just couldn't be gay and a good Catholic. So I chose to be gay. Eventually, I found a church that was gay-welcoming, and once again, my love affair with God has bloomed and is a major part of my life. Feeling loved by God makes it so much easier for me to forgive people when they do me wrong."

Epithumia is a kind of obsessive desire where you find yourself saying things like: "You are my life; I can't live without you" to someone you allegedly "love."

Travis: "I have a history of smothering people: friends, ex-boyfriends. So I really don't want to do that with Justin [his husband]. I am trying hard to not depend on him for everything, but it's hard, because I want to make him my everything, and that's not good for either of us."

Low self-esteem can also cause you to lose yourself in your partner; you don't think very much of yourself and often put yourself down. You may even wonder what your husband sees in you. What can you do about this?

Dear Michael:
    My husband encouraged me to write to you, but I don't know if you can do much. He says I have lousy self-esteem. Maybe he's right. Whenever someone gives me a compliment, I think they're after something and I don't believe them. Doesn't everyone have problems with self-esteem, or is it just me? Do other people feel good about themselves all the time?
    Confused in Colorado

Dear Confused:
    Self-esteem is how we "esteem" ourselves: what we think about ourselves. Obviously, no one thinks they are fabulous 24/7 (do they?), but how do you feel about yourself *most* of the time? Do you usually think you're okay, sometimes really good, other times, not so great? If so, you're normal.

Most people have daily—if not hourly—fluctuations in self-esteem. What is harmful is when you *rarely* see the good in you, that is, you don't ever think you look good, act intelligently, are kind to others, have good qualities—get the picture? It sounds like this may be true for you when you say, "Whenever someone gives me a compliment, I think they're after something and I don't believe them." Could every single person who compliments you want something? Could they *all* be such liars?

See my point?

It sounds like you've got some "cognitive distortion" going on: your brain distorts the input it gets. For example, if someone at work says to you, "That was a great job you did on that project," and your brain distorts the praise and turns it into "They just want something from me," or "I'm not smart enough to do a great job on anything," that's cognitive distortion.

Your brain won't let the truth in; for some reason, your brain "wiring" got messed up somewhere in the past and it won't correctly reroute positive input. (The correct response to a compliment, by the way, is always a simple "thank you," even if the person is a liar. It's clean, easy, and gracious.)

If your self-esteem is messed up because your brain won't let good things in, you've got a problem. Luckily, it's one you can solve. From your e-mail, I'd recommend that you start your change process by becoming aware that (1) you turn compliments into crap, (2) you don't trust what people say to you, and (3) you think everyone wants something from you. These are useful things to know about yourself. Don't beat yourself up for doing this (that always slows down the change process); just notice what you do. Try to observe it from a neutral position.

Once you see what you do, changing it usually involves some introspection.

Questions to Consider

- Has my self-esteem always been this way?
- Is it easy for me to trust people?
- When do I allow myself to receive praise from others?
- What could I do to raise my self-esteem? Could my husband help me with this?
- How can I help my husband raise *his* self-esteem?

Once you've answered these questions, let's get a bit more specific. It's time to do a little detective work; go back in your life and see where these cognitive distortions may have originated.

(A Few More) Questions to Consider

- Look at your past: Who said things to you that damaged your self-esteem?
- What was their motivation?
- When did this happen?
- Is this still affecting you? If so, how?

Part of freeing yourself from past conditioning is to see where all this crap started. It helps to identify how the innocent, trusting child we all started out as (yes, even you hyper-cynical guys) somehow got turned around.

For many of my psychotherapy clients, this is their "aha" moment: they see that something (or a series of events) happened and changed how they saw themselves. They gave up being trusting and open and created psychological defenses to keep people out. This is what is known as the "adaptive self"; it's what we did to survive, to get through tough times. However, it doesn't serve us now to continue this way. I'm not saying to become stupid and gullible. It's good to have a healthy dose of skepticism in life, but it's not helpful to be so over-defended that you don't let anyone into your heart or head.

Losing yourself in your work is another way that many men mess up their marriage. A while back, I read that a Japanese labor bureau determined that one of Toyota's top car engineers—aged forty-five—died from working too many hours. In the two months up to his death, the man averaged more than eighty hours of overtime per month. In Japan, death from overwork even has a name: "karoshi."

This phenomenon is not limited to Japan: recently, two of my clients told me (individually) that they are finding it hard to leave work and go home to their husbands. Work is becoming their life and their husbands are *not* happy. I asked each of these guys, "Why don't you want to go home?" They gave me two different scenarios to justify their workaholism: (#1) "My work is more fulfilling than my life with my husband," and (#2) "With possible layoffs at my company, to keep my job I need to do overtime, overtime, overtime and do it gladly (and with a smile)."

Let's look at scenario #1: What happens when your job becomes the best part of your life? Is this such a bad thing? Doesn't everyone yearn for work they really love? Let's be clear: there's loving what you do, and then there's using work to avoid the parts of your life that are a mess. Some men use work to avoid facing problems in their marriage.

Wouldn't you rather go somewhere on the weekend where people love you—because you work so long (and hard)—or would you rather be home with your husband talking about the problems in your relationship? In the short run, it's understandable. But in the long run, what happens when work squeezes the juice out of the rest of your life and you get lost in your career? When you feel lonely at home or your personal life seems empty, going home can be scary. Work may seem safer. But how long can you put off facing your husband and the possible difficulties in your relationship?

People say that technology frees us to have more leisure time, but is that true? For some of my clients, it feeds their addiction to work. They are those hard-working types who get up in the night to go to the bathroom and seize the moment to check their e-mails and texts, or maybe their cell phone is buzzing away on their nightstand, or under the pillow. This is a great way to frustrate your husband (unless he's doing it too, in which case, I feel sorry for both of you) and lose yourself in your work. This kind of compulsive behavior is linked to depression, but—let's be real here—it can also be linked to climbing the ladder of success.

Let's look at the reality of scenario #2: success at work can be like a drug—addictive and habit forming. But if used like a drug, it's ultimately self-defeating. For example, can you enjoy your success at work? Or is your mantra, "Don't stop, don't slow down"?

It's easy to mock this type of crazy-making ideology, but what if you work in an ultra-aggressive, hyper-competitive environment? To rise to the top in places like this, many "experts" tell you to plan strategically: manipulate the right people, create the right impression, and create a positive image for yourself. According to them (and the books they're selling), doing a really good job isn't enough anymore—career success is all about your image and how you present yourself.

What's a normal, healthy married man to do?

A successful, high-powered executive once told me, "There really are only ten or twelve key decisions you have to get right every year. Concentrate on them, and aim for a success rate of at least 80 percent. Do that and all will be well." It appears that working harder and harder—doing "the wrong thing righter"—does not lead to success at work. "If something comes up that requires seven days of work—then I will do it," this executive told me, "but it rarely does. I think many people just use work as a way of not confronting themselves."

Ah, yes, confronting yourself. This brings us back to the question I posed to my clients—one I suggest that you obsessive, workaholic types ask yourself after your next fifteen-hour day: "Why don't I want to go home?"

What does it mean to be invisible? I made up the below equation to summarize what I often hear from clients.

> • Invisible = Feeling Lost = Merging Too Much into Your Marriage

When we feel invisible, we've usually lost our identity and—not surprisingly—probably resent our husband for it (even though it's not his responsibility).

When we feel invisible, it's as if no one sees us, notices us, or pays attention to us. We feel lost. As a therapist, I hear lots of gay men tell me that they feel "invisible." They walk down the street in a gay neighborhood or go to a gay bar or club and no one sees them. No one makes eye contact. They go to a party and no one talks to them. They go to a gay-friendly church and no one approaches them. Has this ever happened to you? Maybe you don't fit the current gay standards of beauty, so you feel invisible. If you've ever felt "invisible," here are some questions to ask yourself.

Questions to Consider

- Do I want to be seen? If so, by whom?
- How do I want other people to see me?
- How do I see myself?
- What do I think other people are looking for?
- How am I setting myself up for invisibility?

Feeling invisible isn't really about how others perceive us or what we look like, it's largely about how we perceive ourselves.

For some of us, it's a form of self-sabotage. We feel crappy about ourselves, like we don't deserve to be loved or admired or appreciated and—guess what?—that's exactly what we get back from others. Self-love and self-regard play a big part in being "seen." Haven't you encountered people who aren't particularly good-looking or striking, but they seem magnetic? These people draw others to them so easily—how do they do it? I'll bet it's because they feel pretty damned good about themselves most of the time.

From what I've read, 95 percent of how we communicate with other people is nonverbal. We (subconsciously) read their body language, facial expressions, and clothing and get a "hit" from it. We then have an emotional reaction to them, based on that "hit."

If you feel invisible, what do you think you're putting out there in the world on a nonverbal level?

Want to find out? Study yourself in videos and photos. Look at yourself in the mirror (with compassion, please) and see what you get. Is this a man you'd like to get to know? Is this someone you would find interesting? Or is this person someone you'd probably ignore or even avoid? Let's get real here. If you want to shake that cloak of invisibility—you're not Harry Potter, after all—figure out what you're putting out in the world for others to see and experience.

I have clients who are gorgeous who tell me that no one really sees them, and clients who are less than "perfect" who are very popular and desirable. Sure, it helps to be attractive, but it's not enough.

Part of being invisible is not really being 100 percent "there" for your husband (or anyone, actually) to connect with you. Many of us are so distracted by people and things (iPhones, iPads, etc.) that we aren't really available to anyone. Fear is often a factor in this: if we don't trust other people or ourselves, it's hard to be in the present moment. We may be obsessing about the past or worrying about the future, and we miss what's happening right in front of us—and we're likely not enjoying time with our husbands either.

If you feel half-dead much of the time, like your life is one big, boring disappointment, I doubt that you're really living in the present moment. To be in the present moment is both exciting and scary; you never really know what will happen. This is a risk we need to take if we want to be seen, heard, and appreciated by other people.

Another way to stay invisible is to not really listen or pay attention to other people. When you're talking to someone, are you really 100 percent there, or are you only half-available for connection? Many of us go through life missing out on the cues and signals of people around us. We are so preoccupied with ourselves that we *feel* invisible to others. We're afraid to really be there with another person. Maybe we needed this defense in our past, if people were hurtful or aggressive to us. But this kind of once-helpful defense may be keeping people away from you now—letting you feel isolated and invisible.

Invisibility is a choice. If it's no longer what you want, you can begin to choose differently. Start with your husband: let him see you and *really* see him. If you don't usually listen to him very carefully, change that. Practice with him and when you get better at it, start practicing with other people too.

Picking Up the Pieces

I have had clients who told me that, after leaving their husband, they realized that they had no identity outside of the marriage. They'd given themselves away and now had to "find" themselves again. Here is a good example.

Dear Michael:

I am in the process of divorcing my husband and I realize that I have no identity left after being with him. I don't know how to find myself again. He was a very domineering personality and I just gave in and did what he wanted most of the time. I couldn't take it anymore, so now I'm free. But who am I now? I don't have a clue how to find myself. Help!

Desperately Lost in Washington, D.C.

Dear Mr. Lost:

Every man who ends a marriage has to deal with his new post-relationship identity. It's normal to "surrender" a part of ourselves to our husband, but how much should we surrender and how do we get it back if we leave? How do we pick up the pieces of ourselves when we've given ourselves away to our husband, our marriage, or other people's expectations?

It helps to look at motivation: Why did you, Mr. Lost, let your husband dominate you? Was it pleasant to give up control? Perhaps you wanted to please him or maybe you didn't know what you wanted. Since it was truly your choice to give yourself away, it would be helpful to see where that all started in your life.

Questions to Consider

- What *do* I like to do? (If you honestly don't know, go to the next question.)
- What did I used to like to do?
- What have I given up that I miss?
- What positive qualities did I used to have?
- How can I begin to get those back?

Give yourself time to re-create yourself. You don't have to become the man you were before you got married, unless you want to. You can identify the qualities you miss and leave the rest behind. A major life change always gives us opportunities; you may not know who you are, but this is a great time to consider reinventing yourself. You get to make it up.

And don't do it alone. It's way too hard. This is the time to surround yourself with friends, colleagues, and family members who love and support you. You may need to lean on them to get through the coming months.

We don't just wake up one day and realize that we are a completely different person; we lose our identities piece by piece, moment by moment, one misstep at a time, one lie at a time, one pushed-down desire at a time. And when we're ready to find ourselves anew, we do it slowly, thoughtfully, and carefully.

Some people feel that, once they've lost themselves, they'll never be able to "go back." Luckily, the *essence* of you cannot be lost. In my work with clients, I describe the essence of a person as a pilot light in a furnace (I *am* from Ohio, remember). Your pilot light—your essence—may get *very* low and may seem to almost be extinguished, but that cannot ever be true. You can always turn your flame up. Slowly, yes, but you can *always* turn that flame up.

The essence of you may have been waiting a long time to be "turned up," but have no fear, it's just waiting for you to do it.

At some future time, Mr. Lost, I suggest you take a look at why you stayed with this guy for so long. Is this what you felt you deserved? Did the relationship resemble previous relationships, like your parents'? Learn from this relationship so that you don't repeat it again. A good therapist or counselor can help you get to the bottom of that stuff. Get some help and break the pattern.

Don't Lose Yourself in Other People's Expectations: Dare to Be Eccentric

If you live and die by the changing standards of gay culture, you're probably very confused! One way to lose yourself is to *not* question the advice that comes your way. Another way to get lost is to try to obey all the "shoulds" you hear from the people around you. Any advice that someone gives you is what *they* would do (or wish they could do); this often has *no* relationship at all to what's in *your* best interest. Many gay couples try to do everything "right" and end up very confused. They get lost in other people's expectations and, of course, all those people don't agree with each other either. Try to please your parents and best friends and neighbors and you'll realize it's impossible.

Yet we try.

Instead, I recommend that you and your husband take plenty of time to find out what the two of you like and don't like. It's corny and trite to say, "be true to yourselves," but it's no small feat to pull it off.

Dare to be a happily eccentric couple. Some people may think you're strange, but there's nothing like the satisfaction of doing it *your* way—whether anyone else approves of it or not.

Questions to Consider
- In what ways in your marriage "typical"?
- Who are the people in your life that you feel the most pressure to please?
- How have your past relationships been "typical" (or not)?
- How would you like your marriage to be "outside the box"?
- If you have any kind of relationship you wanted, what would you like? Let your mind go free . . .

Keep Reinventing Yourself (and Your Marriage)

We create our own happiness by *reinventing ourselves* over and over again. As maturing men, we all live the archetypical hero's journey: we must leave our families and go out into a largely hostile world where people are bound to give us a hard time.

Like true heroes, we have dragons to slay. These dragons stand in the way of our happiness. However, our dragons are not mythical, but internal; they usually include our own self-hatred, the ways we punish ourselves for not being perfect and our fears of not doing it "right" (e.g., not having enough sex, making enough money, building the right body, or wearing the right clothes).

Our dragons tell us not to trust ourselves, that we are weak and need to give in. They encourage us to get lost in self-doubt and wonder why we're not happier in our marriage or more successful in our careers. These dragons tell us, "You're a loser. Everyone else knows what they're doing, but you don't." And if we listen to them, we get lost.

When my dragons get too loud, I remind myself, "Progress; not perfection." It helps. Happiness rarely comes around the first try. Perseverance is crucial; to be happy, we need a soft heart and a hard ass. A soft heart is the loving-kindness we give to ourselves, to soothe and forgive ourselves as we blunder ahead on our own unique path to greater happiness. On the other hand, we want to be mature adults, not childish or dependent. We need a hard ass, a toughness, a resiliency. We need to know when something is *real* and *important* so we can kick ourselves in the ass when we need to.

We may be scared to change ourselves, our marriages, and our self-definitions; but being scared isn't a valid excuse for being unhappily married. We can still take action while feeling afraid. It won't kill us; it may kill us *not* to.

A half-dead life is more likely to kill us (spiritually, psychically, and physically) than a life of action with fear around the edges. If we're waiting to feel brave so that we can act brave, we're going to be waiting a long time. This is what separates real men (whether they're eighteen or eighty-one) from fifty-year-olds who still act like little boys wanting some kind of magical "daddy" figure who will come and make it all better.

If we're willing to reinvent ourselves and our marriages, we have a much better chance of experiencing happiness. There is definitely a risk, though; with any change, there is always a chance that we may fail. And this is scary. But isn't the alternative—going through life half-alive—even more frightening?

Taking a chance on happiness means taking risks—experimenting—falling down—perhaps not succeeding initially. We need to keep going anyway, especially when it gets uncomfortable (this is when many people quit). For my clients, many of their biggest and best life changes came after they turned forty; it may be that long before we are able to handle the temporary discomfort that comes with risk.

Getting Older Helps

As I get older, I am less willing to sell myself short, less likely to get lost in what other people want, and much more likely to be true to what feels right for me. Listen to the wisdom of these gay elders.

Nick (age sixty-two): "When I was younger, I worried so much about what other people thought of me. I tried so hard to do the right thing, especially with my family and my former partners. Now I'm married to Denny; we both encourage each other not to give a shit when others judge or criticize us. We aspire to be kind and forgiving, but we fuck up a lot. What's great is that now we can laugh at ourselves, learn from our mistakes, and keep going without beating ourselves up."

Ken (age seventy-seven): "I was a lost boy: I grew up in the South on a farm and had no clue about how to be gay or what the possibilities were. It took me many years to find myself and not give myself away to every handsome man who wanted my body. I had to contract HIV to really wake up and start to assert myself in the world. Some of my friends didn't like it. They're not friends anymore."

Jahleel (age eighty-three): "I was married to a woman for many years; that's just what you did back then. I could never have gone against my parents' wishes. I didn't come out until I had grandkids, and they were more accepting than their parents! When I met Hal [his husband], we were both in our sixties. No spring chickens. But we were seasoned and calm and (hopefully) wise, so we've had a great eighteen years together. Thank God we found ourselves while we still had time to enjoy ourselves, and each other."

Have you ever noticed that older people tend to take less bullshit from other people? They aren't willing to suffer fools gladly or pretend they like something when they really don't. More than once I've heard people say, "I can't wait to be older so I don't have to put up with so much crap from people."

Why wait? Start now.

I like getting older because I feel more and more alive all the time. And I appreciate myself, other people, and the world around me more than I used to. I don't take things for granted like I did when I was younger and more self-centered. In my twenties and thirties, I was so unhappy about all the things I didn't have—wealth, fame, a perfect body—that I ignored what I did have—a loving boyfriend, enough money to live reasonably, good health, and a great group of friends.

I often work with clients who tell me, "I'll feel good about myself when I lose twenty pounds" or "When I get a great job/partner/house I'll be happy." Guess what? It doesn't work that way. Putting your happiness in the future is a setup for misery. All we have is the present. And as we age, that present changes.

My present isn't the same as it was when I was thirty or forty; in some ways it's much better. I worry less about what other people think of me; I am more confident; I speak my mind more easily. And yet, in some ways it's harder to be older: I have lingering knee and shoulder injuries, my hair is thinning, my feet hurt from walking on hard surfaces, and gravity keeps trying to pull this body down. Sometimes, it's hard not to wish for things of the past.

Can we live in the present and not pine for a past when things were different? Can we accept where we're at, or are we going to fight it tooth and nail and grieve for what we've lost?

The best part of being older is not getting lost anymore in things you used to obsess over. "Well, I'm not much good at baseball or competitive tennis anymore, but I love walking in the park and I actually pay attention to what I see now," a client in his seventies recently told me. He's got the right idea.

This is one of the most interesting e-mails I've ever received. It really woke me up. See if it doesn't have the same effect on you. I call it: "Let's Be Shallow."

Dear Michael:

I am a really shallow person and I enjoy it. My husband and I like to spend our time focusing on fashion, movies, and music and going out to clubs, bars, circuit parties, and gay cruises. Most of our friends are this way too and we have a blast together. Is there something wrong with this? Should we change if we're happy? What's wrong with shallow anyway?

Shallow and Loving It in Atlanta

Dear Shallow:

Far be it from me to tell anyone how to be happy. Yet if you are writing to me, perhaps there is something not quite so perfect in Shallowville. Maybe I'm wrong, but could you and your husband be looking for something more? Do you feel something missing in your lives? If so, instead of feeling that you *should* change, why not *expand* your lives instead? Keep on doing what you are doing—as long as you both enjoy it and are not hurting yourself or each other—and simply add new things into the mix.

There's nothing wrong with focusing your life on fashion, movies, music, and dancing. You don't say your age, but I have observed that many of my clients focus their lives on this kind of stuff when they are in their twenties and early thirties. This is an ideal time to explore different ways of living and to try many different ideas and philosophies, going to parties, getting to know different types of people, and discovering who we are at any given point in time. This experimentation can be a lot of fun and we can learn a lot about what we like/don't like and who we want to be/don't want to be.

And let's not get stuck with words; one person's definition of shallow may be another's definition of deep. Go easy on yourself and your husband; you don't need to read Proust in French (or English) to be considered a person of depth. If you are a loyal friend, kind to others, give what you can (time, energy, money) to people, animals, and mother earth, and are as honest and respectful as you can be—then, I'd say you are *far* from shallow.

And who says fashion and music and that other stuff you mention can't be enjoyed by people "of substance"? (Cue music from *Downton Abbey*.) The most interesting people around have the most diverse lives, with a wide variety of interests, friends, hobbies, and activities. *These* are usually the marriages that everyone envies.

If you feel "shallow" and there's some unhappiness there, you and your husband might consider expanding your repertoire of interests, activities, and people. Add something new, something unexpected. Try doing the opposite of what you usually do on a Saturday night and see what happens. Go to the ballet instead of the bar, or vice versa. Sit alone at a coffeehouse and watch people instead of going to a restaurant with a bunch of friends. Go to a museum instead of the gym. You get the picture . . .

Why should you and your husband change if you're happy? Most of us change to stop being unhappy or to become happier. If you're both feeling just fine as you are, don't let other people pressure you into changing because they think you're "shallow" or lacking in something. You could also stop labeling yourself as "shallow," which is very self-deprecating. Why not try "happy" or "lively" or "fun-loving" instead?

I don't know anyone who is totally shallow or totally deep, completely happy or completely miserable, always kind to others or always an asshole. The vast majority of us have a wide range of pleasures, desires, and preferences. Why not enjoy a variety of tastes, interests, and lifestyles with your husband? Vive la différence!

Expecting Loneliness

You may be surprised to read this in a book about marriage, but expecting loneliness in your marriage is an important aspect of not losing yourself. Many of my clients are shocked to hear this. They think that being married is going to completely—or, almost completely—eliminate their loneliness.

Not true.

Not everyone you love is going to understand you—your husband included. You can compromise yourself away to satisfy him (and everyone else), or stay true to yourself and realize that loneliness is part of marriage. Instead of trying to "fight" it, I encourage you to *expect* loneliness and let it be your teacher.

Loneliness is a topic that no one wants to talk about.

> Boyd: "I hate feeling so lonely. I thought marriage would change that. But ironically, now when I'm lonely I feel worse than when I was single, because then I expected to be lonely; now, as a married man, I don't."
>
> Augustus: "My loneliness is too depressing; it's so intense at times. My husband can't really take it away, although he tries. I'm so surprised how lonely I feel when he's trying to comfort me, and although I feel his love, I still feel lonely."
>
> Seiji: "Sometimes, there's nothing I can do about my loneliness. My husband asks me if there's anything he can do, and I just say, 'No, thanks.' I know he cares, but this isn't about him—I'm trying to work with it. I'm learning to meditate, so, when I do my meditation, I notice my loneliness. I feel it in my body, and instead of being freaked out by it, I'm trying to make peace with it."

Lots of people feel overwhelmed by their loneliness. They think that they're doing something "wrong" if they feel loneliness in their marriage. But loneliness is a part of life, regardless of how much you are loved or how intimate you and your husband are. Ironically, loneliness—like any difficult emotion—has a lot to teach us.

"Like what?" you may be asking. Well, consider this:

- Loneliness is a choice. Some of my meditation teachers believe that loneliness is a perception, not a reality. It has a lot to do with our self-talk: What do I tell myself when I am alone? Do I scare myself or comfort myself?
- We can avoid or run from loneliness, but only for a while. Even the most handsome, successful, popular men sometimes feel lonely. It's a part of life, so why not learn how to make peace with it?
- Other people aren't the answer. There have been times where I've felt lonelier in the company of others than I have when I was alone. Imagine being at a party, surrounded by laughing, happy strangers and feeling lonely in the midst of it all. Ugh.
- Staying busy or calling other people isn't always helpful. When I did Internet research on this topic, one website told me to stay busy and connected, call other people, join social clubs—that quick-fix kind of stuff. This is only a temporary fix. You can do all that and still feel lonely.
- No one else can take it away. Unfortunately, no other person—no matter how loving and wonderful—can be there for us 24/7. Even if they could, no one else understands exactly what we're going through at all times. Even the best husband or friend will—eventually—let us down.
- Loneliness is almost always temporary. In 99.99 percent of all situations, it passes. The situation changes or we change how we feel about it. The real challenge is taking care of ourselves until it passes.
- How can we work with loneliness so it doesn't terrify us so much?

When I was younger, I felt very lonely at times. I didn't know what to do about it, so I tried a lot of ways *not* to feel it. In the short run, it helps to find other things to do to get your mind "off" it. But a better strategy is to make peace with it. You could tell yourself, "This is temporary, it will pass," and sit down for a minute or two and just feel it. You may cry or feel angry or numb, but let yourself feel it.

Watch what you tell yourself; don't make it worse. If your friends aren't calling and you feel lonely, tell yourself things such as "This is temporary. I know people love me." Affirm positive truths about yourself.

Be willing to accept things as they are. Loneliness tells us that things *should* be different than they are, for example, "My husband should tell me he loves me more often. Why doesn't he? Is there something wrong with me?" This is a sure way to suffer. Instead, tell yourself, "I am willing to accept things just as they are, right now," and see what happens. This is the essence of mindfulness, meditation, yoga, and any kind of meaningful personal/spiritual growth. Loneliness is a part of life for everyone, and it can be a great teacher. Don't fear it; hear it.

Help Your Marriage and Help Yourself: Find Your Own Unique Sense of Humor

Psychological research has found that when people list the qualities they desire in a mate, a good sense of humor consistently shows up near the top. For some of us, a good sense of humor is more important than physical appearance or socioeconomic status. Perhaps life is so hard that a humorless husband is too much to bear. When the road gets rough, it's great to be with a man you can laugh with.

Humor can defuse tense situations and change the mood from serious and heavy to lighter and more balanced. A good sense of humor is a tangible asset—but can it be cultivated? If you're pretty humorless, are you doomed to be this way forever? Fortunately, no. A sense of humor can be developed just like any other personality trait. This is great news, particularly for those of us who have been told, "You have no sense of humor" or asked, "Where's your sense of humor?"

Ironically, having a good sense of humor is serious business. Humor is no silly little thing; it's part of your life force, right up there with breathing and eating. Just for a moment, imagine that you are having trouble breathing. It has been proven that telling a joke to hospital patients who suffer from asthma or respiratory problems helps them breathe more easily. Humor lowers panicky feelings that contribute to poor breathing.

A well-developed sense of humor has been linked to improved all-around physical and mental health in study after study; it strengthens immune systems, lowers blood pressure, and reduces stress on the organs and muscles—and it certainly makes your marriage a whole lot better!

Take a few minutes and get in touch with your own sense of humor (or lack of it) and ask yourself:

Questions to Consider

- When was the last time you laughed? I mean *really* laughed—a loud, spontaneous, big belly laugh.
- Make a list of things that you find funny. It can be a person, a TV show, movie, comedian, or a comic strip—it doesn't matter, just write them down.
- Can you laugh at yourself? When was the last time you did something "weird" and were able to laugh at yourself?
- Do you and your husband have a similar sense of humor? A complementary sense of humor? How often do you both laugh together?

If it's difficult for you to answer these questions, I urge you to spend some time cultivating your sense of humor—alone and with your husband. Not only is it good for your health; it also makes you more attractive to each other. Men who can laugh at themselves tell the world (and their husbands) that they love themselves enough that they don't have to pretend to be perfect—that it's okay to fall on their butt now and then, grin sheepishly, get up, and move on.

Humor is innately anti-perfectionistic. Aspiring to perfectionism is a great way to lose yourself in unrealistic expectations and it's usually *tremendously* frustrating for our husbands. Unlike perfectionists, men with a well-developed sense of humor know they're totally human, will inevitably mess up something important and can appear vulnerable when they do.

Humor is a form of kindness to yourself and everyone around you. Research shows that men with a well-developed sense of humor live longer, much happier lives. We're more pleasant to be around because we're less demanding of our husbands and others. We make better parents, bosses, friends, and partners.

All of this may sound impossible for you perfectionist guys. Perfectionists are hard on themselves and rarely see the humor in their mistakes; instead, they berate themselves for not doing everything perfectly. But perfectionism is a *learned* characteristic and can be *unlearned*.

Wherever you are in your life, you can improve your sense of humor; it's not a fixed quality. Start small; be willing to laugh at little things that you or your husband find funny. It can be something you do or something he does. (Note: make sure that you are laughing *with* your husband, not *at* him, and that your humor is kind, not punishing.)

Why not take on improving the humor in your marriage as a fun experiment for the two of you? You can watch funny movies or videos. Tell each other jokes. Tell each other about funny things you saw or read about. Like any skill, it takes practice. Don't give up after one or two tries and say, "I can't do it." Persist and experiment. After all, it's not brain surgery; have some fun with it!

The Ultimate Loss of Self: Becoming Your Husband's Caretaker

Dear Michael:

My husband has developed cancer and requires a great deal of care and attention from me. We've been together for twenty-three years. Tom was really healthy up until about a year ago. Now, he is bedridden and in great pain (he has bone cancer) and I have become a full-time caretaker. All our plans to travel in our retirement years (he's sixty-eight and I'm sixty-two) are gone.

I feel completely lost. This is not what I signed up for. I feel like I'm losing my identity and becoming nothing but "Tom's caretaker." We both have adult children and grandchildren (with our ex-wives) who live out of state, but they say they want to help. What should I do?

Losing it in Palm Springs

Dear Mr. Losing It:

I used to work for a large hospice organization where I learned a great deal about caring for ailing or ill partners. Here are some things to consider if you want to care for your husband but don't want to lose yourself.

As a caretaker, your #1 priority is to take good care of yourself. Look at your family history; do you have a pattern of always being the caretaker, the one who makes sure that everyone is doing okay? It's helpful to know yourself and not fall into old dysfunctional family patterns. How can you balance the needs of your husband, your kids, and yourself? Consider these ideas.

- Don't do it all alone. Bring your husband, children, and grandchildren into this; let them know just what you're dealing with. If you don't tell them what's going on, how can they pitch in and help?
- At the hospice where I used to work, I facilitated family meetings when a family member was ill or dying. Everyone in the family gets together—in person or via Skype—and does specific problem solving; in this case, the focus would be how to best assist you and Tom with health/financial/ quality of life concerns. The result of a family meeting is a "family plan" that is specific as to who will do what for whom and when, for example, child #1 will stay with you and Tom once a month for a week, child #2 will call Tom twice a week and visit in person once a month for three days.
- Get help. Make a list of who can help you care for Tom. Find out what's available in your area. Do you have neighbors you're close to? Does Tom have friends he sees regularly? Do you two belong to any social groups, bridge clubs, senior centers? These are all resources that you and your family can tap into so you don't end up burning yourself out.
- Get information. In your family meeting, allow everyone to talk openly and honestly with you and Tom to find out what you need and what they can offer. If you haven't already, have a heart-to-heart talk with Tom's doctors (with his permission). Does he have a will? A durable power of attorney for healthcare? Talk with him about these important documents. Consult with an attorney if necessary.
- Get respite for yourself. You can't do this alone. Does Tom qualify for hospice or palliative services? For Meals on Wheels? For other respite care (to give you a break)? Much of this information is available on the Internet. Let your friends, children, and grandchildren (if they're old enough) help you with this. People feel less helpless when they are doing something constructive, so find something constructive for everyone to do. Make sure that the family plan is *specific*. You can always adjust it later, but make sure that everyone involved knows what they will do and when.
- Be flexible. Situations change; people get sicker (or healthier). Can you anticipate the future, discuss possible scenarios, and get everyone involved in talking about what the options are and how you, Tom, and your family will choose from among them?

- Monitor your caretaker tendencies. You can't do it all, no matter how much you (or they) think you should. Get a periodic reality check from your husband and kids. All caretakers need to increase their self-care. Get a massage now and then, talk with a therapist (or someone objective to "vent" to), get away for an occasional day or weekend with Tom (if he can travel) or go alone or with a friend (if he can't). Find a few minutes for yourself every day: read, garden, take a bubble bath, rent a funny video, and watch it alone or with Tom. Go for a fifteen-minute drive in the car, buy yourself some new clothes, walk around the block—you know!

And, dear readers, don't ignore this topic because you're young and healthy. The best time to talk about the future with your husband is when things are going well and you're both healthy and financially solid. The worst time is when something dramatic (and traumatic) happens and no one has thought ahead or made any tentative plans for health emergencies, legal matters, durable power of attorney for healthcare, wills, and living trusts. Being proactive now can spare you a lot of grief and panic in the future.

God willing, we'll all live long enough to age gracefully and die peacefully. Planning ahead really helps.

Conclusion

I have never written a book before, so this has been quite an adventure. This adventure started when, as a young gay boy, I dreamed of the prince who would carry me away on his horse, make me happy, and take care of me forever.

Reality appeared shortly after and I realized that I was going to have to be that prince if I ever wanted my dream to come true. I never, as a young gay boy, imagined that I would be able to legally marry that prince someday. As someone born in 1953, it wasn't even within my realm of possibilities.

And here we are, now, in 2017, with marriage to that prince not only possible, but very real. What do we want to do with this opportunity, now that we've finally got it?

That's the question that motivated this book.

I have been giving workshops on "Monogamy or Open Relationship?" for many years, long before gay marriage was legal. While marriage wasn't a possibility then, the questions in those workshops were basically the same as those in this book: As gay men, do we choose the monogamy of heterosexual marriage as our model or do we prefer an open marriage? There are pros and cons to each option; in my mind, neither is "better," but they sure are different.

The order of the chapters in this book changed as I wrote it. Initially, it was all about open or monogamous marriage. But, as I wrote and researched, it became clear to me that there are challenges to gay marriage that are independent of the monogamy question. I have seen, as a psychotherapist for gay couples for many years now, that "handbooks" for heterosexual marriage don't really apply to our marriages in several significant ways.

Our marriages are more "designed" than "assumed." We don't have to mimic our straight friends and relatives in their marriages. As gay men, we are used to forging our own paths and defining our relationships on our own terms. So it's quite a paradox to be "given" legal marriage as an option, when, for many of us, heterosexual marriage is not the best model.

The paradox continues: heterosexual, "traditional" marriage has many facets and dimensions, some of them bound to be good and helpful for us. It makes no sense to throw out the baby with the bathwater, as my grandma used to say. Why not design our own marriages by carefully and consciously critiquing heterosexual marriage, taking what works for us, and letting the rest go?

That is what this book invites you and your husband (or future husband) to do.

I have also observed that relationships between two men typically have a lot of conflict and competition, in ways that opposite-sex and lesbian relationships do not. I cannot determine the exact cause or source of this conflict; there are some who say it is biological (the testosterone question), while others claim it's more cultural—that we, as men, are trained to be this way. We are trained to compete with each other; we are trained to win, to want to be the best. This is how we've been socialized, isn't it?

And yet, that too is changing. When I work with young gay (and bi, straight, and trans) men, I see a sea change ahead. More and more often, I'm meeting young men who *don't* make all those traditional assumptions about what a man "is" and who we "should" be. My younger clients inspired and encouraged me to write the chapter about redefining gender roles.

At this point in time, we have an amazing opportunity as married gay men to determine who we are as two men, married to each other. How do *we* divvy up the household tasks? How do *we* decide who is the more nurturing one? The more aggressive one? The more career-oriented one? The more childcare-oriented one?

I am *very* excited by the possibilities that lie before us. We have the opportunity to redefine what marriage is—and not just for us. By doing so, we show our heterosexual brothers and sisters that they can do the same. Once again, as gay people, we can create new structures and paradigms that serve not only us, but *all* people.

It's time to take a good look at marriage as a cultural institution. It's not doing very well for about half of us. For far too long, many of us have just been going along with the same old assumptions and paradigms, saying some version of, "Well, let's give it our best shot and see what happens."

This book encourages everyone, not just gay men, to take a good look at this formidable institution called marriage and begin to ask some *big*, meaningful questions, such as

- How do you decide whether to choose monogamy or an open relationship?
- What happens if you don't get support for your marriage from people around you, important people, like your friends, family, and community?
- If you are married and you both want children, how do you and your husband want to do parenting?

These are not just questions for gay couples; they are questions for all couples; my polyamorous straight clients are dealing with the same stuff. It's not just us, my brothers—*all* people can benefit by questioning the underpinnings of marriage and experimenting with its structure.

I remember living in Paris in the early 1980s, and noticing how heterosexuals in the upper classes typically had a wife (or husband) and a lover. This wasn't unusual; in many circles, it was the norm. I once asked a wonderfully wise and handsome man, with whom I had a wild and passionate affair, why he was still married to a woman. He told me, "You Americans are so conservative, you pretend to love monogamy, but, in your heart, you would love the opportunity to live as we do."

Well, that pretty much shut me up for quite some time. I kept asking myself, "Is he right?" As someone from a small town in Ohio, I was not raised with the mores of my married French lover, so this was quite a jolt for me. I remember getting very defensive with "Michel" (as I'll call him here) and saying, "Oh, you French people, you always assume you know everything and do everything better than anyone else. Get over yourself, Mr. Know-It-All."

It has taken me about thirty-five years to process the questions that Michel posed to me in his lovely flat on Rue Victor Hugo, while his wife was "in the States," working in Atlanta. In a very long and winding path, this book is a result of my conversations with him. Merci, Michel.

While I considered nonmonogamy important to explore in this book, I am also very clear that I do *not* want to denigrate or invalidate monogamous relationships. I know many gay, bi, lesbian, trans, and straight couples who have solid, loving monogamous relationships. To look down upon them would be foolish and naïve. *There is no one form of marriage that is "the best."* Let's be clear about that. That's why this book looks at *both* open and monogamous marriage; each has its own unique gifts and challenges for us.

In this book we followed two married couples: Tomas and Larry, representing a harmonious open marriage, and Ethan and Jake, representing a fulfilling monogamous marriage. They're an amalgam of hundreds of real couples I've worked with. Each couple experienced the joys and difficulties of their double testosterone marriage, showing you and your husband options and possibilities for your own marriage.

A marriage is only as strong as the two individuals. A great marriage—not just a good one—is one where each man does his *own* inner work and supports his husband to do the same. I've seen this kind of relationship in many of the gay marriages—both open and monogamous—that I've had the pleasure to work with.

Your gay marriage can be amazing, high-functioning, and extremely fulfilling—*if* you and your husband are willing to do the work. When you and your husband work on your own psychological baggage, you end up a much stronger couple who have *more* to give each other and are *less* needy. Two strong, happy men together is a beautiful, powerful thing.

We can set a new standard of what marriage can be—it's *never* before been possible to see what a marriage of two men can be. We can do the work, reap the rewards, and take the institution of marriage to a new level of happiness and satisfaction.

Two men together—each strong on his own—can do and be anything.

We need not imitate hetero-normative marriage—we can redefine marriage itself—and provide all couples—gay, bi, lesbian, trans, and straight—with a new model/paradigm for relationships.

Every now and then, in history, there's an opportunity to take something to the next level. My brothers—this is our moment. This is our chance to help make marriage even better.

Forgive my idealism, for, you see, I believe in us.

Acknowledgments

This book wasn't my idea. Really.

I started offering workshops for gay, bisexual, and transgender men about eighteen years ago. I really enjoy facilitating workshops, which is great because for the longest time I never charged for them. After a couple of years of doing these workshops, I noticed a familiar pattern: after the workshop ended, there were always a few guys who came up to me and said (in whispered tones), "You've got to put this stuff in a book."

My response was always to be kind and acknowledge them with some version of "Yeah, yeah, yeah. You're very kind. Thank you so much." And then immediately forget the idea. They might think it was a great idea, but I didn't. I had no desire to write a book. The idea sounded like no fun and way too much work.

About fifteen years ago I started writing my advice column, "Life Beyond Therapy" in local LGBT newspapers. I asked readers to send in questions. Boy, did they ever! I wonder if Dear Abby ever got some of the questions I got (don't worry, I put the best ones in this book).

I don't know if you've ever written a book. If you have, good for you; you can skip this page. For the rest of you, do you know what a strange ride it is to write a book? Allow me to explain.

About five years ago, a writer friend of mine recommended me to a gay publisher (no names, please) as a "potential" author. The gay publisher asked me to submit an idea for a book. I did. They liked it. I was in shock. Omigod, could this really happen?

Well, not really. What happened next is straight out of David Sedaris: the gay publisher assigned me to an editor, who was very encouraging and wanted me to send him new stuff almost every day. So I worked like a fiend, writing, rewriting, rerewriting (is that a word?) for weeks until, finally, it seemed like we were getting close to something.

As if.

One day I got a strange e-mail from the editor, telling me he had resigned from the publisher and suggesting I contact a writer's agent he knew. I was in shock. It was like being engaged to a fabulous guy, going through all the bridal (groom-al?) showers to get all the toasters and rainbow-colored appliances my future husband and I would ever need, and then being dumped by said future husband just before getting fitted for my tux.

It gets worse. Do you know why Mr. Editor dumped me? So he could quit the publishing business and go into a Zen Ashram. My book was sacrificed for his peace of mind? How unfair.

So I pouted. For about two years (I'm good at pouting). Then I woke up and realized, I can still write this book.

And I did. And you're reading it.

This book wouldn't have happened without all the guys who came to my workshops and e-mailed me after reading my "Life Beyond Therapy" columns. It was you guys who kept nudging me toward authordom. Thank you. Really.

And thanks to my soul brother Stephen Caudana, who has always believed in this book and has loved me consistently. Much gratitude to my agent Claire Gerus for her belief in my writing talents and to my editor Suzanne Staszak-Silva at Rowman & Littlefield for her unending patience with my hundreds of questions.

Kudos also to Rowman & Littlefield production coordinator Elaine Mc-Garraugh for all her wisdom, the R&L design department for a beautiful cover design and the terrific copyediting talents of Jo-Ann Parks. This book is *so* much better because of you all.

And a big shout-out of appreciation to some special folks who've encouraged me along the way: Joe Lonegran, Edwina Foster, Daniel Ostroff, Paula Buckley, Curtis Taylor, D'Andra La Pierre, Ted Kerkelis, Charlotte Knabel (who taught me all about editing), Jim Curtan, Claudia Bolognesi, David Kobosa, Marie Schilling, Jim Watters, Gail Braverman, Aman and Sunny Keays, my father (for inspiring me to be true to myself), my mother (for encouraging me to be humble), Patty Eichelberger, Craig Arnoff, Eleanor Johnson, Joerg Claus, Anne Lamott (who gave me permission to write "shitty first drafts"), and my Uncle Bob, who loved me—a confused, frightened young gay boy—just as I was, when I felt so unworthy of anything remotely approaching love.

I am also very grateful to the many gay periodicals that have run my work over the years, especially *Gay San Diego*; *The Erie Gay News* (New York, Pennsylvania, and Ohio); *The Gayzette* (Omaha and Lincoln, Nebraska); *The Letter* (Kentucky, Ohio, Indiana, and Illinois); *Out & About* (Nashville, Knoxville, Memphis, and Chattanooga, Tennessee); *The Gay & Lesbian Times* (Southern California); *The Bottom Line* (Palm Springs); *Buzz* (Southern California); and the "Out in America" cities network (174 city-sites across North America and Great Britain).

Notes

Chapter Three

1. "Same-sex and Different-sex Parent Households and Child Health Outcomes: Findings from the National Survey of Children's Health." The study was recently published in the *Journal of Developmental and Behavioral Pediatrics*, the official journal of the Society for Developmental and Behavioral Pediatrics. From out.com, accessed April 17, 2016.

2. Ibid.

Chapter Four

1. Spike W. S. Lee and Norbert Schwarz, "Framing Love: When It Hurts to Think We Were Made for Each Other," *Journal of Experimental Social Psychology* 54 (September 2014): 61–67.

2. Laura E. VanderDrift, Juan E. Wilson, and Christopher R. Agnew, "On the Benefits of Valuing Being Friends for Non-Marital Romantic Partners," *Journal of Social and Personal Relationships* (July 2012), doi 10.1177/0265407512453009.

Chapter Five

1. PrEP stands for Pre-Exposure Prophylaxis. It's the use of anti-HIV medication that keeps HIV negative people from becoming infected. As I understand it, the medication interferes with HIV's ability to copy itself in your body after you've been exposed. For more information, check out www.aids.gov or http://myprepexperience.blogspot.com.

Chapter Seven

1. Carolyn Myss, *Why People Don't Heal and How They Can* (Easton, PA: Harmony, 1998).

Index

marriage: from affair, 226; as car buying, 135–36; children in, 125; community against, 84; as cultural institution, 260; for dependability, 112; emotional monogamy cornerstone of, 137; ending of, 227–28; family-of-origin issues influence on, 216–17; financial benefits of, 18; healthy boundaries for, 50–51; hetero-normativity defining of, 1; identity from, 244–45; leaving of, 226; for loneliness, 251; love motivation for, 16–17; as overlapping circles, 236; as polishing gemstones, 15; prince for, 259; questioning of, 95, 261; reinventing from, 245; retirement influence on, 218; romanticizing of, 80; self-soothing influence on, 197; youthfulness for, 202

marriage list, 12–13

meditation: for centering, 162–63; for health, 163; for silence, 45; time spent on, 164; *You Can Heal Your Life* on, 163; for youthfulness, 202

men, gender-based roles of, 58–59

mental health: body obsession and, 151–52; sex life for, 99; sex-oriented work and, 183

mental stimulation, 219

merging, 229–31

Middle Path, 37–38

mid-life crisis, 153

mind, state of, 132, 140–41, 214. *See also* monkey mind

mirror work, 200–201, 215

moderation, for addiction, 203–4

mom: emotional balance of, 192; hyper-responsible from, 230; relationship role as, 216

money: children influence on, 125; "creating and adjusting" for, 125; enough of, 212–13; expectations of, 124

monkey mind, 45

monogamous marriage: boredom of, 14–15, 169–70; challenges of, 168–69;

choice of, 259; complacency in, 175; disrespectful of, 91–92; emotional stability in, 187; exploration of, 167; family for, 86–87; insecurity in, 110; jealousy in, 110; losing yourself in, 171; love of, 261; myths of, 224; sex life in, 66–67; spontaneity of, 187, 220; unresolved issues from, 168; validation of, 261–62

monogamy: "creating and adjusting" for, 130–31; of double testosterone marriage, 2; gay men for, 91; security of, 3. *See also* emotional monogamy; sexual monogamy

motivation: for domination, 245; for drama, 52; for parenting, 224; for sex parties, 147

narcissism, 151, 230

negative stereotypes, 68

negative stories, 131–33

negotiating, 109–10, 130–31

neurosis, 151

"neutral" state, 53, 75

non-drinking life, 54

nurturing, 199

old. *See* aging

open marriage: adaptability of, 119–20; Alexander on, 138; alone in, 143–44; balance of, 137–39; check-in night for, 120; choice of, 259; closing of, 113–14, 116; communication in, 107, 113; community and, 88–90; consideration of, 115; "creating and adjusting" in, 123–24, 128; emotional ugliness and, 156–57; family against, 85–87; friends against, 85–86; happiness in, 120, 127–28, 131; high-maintenance experience of, 123; honesty in, 113, 128; husband against, 112–13; insecurity in, 108–9; jealousy in, 108–9; job loss influence on, 116–17; leather community for, 106–7; lying about, 89; on marriage list, 12–13; as Maserati, 135–36; "other" man feelings in, 115–16; as process, 135; rigidity and, 129–30; romance in, 158–59; rules in, 118–19; sex life in, 66, 88; sexual freedom in, 107; transition to, 2

open relationships: exploration of, 4; for heterosexual marriage, 87; secret of, 87–88; from "Three-Year Itch," 173

optimism, 194, 198

orgastic potency, 146

"other" man feelings, 115–16

paranoia, 236

parenting: abandonment and, 235; by gay dad, 24; gender-based roles for, 72; motivation for, 224; rules set by, 74–75; in same-sex marriage, 76, 267n1; stepdad role in, 74; of teenager, 73–74

parenting group, 24, 75

parents: affair by, 127; "creating and adjusting" as, 127; gay men as, 20; partner resemblance of, 193, 216; perfectionism from, 41–42; relationship influenced by, 216. See also same-sex parents

partner: against "creating and adjusting," 130; desire balancing with, 140; parents resemblance for, 193, 216. See also sexual partner

patience, 43–44

"paying attention" exercise, 163, 202–3

peace: acceptance from, 44, 216; for competition, 43; drama against, 51–52; empathy from, 44; with loneliness, 253

people-pleaser, 49–50, 233

perfectionism: compassion for, 42; competition from, 41; humor against, 254–55; husband influenced by, 42–43; from parents, 41–42

perseverance, 247–48

personality: abandonment influenced by, 234; embarrassment from, 70; in emotional monogamy, 162; as subconscious, 234

personal responsibility, 110, 112, 121–22

Philautia, 178, 237

physical beauty: as assembled parts, 150; happiness and, 183–84; hook-up apps for, 148–49; humor over, 253; husband and, 182; "the man machine" for, 150

physical expression, 138–39, 141

plastic surgery, 207, 214

Platonic, 178, 237–38

polyamorous community, 90

possessiveness, 111

power struggle, 13–14

Pragma, 178, 237

precious stories, 132–33

premarital counseling, 12, 14

psychological attachment theory, 193

rebelling, 75

reflective listening, 52

Reich, Wilhelm, 146

reinventing: of cultural institution, 1, 261; happiness from, 247–48; from marriage, 245; support network for, 245

rejection, 112, 161

relationship: abandonment addressed in, 232–33; adjustments for, 124; aging influence on, 220–21; beliefs influence on, 177; couple's counseling for, 227; as creation, 123; emotional bonds in, 140; energy for, 159–60; expected changes in, 129; Freud on, 216; friendship in, 82; genitals emphasized in, 142; grudge in, 227–28; healthy distance in, 231; internalized homophobia in, 67; mom role in, 216; parents influence on, 216; renewal of, 157–58; soul mate influence on, 81; three musketeers of, 140–42

resentment, 181, 229

resilience, 197–99

sexual compatibility, 150
sexual freedom: case study of, 106; of
    heterosexual marriage, 101; from leather
    community, 106–7
sexually addictive behavior, 142–43, 152
shallowness, 250–51
sharing phase, 101
silence, 45–46
smothering, 122, 192
social connection, 220
soul mate: friendship replaced by, 82–83;
    honeymoon phase of, 79; illusion of,
    174; relationship influenced by, 81; self-
    opinion influence on, 80–81
spiritual connection, 219
spontaneity, 187, 213, 220
stability, 188. See also emotional stability
status, in community, 118
stepdad, 74–75
stereotypes. See negative stereotypes; tradi-
    tional stereotypes
Storge, 178, 237
stories, 39. See also negative stories; precious
    stories
subconscious, 132, 234
suicide, 69
superego, 37–38
superficiality, 155–56
support network, 198, 245
sympathetic nervous system, 52

technology, 241–42
teenager, 73–75
temporary assets, 183

tenderness, 184–86
testosterone, 1, 4–6
Three Musketeers (Dumas), 140
"Three-Year Itch," 172–74
time. See alone time
time monitoring, 149
"time out," 225–26
traditional stereotypes, 60–61
trial separation, 228
trust, 111, 181
truth, 54, 110

ugliness: from aging, 213; fat and, 213; of
    intimacy, 155–56; as state of mind, 214.
    See also emotional ugliness
unresolved issues, 168, 187–88

validation: from hook-up apps, 149–50; of
    monogamous marriage, 261–62
video games, 194, 217
vulnerability: for anger, 209; arguments and,
    209–10; fear of, 208; opposites attract
    for, 234; unresolved issues from, 187–88

widowed, 19–20
work: confrontation replaced by, 24;
    happiness from, 71; husband replaced by,
    241; retirement from, 218; technology
    and, 241–42. See also job loss; mirror
    work; sex-oriented work
writing, 48. See also book writing

younger men, 154–55, 207
youthfulness, 202, 204

About the Author

Michael Dale Kimmel, CBT, MSW, LCSW, is a psychotherapist in private practice with a long history of creating and facilitating innovative workshops for the gay community. His website—www.lifebeyondtherapy.com—has received over 22,000,000 hits and 1,500,000 visitors since its debut. He has offered workshops for gay communities all over California on a variety of topics.

Currently, he writes the "Life Beyond Therapy" column for *Gay San Diego*, the *Erie Gay News*, the *Gayzette* and *The Letter*. He has been a consultant on gay-related issues for Southern California news programs during the past decade and, in recent years, has written for publications including *Buzz*, *Lavender Lens*, *LGBT Weekly*, *The Bottom Line*, *The Gay and Lesbian Times*, Counselingmen .com, *Expression* magazine, *Gay News Network*, Gayfriendlytherapists.com, *Pink News*, Positivearticles.com, *Pulp*, *Rage*, *Sarah Lawrence College Magazine*, and SDGLN.com (San Diego Gay and Lesbian News).